RICHARD FARMER,
Master of Emmanuel College, Cambridge

RICHARD FARMER,
Master of Emmanuel College, Cambridge
A Forgotten Shakespearean

Arthur Sherbo

Newark: University of Delaware Press
London and Toronto: Associated University Presses

© 1992 by Associated University Presses, Inc.

All rights reserved. Authorization to photocopy items for internal or personal use, or the internal or personal use of specific clients, is granted by the copyright owner, provided that a base fee of $10.00, plus eight cents per page, per copy is paid directly to the Copyright Clearance Center, 27 Congress Street, Salem, Massachusetts 01970. [0-87413-444-7/92 $10.00 + 8¢ pp, pc.]

Associated University Presses
440 Forsgate Drive
Cranbury, NJ 08512

Associated University Presses
25 Sicilian Avenue
London WC1A 2QH, England

Associated University Presses
P.O. Box 39, Clarkson Pstl. Stn.
Mississauga, Ontario,
L5J 3X9 Canada

The paper used in this publication meets the requirements of the American National Standard for Permanence of Paper for Printed Library Materials Z39.48-1984.

Library of Congress Cataloging-in-Publication Data

Sherbo, Arthur, 1918–
    Richard Farmer, Master of Emmanuel College, Cambridge : a forgotten Shakespearean / Arthur Sherbo.
        p.   cm.
    Includes bibliographical references and index.
    ISBN 0-87413-444-7 (alk. paper)
    1. Farmer, Richard, 1735–1797.   2. Shakespeare, William, 1564–1616—Criticism and interpretation—History—18th century. 3. Shakespeare, William, 1564–1616—Editors.   4. Emmanuel College (University of Cambridge)—Biography.   5. Literary historians—Great Britain—Biography.   6. Editors—Great Britain—Biography.
    I. Title.
    PR2972.F3S53   1992
    822.3'3—dc20
    [B]   91-58086
                                                                       CIP

PRINTED IN THE UNITED STATES OF AMERICA

For David, Michael, Patrick,
Rachael, and Nicholas—
grand children all

Contents

List of Abbreviations	9
Acknowledgments	11
1. Early Years	15
2. Master of Emmanuel College	37
3. Later Academic Career	61
4. The Abortive History of Leicester	84
5. The Essay on the Learning of Shakespeare	94
6. A Letter . . . to Mr. Steevens	120
7. Further Notes on Shakespeare	139
8. Summing Up	167
Notes	202
Index	211

Abbreviations

Diaries	*Isaac Reed Diaries, 1762–1804,* ed. Claude E. Jones, 1946
Folger	Folger C.b.10 Letters to and from George Steevens
GM	*Gentleman's Magazine*
Letters	*The Percy Letters,* 8 vols., by various editors, 1944–85
Life	James Boswell, *Life of Johnson,* ed. G. B. Hill, revised and enlarged by L. F. Powell, 6 vols., 1934–50
Lit. Anecd.	John Nichols, *Literary Anecdotes of the Eighteenth Century,* 9 vols., 1812–15
Lit. Illustr.	John Nichols, *Illustrations of the Literary History of the Eighteenth Century,* 8 vols., 1817–58
Walpole	The Yale Edition of the Correspondence of Horace Walpole

Acknowledgments

Adam J. N. Goodwin, Assistant Keeper of Archives, the Leicestershire Record Office, answered my query about Farmer's date of birth and about the sermon he delivered in Leicester. Dr. Margaret Smith very obligingly did legwork for me in Oxford. Dr. David Fairer, Lecturer in English, Leeds University, shared his knowledge of Thomas Warton with me. Professor Bertram H. Davis of the State University of Florida in Tallahassee was of invaluable assistance in the matter of the Farmer–Percy relationship. Miss Lorraine Hart again overcame all the difficulties of my hieroglyphics. The staffs of Emmanuel College Library, the Rare Books Room of the Cambridge University Library, and the Special Collections department of the Michigan State University Library contributed their indispensable cooperation. Finally, Dr. Frank Stubbings, former librarian of the Emmanuel College Library, acted as my guide and mentor. If there are errors in this work, they are there despite his guidance and despite the help of the others named.

Quotation of materials from the Bodleian Library, Cambridge University Library, Folger Shakespeare Library, Leicestershire Record Office, and the James Marshall and Marie-Louise Osborn Collection at Yale University is by permission.

RICHARD FARMER,
Master of Emmanuel College,
Cambridge

1

Early Years

On Tuesday 5 October 1790 Isaac Reed, on one of his annual visits to Emmanuel College, Cambridge, where he was the guest of the Master, Richard Farmer, recorded in his diary that "Dr. Farmer said this Evening he was born 4th May, 1735" (185). All biographical accounts of Farmer give his birth date as 28 August 1735 when they do not simply record the year of his birth. George Dyer, for example, writing the account of Farmer in the *Annual Necrology* for 1797 and 1798 contented himself with the year date, and he knew Farmer very well, having entered Emmanuel in 1774, "Where he read hard and was in favour with Richard Farmer" (*DNB, sub* Dyer). John Nichols, another of Farmer's friends, wrote the obituary notice for the *GM* and gave only the year (1797.ii.805). Years later, in 1812, in his account of Farmer in his *Literary Anecdotes*, Nichols gave the 28 August 1735 date (II.619), despite the fact that John Heydrick, who provided him with a pedigree of the Farmer family for his *History and Antiquities of the County of Leicestershire,* gave only the year date (IV.ii.1811, 950). Heydrick appended a note to the pedigree that reads, in part, "I know nothing further of the Farmer Pedigree than I have set out and stated. I was glad of the opportunity of shewing my respect to the memory of my old friend and school fellow Dr. Farmer, whom I highly regard, and to his relatives, for whom I have an esteem." Heydrick, Farmer's contemporary at school, did not know the month and day of Farmer's birth. Nichols is then the sole authority for the August date, having in some fashion come upon it after 1797 and before 1812. According to the Emmanuel College "Wager Book, 1769–85," John Askew, Fellow of the College, on an unspecified day in 1769, wagered with Farmer "more than 34" (13). Here, as with many (even most) of the wagers recorded, the immediate company knew the exact nature of the wager, but today one must conjecture. I believe the wager had to do with Farmer's age, i.e., that he was over thirty-four. He was born in 1735, lending credence to the conjecture. On page 9 of the wager book, and hence earlier than the wager, is the entry "Mr. Farmer to treat wth Wine, ye 15th of May, 1769." The

16 Early Years

reason for the treat is not given. However, in 1774, one entry reads "Farmer Birthday 15th of May 1774 NB: 40th year" (84), for which event Farmer gave two bottles of wine. After the College Audit of 21 March 1775, the date, incidentally, when Farmer was elected Master, another entry reads "The Master birthday 15th of May 1775," which cost him another two bottles (106). The celebration of his birthday was not recorded again until 1795 and then again in 1796 and 1797; on the latter occasion he gave "Four bottles of old Port.[1] What is more, on two occasions there are lists of the birthdays of the Master and Fellows, and Farmer's date is May 15.[2] John Nichols states that Farmer's "native parish" was St. Mary's,[3] and recourse to the parish record reveals that Farmer was baptized May 6. In 1790, when he told Reed his birthday was May 4, he was referring to the so-called "old style" dating, the difference between it and "new style" being eleven days. Hence, May 15 was the date of his birth—new style.

The most detailed account of Farmer's life is still that of John Nichols, despite the error in the date of Farmer's birth. While no precise date can be given for the first meeting between the two, it must have been in the latter part of the 1770s, by which time Nichols had edited three volumes of Swift's works as well as the *Original Works* of William King. Indeed, the account of Nichols in the *Dictionary of National Biography* includes Farmer among other notables who "had already been attracted by the young man's antiquarian tastes" as a result of those publications. Farmer had issued proposals for a "History and Antiquities of the Town of Leicester" as early as May 1766. And in 1775, when he became Master of Emmanuel, he gave Nichols all the plates and notes for the abandoned *History* of Leicester, evidence of an early acquaintanceship. By September 1782, the two were on terms of intimacy, their mutual friend Isaac Reed recording that on Saturday, September 28, while he was on his first visit to Emmanuel College, in "The Afternoon Mr. Nichols came from London and he, Dr. Farmer, Dr. Pennington and myself played at Cards until 10 o'clock, when we went home and supped in the Parlour" (121). Subsequently Farmer and Nichols met Reed at Sturbridge Fair where they ate pork at a booth and then went to the theater where they saw *As You Like It* and *Tom Thumb* (122). Much, then, of any biographical account of Farmer must depend on Nichol's sketch of his friend in the *Literary Anecdotes*—a sketch little changed from the obituary notice Nichols wrote in the *GM* on Farmer's death, but dependent upon George Dyer's account of Farmer in the *Annual Necrology* for 1797–98.

In his account of the Farmer family of Radcliffe Culey, Leicester, Nichols wrote, "The family of *Farmer* was of considerable note here at

Early Years

17

the beginning of the 16th century; and in 1619 *Bartholomew Farmer, gent.* entered the family pedigree, being then 72 years old." John Farmer served as chief constable at Ratcliffe in 1630, and in 1663 George Farmer had a grant of arms. In 1706 "John Farmer, gent." undertook to pay £800 "into the hands of trustees" to buy certain lands.[4] The Farmer family was one of means. E. S. Shuckburgh was of the opinion that "Farmer's hand" in Nichol's *History* was "evident from the very elaborate account of his own family and the village in which they possessed land (Ratcliffe Culey), which it contains."[5] True or not, in the pedigree of the Farmer family in Nichols's *History* (IV.ii.950–51) there is solid evidence of Farmer's hand in the form of a spate of notes found among his papers and reprinted by John Heydrick, who provided the pedigree. Heydrick, friend and school-fellow of Farmer's, also affirmed the correctness and antiquity of a pedigree of the family which Farmer had reproduced from "MS Bibl. Harl. No. 1174. sec. 180." The pedigree in Nichol's *History* shows that Farmer's father, also named Richard, married "Hannah, daughter of John Knibb, born 1712; married at Bricklow Jan. 4, 1732–3; died Dec. 14, 1808, in her 97th year," outliving her son Richard by some eleven years. Richard and Hannah had five sons and four daughters; their firstborn son, John, died when he was eleven days old. Richard was the secondborn child; two of his brothers and three of his sisters survived him. Joseph Cradock, Farmer's schoolfellow, wrote of the Farmer family that his "father dealt largely in malt, more advantageously, I believe, for his customers than for himself. He was always considered a strictly honest man." One of Farmer's brothers was "an officer in the Leicestershire militia," while "another was in trade at Leicester"; "and there was a third, who caused much uneasiness to his parents. He was clever, but very extravagant, and often caused embarrassments to them, who always endeavoured, if possible, to extricate him from pecuniary difficulties." This third brother, unnamed, as were the other two, greatly annoyed Richard "by writing his name Fermor [the family name of the Earl and Countess of Pomfret], and endeavouring to engraft himself on the Pomfret family." Cradock added, "Farmer of Emmanuel" was "the last man who would ever have wished to presume on any family distinction."[6] It should be noted, however, that Farmer must have felt some distant kinship with the Fermors, because, among other things, he noted, in an extant manuscript collection of miscellaneous jottings, "English Baronetage 5 vols." with three more notations, one of them to the "Family of Fermor, 409, 380" in volume V (actually IV) and a quotation of one sentence from page 209 in the 1741 edition, that used by him.[7]

It is a commonplace that a schoolmaster may exert a considerable

18   Early Years

and lasting effect upon a student. Had the young Richard Farmer not
had the good luck to spend many of his formative years under the
tutelage of the Rev. Mr. Gerrard Andrewes and his assistants at the
Free Grammar School of Leicester, his subsequent career might have
been vastly different. Andrewes was of Balliol College, Oxford, an
"elegant classic," so described by Joseph Cradock, a contemporary of
Farmer's at the Free School.[8] Andrewes was Headmaster from 1739 to
1762 and vicar of St. Nicholas's, Leicester, from 1757 to 1764, the
year of his death. The fullest account of him is in John Nichols's
History and Antiquities of the County of Leicestershire, where his
abilities as a divine are highly praised. Nichols continues:

> He also filled with distinguished credit the office of the Master of the Free-
> school of the town of Leicester; which, under his superintendance, was a
> seminary of great repute; not only the sons of the first families in those
> parts were placed under his care, but numbers from much greater dis-
> tances also received the rudiments of education that reflected him or his
> abilities. Among these was the present Earl of Stamford; and, not to
> mention many others, the late Dr. Halifax, Bishop of St. Asaph, and Dr.
> Farmer, the late worthy Master of Emmanuel College, Cambridge, were
> contemporaries under his instruction. Cheerful in his deportment and
> destitute of tyranny, his school was a scene of lively obedience. Beloved by
> the boys for his free and gentle treatment, his precepts were readily
> received, and the task dispatched with alacrity.[9]

The course of studies at Leicester was that which obtained in the
grammar schools elsewhere in England, with an emphasis upon Latin
and Greek. Richard Farmer's later career as student, Fellow, and
finally Master of Emmanuel College, demonstrates the benefits he
derived from his years with the Rev. Mr. Andrewes, and it was almost
surely Andrewes who started Farmer collecting black-letter literature.
Cradock, in the first form when Farmer was about to leave for
Emmanuel College, states that Farmer had already "begun to collect
scarce black-letter books." Leicester, according to Cradock's
Memoirs, had a distinguished group of literary men and book collec-
tors, among the latter, "the Rev. Mr. Simmonds, vicar of St. Mary's,
[who] had made no inconsiderable progress in a collection of very
rare editions of books, from which Farmer derived considerable ad-
vantages." "Literature," according to Cradock, "at that time was
much the discussion at Leicester. John Whiston, the London bookseller, passed part of the summer with Mr. Jackson [a Greek scholar].
Samuel Carte, a learned ecclesiastical lawyer, brother to the historian,
visited my father"(I.4—5).
But it was probably Simmonds who exerted the most influence on

Early Years   19

young Farmer. In John Nichols's list of the Vicars of the Church of St. Mary de Castro, John Simmonds is described as "M.A. Oct. 17, 1768; died Aug. 29, 1788" with a footnote reference to his epitaph. The epitaph reads in part: "He was a man of exemplary piety and universal beneficence . . . enforcing by his own example the precepts of that most holy Gospel of which he was a minister. In the discharge of all Christian duties none was more assiduous; within the circle of his acquaintance none more esteemed." William Bickerstaffe, Simmonds's curate at St. Mary's, added a ten-line poem ending "Simmonds is dead, and Charity is no more."[10] Simmonds's library was of sufficient size and worth as to be sold at auction, the sale catalog being dated 6 July 1779.[11] Farmer was indeed fortunate to be educated by Andrewes and encouraged in his love of books by Simmonds, both men noted for their religiosity. What is more, Leicester boasted of a library rich in old books, which were accessible to the young reader.[12]

Not much biographical information about Richard Farmer's pre-Emmanuel years has survived. One important exception is what Thomas Martyn, friend and contemporary of Farmer at Emmanuel, added to John Nichols's account of Farmer in the *Literary Anecdotes*. Nichols had noted that Farmer had wanted to marry Sir Thomas Hatton's daughter but had been refused (II.637). Martyn, referring to this, wrote that Farmer

> suffered a disappointment in love very early in life (see p. 637). From his first coming to College he always gave Miss Benskin as a toast, and never could mention her name without evident feelings of the most ardent affection. We were then so intimate that his joys and sorrows were poured into my bosom. After a lapse of almost 60 years, it is no wonder if I do not correctly remember how the connexion terminated; but I have some notion that at length she married another person, there being little prospect of a connexion with Dr. Farmer speedily taking place. But as she was a Leicester girl, Mr. Nichols may perhaps know this circumstance better than I do. This I am certain of, that the disappointment affected his mind very deeply, and was the source of his peculiarities. (VII.420–21)

Both Farmer and Martyn were seventeen when they were admitted to Emmanuel, and while the lapse of some sixty years probably colored Martyn's account, it is possible that Farmer either suffered a great disappointment or dramatized his sorrow. In his *History* of Leicestershire Nichols records that a Thomas Benskin was one of the executors of the will of Thomas Stavely, dated 21 September 1702 (I.ii.351). Four members of the Benskin family of Stony Stanton are buried in the church there (IV.ii.972), and there were other Benskins

20 Early Years

in Seagrave and Reresby. Possibly Farmer had little good fortune with the fairer sex because although John Gilbert Cooper "discovered the rising talents of Farmer, and always gave him encouragement," Craddock added "(to use a once fashionable phrase) Farmer was not a produceable young man."[13]

Neither Andrewes nor Simmonds, Farmer's early preceptors, attended Emmanuel College, but some members of the Farmer family of Leicestershire preceded Richard there. *Alumni Cantabrigienses* listed admissions in 1623 (Seth), 1633 (Roger), 1641 (Thomas), and 1660 (Thomas). For the record, Richard's brother John followed him to Emmanuel, admitted as a pensioner on 30 June 1757 and awarded the B.A. degree in 1761, as did Farmer's nephew, Thomas, who was admitted in 1790, and who became a Fellow of the College in 1797, the year of his uncle's death.

Alumni Cantabrigienses gives the date of Farmer's admission to Emmanuel as pensioner as 12 April 1753, while the account in the *DNB* has it simply as "about 1753." Thomas Martyn, born the same year as Farmer, entered Emmanuel as pensioner on 24 June 1752 and was thus part of the relatively small number of students contemporary with Farmer. D. A. Winstanley states that Emmanuel admissions for the years 1733 to 1767 averaged "about nine or ten," so that the undergraduates were a small society unto themselves.[14] John Nichols had written that Farmer entered Emmanuel "about 1753," and Martyn claimed that Farmer was admitted, "not in 1753, but in October 1752, and came into residence at the same time," that is, at the same time Martyn was admitted to the College. "Though he arrived within a few days after me, yet he was a year my junior, because he had not been admitted before the Commencement. We were near neighbours in Bungay-court, and almost always together."[15] The Emmanuel College admissions record is, however, unambiguous; Farmer was admitted on 12 April 1753.

Undergraduate academic life in the eighteenth century was marred by drunkenness, sexual license, and physical violence. An extreme instance of such violence is reported in the *GM* for April 1751, two years before Farmer's admission to Emmanuel.

Cambridge, March 31. On the 21st a woman and her maid servant going to the conduit for water were met by some scholars, just coming from the sign of the tuns, who knocking the mistress down the maid ran home and bolted herself in, but they pursued, broke the door open, and on her struggling to prevent ravishment, thrust a stick up her body, and otherwise abus'd her. On *April* 7. 5 scholars were produced before her in the presence of the vice chancellor, &c. where she fixed on two, and acquitted

Early Years

the others; the offenders are secured, and the girl's father is to prosecute them at the expence of the university. (183)

It is to Farmer's credit and to that of the majority of the students of Cambridge University that their undergraduate years were without reproach. Indeed, George Dyer wrote that Farmer "while an undergraduate, was neither distinguished for any gross vices, nor for any extraordinary qualities. He was, however, known to be a man of reading, distinguished rather for sprightly parts, than profound speculations, and much esteemed in the circle of his friends" (393).

Farmer, admitted to Emmanuel as pensioner on 12 April 1753, was to remain in Cambridge and Emmanuel for the rest of his life. With the inevitable exceptions of character, circumstances, and opportunities, his career epitomizes academic life in the eighteenth century. One year after his admission, on 25 April 1754 and until 21 April 1759, he enjoyed a common scholarship, while at much the same time, from 19 October 1753 to 26 April 1759, he also held a scholarship under a grant from Francis Ash, one condition of the latter being that it be held only until the scholar proceeded Master of Arts. Some of the conditions of the Ash scholarship are very interesting, particularly that which required each of the ten exhibitioners every year to "pronounce an oration upon such subject &c at such time as ye Master of the College shall appoint." Another was that all exhibitioners be designed for the ministry. Each received ten pounds annually in quarterly payments. That young Farmer was well thought of by the Master and Fellows of Emmanuel is further evidenced by his also holding a Whichcote scholarship from 13 March 1756 to 26 April 1761, although this yielded much less than the other two, the revenue from the grant being divided among the Master, the Fellows, and the Scholars.[16] Being of a versifying bent, he was asked as an undergraduate to contribute to a volume of poems celebrating the laying of a stone for the new University library in 1755.

Farmer became a Bachelor of Arts in 1757, ranked a senior optime, i.e., of the second class in the Mathematical Tripos. Nichols stated that "the degree, though not of the first class, procured him notice in College; and he successfully contested the silver cup given at Emmanuel to the best graduate of that year with Mr. Wanley Sawbridge, brother to the Alderman" (*Lit. Anecd.* II.620). Thomas Martyn claimed that there had been "no contest between him [Farmer] and Sawbridge for the cup; Farmer had it of course, as senior in the Proctor's list" (*Lit. Anecd.,* VIII.420). William Chafin wrote that Farmer "succeeded me in gaining the cup, which had been unclaimed for 2 or 3 years, therefore it was much larger than it otherwise would

22   Early Years

have been; and the Doctor prided himself much in the possession of it" (*Lit. Illustr.*, VI.201). In any event, on 26 April 1759, at which time his scholarships came to an end, Farmer became a Fellow of Mr. Gillingham's Foundation. The Fellowship was "additional to the existing twelve, and to be paid by the estate left expressly for it."[17] For Farmer the Fellowship was but a temporary step in his progress, for the next year he proceeded M.A. and became a Foundation Fellow, Tutor, and possibly one of the curates of Swavesey Church. On October 1 of the same year he was elected Lecturer and Hebrew Lecturer, positions he was to hold again in 1766 and 1771, having been one of four sublecturers in 1759 and 1762. It was in 1760, soon after the coronation of George III, that Joseph Cradock "attended an able Lecture by Mr. Farmer, on Aristophanes" (*Memoirs*, I.13). Dyer stated that the "first books that he [Farmer] lectured in were Euclid's Elements, Aristophanes, Tully's Offices, the Amphictyon [*sic*] of Plautus, and Hurd's Horace. In later periods he lectured in Quintillian, Grotius de Veritate Religionis Christianae, and the Greek Testament." The same authority noted that "By his pupils, as formerly by his fellow students, he was generally esteemed, though his want of punctuality exposed him to frequent censure from their parents" (393). In 1765, and again in 1769 and 1773, he became Steward, while in 1766, 1771, and 1778 he was elected Dean and Greek Lecturer. By 1775, when he was elected Master, he had held most of the College offices.[18]

From 1760, when he became a Fellow of the College, to 1775, when he was elected Master and subsequently Vice-Chancellor of the University, other events, both in and outside of the University, were taking place. On 15 February 1761 Farmer was ordained priest at Ely, taking his Bachelor of Divinity degree in 1767, the statutory seven years after proceeding Master of Arts. On 19 May 1763 he was elected a Fellow of the Society of Antiquaries, doubtless because it was known that he was gathering materials for a history of the city and antiquities of Leicester. Elected on the same day were Samuel Felton and James Petit Andrews. Felton was to arouse controversy later in the century with his purchase of the alleged only genuine portrait of Shakespeare. Andrews was both an antiquary and a historian; his *Anecdotes, Ancient and Modern* (1789) would have endeared him to Farmer. The Master and Fellows of Emmanuel met on 23 May 1765 and "unanimously elected" Farmer "Proctor of the University &. Mr Blackall Moderator, for ye Year ensuing" (Order Book, 60), by which election Farmer was designated as their choice of Proctor, the actual election being by the Senate on October 10 each year, with two Colleges nominating candidates for the office according to a fixed cycle.[19] In

Early Years

23

1769 Farmer became one of the twelve Preachers at the Chapel Royal at Whitehall. Dyer wrote that while in London to fulfill his duties as one of the Whitehall preachers, Farmer's "place of residence was usually the house of Dr. Anthony Askew, a physician of Queensquare, Bloomsbury, formerly of Emanuel College, Cambridge. This gentleman was a respectable scholar, more particularly distinguished by his acquaintance with Greek literature, and possessed of a liberal and communicative spirit." Askew, Dyer added, had "a magnificent library of printed books, enriched by a most valuable collection of manuscripts" (394). Askew died in 1774, and while his library, i.e. his books, was put up for sale in 1775, it was not until 1785 that his manuscripts were sold, with Farmer buying heavily for the University library.

In 1774 Farmer was elected Lady Margaret Preacher, an office that brought him £10 per year and that he kept until 1782. It is curious that Farmer followed Henry Hubbard, Lady Margaret Preacher from 1752–74, in this office of the University as well as Tutor at Emmanuel, and it was Hubbard who was offered the Mastership of Emmanuel in 1775 and declined it because, according to Nichols, of "age and infirmities." William Cole, whom Nichols quotes, wrote of Hubbard, "who, having with his wonted moderation and disinterestedness, declined that honour, gave his full suffrage to his friend Mr. Farmer" (*Lit. Anecd.*, II.629 and n.). Hubbard was the mathematical tutor when Farmer was admitted to Emmanuel. It was in 1775, the year that he became Master of his College and Vice-Chancellor of the University, that Farmer became a Doctor of Divinity, a degree "not lightly acquired, for in keeping his act the candidate was expected to attain a standard of scholarship worthy of the highest intellectual honour which the University could confer. His learning and adroitness were severely tested; and, if he was a scholar of established reputation, it was customary, at least in the eighteenth century, for the Regius Professor of Divinity to oppose him in person."[20] In 1775 the Regius Professor of Divinity was Zachary Brooke, Fellow of St. John's, remembered, when remembered at all, for his *Defensio miraculorum quae in ecclesia christiana facta esse perhibentur post tempora Apostolorum*, published in Cambridge in 1748. Cole wrote of Brooke's book that he had "distinguished himself by writing against Dr. [Conyers] Middleton, but in a language that made it less taken notice of than had it been in English" (*Lit. Illustr.*, IV.371n.). It was in February 1775, soon before Farmer became Master, that he went to Lichfield to present the College's congratulatory letter to the Bishop of Lichfield and Coventry on his promotion to that office.

On 27 June 1778 John Barnardiston, principal librarian of the

24   Early Years

University, died, and Farmer was elected librarian. The other candidate for the post was Francis Wilcox, also a Fellow of Emmanuel.[21] Farmer held the post until his death in 1797. Two years after his election as librarian he was "collated by Bp. Hurd, then Bishop of Lichfield and Coventry, to the Prebend of Andrews, and the Chancellorship annexed, founded in the Cathedral Church of Lichfield, vacant by the death of Dr. Green, Dean of Salisbury," according to Nichols (*Lit. Anecd.,* II.632). Richard Hurd, an Emmanuel man, had been nominated to the See of Lichfield and Coventry on 30 December 1774 and consecrated on 12 February 1775. Two days later Farmer and Askew had borne the College's congratulatory letter to the new Bishop,[22] one circumstance which doubtless led to the somewhat biased accusation that Farmer rose in the church through the influence of Hurd and other friends in high places. Dyer stated that "Dr. Farmer's literary character, and particularly his reputation justly acquired by his Essay on the learning of Shakespeare, which could hardly be diminished by his good friend at court, Dr. Hurd, were favourable circumstances to him on his way to preferment," adding that Farmer's "ecclesiastical honours were connected with his political conduct at Cambridge" (399). Two years after his collation to the Chancellorship of Lichfield, Farmer was installed as Prebendary of Canterbury Cathedral in March 1782, "through the recommendation of Lord North, then Premier," according to George Gleig in the *Encyclopedia Britannica* (1797, vol. I of Supplement, 641)—another supposed instance of strings being pulled. It was when he went to kiss hands at Court for this last preferment that the King very politely asked,

> "Whether the University was flourishing, and what Noblemen were resident; and told him, that he could wish every one of that rank had as good principles instilled into them as the Earl of Westmorland." Dr. Farmer had before told Mr. Cole, that Charles Fox, the vehement haranguer in Parliament against the Court, had publicly reflected upon him, as breeding up the Earl, his pupil, in Emanuel and Tory principles: the mention, therefore, of this Earl to Dr. Farmer was as polite as *a propos.* The Queen, who came to him in her broken English, accosted him thus—"Doctour! in what part of the Kingdom, do you reside?"—"Always at Cambridge, Madam."—"Oh, College!" replied her Majesty, and gave him joy of his preferment. (*Lit. Anecd.,* II.633–34)

John Fane, tenth Earl of Westmorland, was admitted to Emmanuel College on 25 January 1776 at age seventeen and was made Master of Arts in Right of Nobility in 1778. Since Farmer had become Master in 1775, the Earl could not properly be called his pupil, although

Early Years 25

influence of the one on the other was not impossible. William Bennet, later Bishop of Cloyne, was the Earl's tutor.

The Earl of Westmorland became a friend of William Pitt's while at Cambridge. Both men were born in 1759. Pitt was admitted to Pembroke College in 1773 at the tender age of thirteen; matriculated Michaelmas term 1775; and was made Master of Arts the following year. Hence, the two could not have had too much time together at Cambridge, although, according to the *DNB*, they became friends for life. Seven years after becoming a Prebendary of Canterbury Cathedral, Farmer, according to Gleig, resigned the Prebend "on being preferred by the late Mr. Pitt, then Premier, to a Residentiary of St. Paul's." Nichols, who quotes Gleig, is, however, the source for the following anecdote that he quotes in his *Literary Anecdotes:* "In an hour or two after he received the official information of his appointment, I met him near Amen Corner; and he pleasantly observed to me, "I could now, if I thought proper, cheat the Minister; for I have in my pocket an appointment to the Residentiary of St. Paul's, without having resigned the Prebend of Canterbury' " (II.634). Those who saw Farmer's ecclesiastical preferments as resulting from a form of old boys' network could point to the Earl of Westmorland, indoctrinated at Emmanuel, and his friendship with Pitt. The letter in which Pitt as much as assured Farmer of a Residentiaryship of St. Paul's is extant. It is addressed from Downing Street and dated Feb. 6, 1788. "Dear Sir," he wrote,

> As one of the Residentiaryships of Sr Pauls will before long become vacant by the appointment of the Bishop of Carlisle to the Deanery of Windsor, and as that Preferment is certainly more eligible than the State you at present hold at Canterbury, I shall be happy if you will give me Leave to recommend you to the King, to succeed both, and think myself fortunate in an opportunity of shewing the Regard & Esteem with which I am, Dear Sir,
>
> Your most obedient
and faithful Servant
W Pitt
>
> Revd Dr Farmer (Bodleian MS Eng lett c 144 f. 200^r)

One significant result of Farmer's becoming a Residentiary of St. Paul's became known through a letter that Michael Lort, Farmer's friend, wrote to Bishop Percy on 21 May 1788. Lort feared an earlier letter to Percy had miscarried:

> for I think I mentioned in it our friend Dr. Farmer's succeeding Dr. Douglas in a residentiaryship of St. Paul's, supposed now to be worth

26   Early Years

1,000l. a year, on the strength of which he renewed his proposals of
marriage to Miss Hatton, whose father, the late Sr. T. Hatton, had resisted
the former proposals; but now the young lady and her mother very readily
acceded to them, and the former was ushered to Amen Corner to give
directions about the house, and to a painter to sit for her picture. But so it
happens, that the lover's cold fit is come on, and he has absolutely declined
all further proceedings. No good reason has yet been publicly assigned, so
that all his friends, as well as the lady's, are much hurt, none more than
G. Steevens, the common friend of both, under whose guidance and
direction the whole business has proceeded, and was to have been completed. (*Lit. Illustr.*, VII. 495)

Lort, although the only authority for this story, must be believed, for
he was intimate with both Farmer and Steevens. Indeed, Reed records
a number of occasions when he, Lort, Farmer, and Steevens dined
together or visited some popular London locale.[23]

Gleig, least reliable of authorities, wrote that "In early life, at least
before he [Farmer] was advanced in years, he had felt the power of
love, and had suffered such a disappointment as sunk deep in his
mind and for a time threatened his understanding" (641). Henry
Meen, Fellow of Emmanuel, a friend of Farmer's, corrected Gleig: "It
was not at an early, but at an advanced, though not a very late, period,
that an attachment of the kind here alluded to was formed."[24] Dyer
says nothing about any romantic attachments, simply recording that
"While curate of Swavesey, Farmer formed an intimacy with Sir
Thomas Hatton, a good-humoured county gentleman, of Madingly in
Cambridgeshire. In the year 1767 he took the degree of bachelor of
divinity" (*Annual Necrology*, 394). On the same page on which he
quoted Gleig on Farmer's disappointment in love, Nichols added a
footnote,

> This attachment, formed whilst curate of Swavesey, when his situation in
> life was inadequate to the union, continued for many years unimpaired:
> and, when his fame and fortune rendered his situation in life at least
> adequate to the rank of the object of his affections, he began to think
> seriously of Matrimony; but, on mature reflexion, found that his habits of
> life were then too deeply rooted to be changed into those of domestic
> arrangements with any probable chance of perfect happiness to either
> party.—Mr. Cole, however, says, "Dr. Colman told me, May 3, 1782, that
> he had it from sufficient authority, that Sir Thomas Hatton had refused his
> eldest daughter to Dr. Farmer, but on what foundation he knew not. The
> lady is 27 or 28, and Dr. Farmer about 47 or 48. It will probably be a
> great mortification to both, as to every one it seemed that their regard for
> each other was reciprocal. Dr. Farmer's preferment is equal to 800l. *per
> annum;* and I guess the lady's fortune, there being six daughters and two
> sons, not very great" (*Lit. Anecd.*, II.637).

Early Years   27

Nichols does not mention the Hattons, but his reference to the Swavesey curacy plus the naming of names in Cole's manuscript note makes it clear that he too was referring to them. It will be noted that Lort told Percy that Farmer "renewed his proposals of marriage to Miss Hatton, whose father, the late Sir T. Hatton, had resisted the former proposals." Thanks to Cole's note one can approximate the time of the first proposals, i.e., 1782 or 1783 when Farmer was about forty-seven or forty-eight.[25] Reed records only one time when he, Farmer, and Sir Thomas Hatton were in the same company, at a dinner given by Steevens in Cambridge on 16 September 1782. On two later occasions, 1786 and 1787, Reed dined at Sir Thomas's; Farmer was not of the company.[26] Sir Thomas must, however, have been in Farmer's company more often, as he appears in the Emmanuel Parlour Book as a wagerer in 1783.[27]

There is another, much later account of the whole affair, this one by Gunning, writing his *Reminiscences,*

> It was about this period that a circumstance occurred which caused Farmer considerable uneasiness, nor did he ever completely get over it. It had been long whispered in the University, that Farmer had made proposals to a daughter of Sir Thomas Hatton; that he was accepted by the lady, but that the father (although on the most intimate terms with Farmer) positively refused his sanction to their marriage. When the Baronet died, it was fully expected that the engagement would be made public; but, to the surprise of all who knew the parties, it was terminated in the most unexpected manner. Farmer employed Harwood to communicate to the lady his change of sentiments. A more unsuitable ambassador could not have been selected to make a communication of so delicate a nature; though it was a prevailing opinion that Farmer could scarcely have employed a more *willing* envoy, as Harwood was for the most part a resident at the Lodge, and his position there must have been considerably changed by Farmer's marriage. Both Harwood and Farmer were attacked with epigrams without end, to which (although the Public Orator could not miss so fair an opportunity of attacking Harwood) Tweddell was the principal contributor. (I.167–68)

Sir Thomas died on 7 November 1787, and Farmer wasted no time in renewing his suit. Busick Harwood, who had become Profesor of Anatomy in 1785, had migrated from Christ's College to Emmanuel and was often in Farmer's company. Gunning wrote of him that "his conversation was profligate and licentious to the extreme" (*Reminiscences,* I.48). John Tweddell, Fellow of Trinity, was no friend of Farmer's.[28] The Public Orator was William Lort Mansell, "generally known as the chief wit and mimic of academic society."

Thomas Martyn, writing sixty years after leaving Emmanuel, maintained that it was the impossibility of Farmer's marrying Miss Benskin

28   Early Years

(see page 19) that "affected his mind very deeply, and was the source of his peculiarities. Of his later connexion with Miss Hatton I cannot speak with the same certainty, because at the time I did not reside in the University, and our intimacy had ceased . . . Dr. Colman was likely to know the truth of the affair with Miss Hatton" (*Lit. Anecd.*, VIII.421). William Colman was admitted a sizar at Corpus Christi College, Cambridge, in 1745 and became a Doctor of Divinity in 1778. In 1759 he was Vicar of St. Benet's, Cambridge, and was elected Master of Corpus Christi 25 June 1778. He was twice Vice-Chancellor, in 1779–80 and 1793–94, his career somewhat parelleling Farmer's. He and Farmer were friends and their names were sometimes linked, as when Cole, friend to both, told Richard Gough that if he visited Cambridge in 1779, he would insure that Colman, Farmer, and Robert Masters of Corpus Christi would meet him (*Lit. Anecd.*, I.681). That same year, Cole, writing to Walpole, told him that he had sent copies of Walpole's Letter to the editor of the *GM* on the Chatterton controversy to Colman, Farmer, and Doctor Glynn (Walpole, II.149). And it was in a letter from Cole to Walpole, dated 10 March 1780 that he told him of "a curious double mistake of Dr Kippis":

> On the last day of February the Masters of Benet [i.e. Colman, Benet being the old name for Corpus Christi] and Emmanuel calling in here [Milton] on their ride, seeing the *Biographia* [*Britannica*, edited by Kippis] on the table, on my mentioning Bishop Bull, they turned to look at it, and fell upon Eustace Budgell, p. 693, where seeing the epitaph and epigram (which stand glaringly in view) produced by Dr Kippis as specimens of the fine taste and poetical abilities of Mr Budgell, Dr Farmer read them aloud. After a moment's pausing, he said that the epitaph, he was sure, was the last two lines of that made on Queen Elizabeth, and is on her tomb in Westminster Abbey, recorded by Camden in his *Remains*. . . . Dr Colman averred that the distich or epigram on the bad dancers to good music was by Mr George Jeffries of Trinity College, and published in some miscellaneous poetry which he had by him (Walpole, II.202).

Reed records only two occasions in which he was in the company of the two, once in London in April 1783 when they dined at Holyland's Coffee house (125) and once in October 1793 in Cambridge when they dined in Emmanuel College Hall (201). Colman, who told Cole, "from sufficient authority," of Sir Thomas Hatton's refusing his daughter to Farmer, said nothing of any great emotional effect on Farmer. Cole thought it would "probably be a great mortification" to both Farmer and Miss Hatton, but that, too, does not point to dire emotional or psychological consequences. Hence it is only Gleig, who

Early Years 29

barely knew Farmer, and Martyn, writing, as he said, sixty years after the event, and naming Miss Benskin, not Miss Hatton, who are the sources for the alleged devastating effect Farmer's amorous reversals had upon him.

Dyer, Reed, and Nichols all laud Farmer for his active role in the movement to introduce sculpture into St. Paul's Cathedral during his term as Residentiary. Reed wrote that if Farmer "was not the first mover, he was certainly the most strenuous advocate for promoting the art of Sculpture, by the introduction of Statuary into the Metropolitan Cathedral: and many of the regulations on the subject were suggested by him, and adopted in consequence of his recommendation." Nichols, describing himself as "an active agent" in promoting a statue of John Howard, the prison reformer, testified to "the readiness with which the Right Reverend the Dean and the rest of the Dignitaries of the Cathedral (Dr. Jeffreys, Dr. Farmer, and Dr. Jackson) acceded to the proposal." Dyer also maintained that the public was "principally indebted to the exertions of Dr Farmer" for the introduction of sculpture into what Reed, possibly recalling Farmer's own description of St. Paul's, described as "the most beautiful stone quarry in Europe" because of "the desolate state of the fabric." Dyer's is the most circumstantial account of the matter. "The idea," he wrote,

> was first started in a conversation at Mr. Tuffin's, in Lower Thames-street, at which Mr. Romney, Mr. Banks the statuary, Mr. Horne Tooke, Mr. Sharpe, and Mr. Seward, were present. It was forwarded by Farmer to the Chapter, and, as if it was intended to bear testimony to the liberal party among whom the idea was first started, the statues first erected in St. Paul's have been those of Mr. Howard and Dr. Johnson.[29]

Romney, Sharpe, and Seward belonged to one or another of the two clubs of which Farmer was a member. Farmer's interest in prints and portraits, sufficiently attested to in the sale catalog of his library, extended to sister arts.[30]

It is on good authority that Pitt twice offered Farmer a Bishopric, although Gleig, whom Nichols quotes, mentions only one offer, and that made "as a reward for the constitutional principles which he was at pains to propagate, not only in his college, but as far as his influence went, through the whole University." Dyer's is the fullest account of those last two preferments—Canterbury and St. Paul's:

> Dr. Farmer had not yet arrived at the zenith of his prosperity, and, indeed, declined being raised to that point, to which the present minister was inclined to advance him. The offer of a bishoprick was twice made him by Mr. Pitt: the promise, at least, of his influence, made personally, as

30   Early Years

well as by letter, may be, as it always is, considered as the sure forerunner
of advancement.

But the truth is, the solemnity and formality of the episcopal character
would have sat but awkwardly on Farmer. He chose to move without
restraint and to enjoy himself without responsibility: to use his own
language to a friend, "One that enjoyed the theatre, and the Queen's
Head, in the evening, would have made but an indifferent bishop."

A piece of preferment, however, was soon conferred on him by Mr. Pitt,
no less agreeable to his taste, in point of situation, than valuable in point
of income, a residentiaryship of St. Paul's. This was given him in exchange
for the prebend of Canterbury. It was agreeable to his taste, as requiring
three months in residence in the capitol, and only three, in the year;
enabling him to enjoy in succession his literary clubs in London, and his
literary retreat at Cambridge. It was valuable, for its clear income is twelve
or fourteen hundred a year, besides perquisites, which, though not easily
ascertained, are considerable.

The ingenious, good-humoured doctor now expressed himself in terms
of perfect satisfaction. He looked for nothing higher. He enjoyed a plentiful income himself, and, possessing with it a considerable share of
patronage, had the means (an important consideration to a kind-hearted
man) of rendering essential services to his friends.

Independently, therefore, of the political principles originally imbibed
by Dr. Farmer, it was natural enough for him to express, and, in his
conduct through life, to exhibit, a warm attachment to Mr. Pitt, and to
support with great cordiality the measures of his administration. (398–
99)

That the offer was made twice is corroborated by both Reed and
Henry Meen, the latter writing that Farmer "declined both an Irish
and English bishoprick" (*European Magazine*, February 1800, 116),
and the former specifying that Farmer "might have had the Bishoprick
of Dromore in exchange with Ekins for his Prebend of Canterb.ʸ If he
had chose it" (Folger MS. M.A. 138, fol. 17ʳ). Jeffery Ekins was
installed Dean of Carlisle when Thomas Percy became Bishop of
Dromore in 1782, which suggests Ekins would have gone to Canterbury, Percy would have remained Dean of Carlisle, and Farmer would
have gone to Ireland. Ekins, who was created Doctor of Divinity at
Cambridge in 1781, must have been rumored to be about to be
offered the Deanship of Carlisle when the offer to Farmer was made.
Since the notebook in which Reed made his statement is labeled
"Memoranda taken at Cambridge During my stay in Emanuel Col-
lege. Sept.ʳ 1784," there is the very strong probability that his infor-
mant was Farmer himself. Unfortunately, the entry "M. 27th
[September] Set off for Cambridge with Mr. Steevens" followed by
"W. 20th Octr. At Covent Garden. Saw *The Hypocrite*" in Reed's

Early Years

31

diary for 1784 (134) reveals nothing about his stay at Emmanuel that year.

The last two notable events of Farmer's career were his election to a Fellowship of the Royal Society on 1 March 1791 and his being admitted *ad eundem gradum*, i.e., as Doctor of Divinity, at Oxford. These are the bare bones, to be fleshed out with detailed accounts of his early efforts at belles lettres, his tenure as Master of Emmanuel, his two terms as Vice-Chancellor of the University, his health, and related matters.

There is but one extant published undergraduate poetic effusion by Farmer, a poem published in a collection compiled for the occasion of the laying of the foundation stone for the east front of the University library by the Duke of Newcastle, Chancellor of the University, on 30 April 1755.[31] There are thirty poems of varying length, both in Latin and English, a number of them by undergraduates. George Dyer, a prejudiced judge because of his friendship with Farmer, wrote of Farmer's effort that it was "very poetical, and to me it appeared to surpass every one I read in that collection for classical elegance," an opinion he later qualified, "Not setting up for the Arbiter Elegantarium of every thing in the Cambridge poems addressed to the Duke of Newcastle, I allude, in a way of comparison, only to the few copies of verses that I have read in that collection."[32] While twenty of the fifty-two lines of the poem are quoted elsewhere,[33] it may be well to quote the whole poem that it may be judged in its entirety.

> HASTE, young-eyed May! and gently pour
> From bosom green thy balmy store:
> Bid violets paint their azure beds,
> And daffodils with bending heads,
> And tulip gilt, and primrose fair
> Sweetly catch the laughing air.
> Bring Joy along, thy eldest born,
> And Plenty with her flowing horn;
> Whilst Birds of many a various wing
> To *Cam* in wildest woodnotes sing,
> Who sees approach his *sedgy* Throne
> The State's great Patron, and his own.
>   Hail, PELHAM by whose fav'rite hand
> *Peace* yet strews olive round the land:
> See, EUROPE's groans betray despair;
> Her trembling Ballance asks thy care:
> And if no human art can guide
> The pendant weight on either side,
> If sacred GEORGE at length shall cease
> To bid the world be blest in Peace,

Early Years

Of crowns in vain shall *Lewis* dream;
His scale shall mount, and kick the beam.
  Whenc then, *Britannia*, the big tear,
Lest Song detain thy Patriot's ear?
His noble breast at once is free
To guard the well-lov'd Muse, and Thee.
See, *Learning* marks his chosen way
With many a beam of early day;
And louring *Ignorance* gives place
To Science, with averted Face;
Whilst PELHAM bids the column rise,
And tell his bounty to the skies.
Now smiles old *Cam,* and scatter'd finds
His *Gothic* dust the sport of winds;
Nor envy *Isis,* who erewhile
Boasted her Mausolean Pile.
On Domes depends not PELHAM's name:
But be *They* founded on *His* fame!
Haste, ye Muses, to prepare,
Sweet flowrets for your Guardian's hair;
Beneath His banner safe engage,
And brave the *Vandals* of the age.
For Him your choicest lawrels bring,
Who lifts ev'n Me on Fancy's wing:
For Him let Nature's face be gay,
All be mirth, and holyday!
But when the ruddy Eve steals on,
And tips the grove with mantle brown;
When swings the solemn *Curfeu* slow,
Far absent be, thou Bird of woe!
Nor close the day with hoarseness drear,
This fairest daughter of the year!
                    Richard Farmer, Scholar of Emmanuel College

This is neither better nor worse than many of the verses printed in the *GM* in mid-century. The influence, if the word be not too grandiose, of Milton is not far to seek.

The year before entering university Farmer attempted a work on a grandiose scale, no less than a tragedy in three acts entitled, "Charles the Bold, Duke of Burgundy." The manuscript in Farmer's hand, Cambridge University Library shelf mark Add. 4494, has the following on the fly leaf, reading from top to bottom, "These *childish* performances are in many hands. I wish they were all burnt, lest some Rogue or Fool should hereafter reprint them." "Liber Rich.[d] Farmer 1752." "Thos. Farmer Cooke. 1854." The first must have been written some years after the play was written and possibly performed.

Early Years

Thomas Farmer Cooke was Richard's grandnephew. Immediately after the title-page, the lower third of which had been torn off, is a prefatory statement, "To my much beloved & worthy Sc^hoolfellows, The Company of Performers," which reads,

> Gentlemen
>
> I shan't enter into many Apologies for the Following Trifle, since if It is tolerable, It does not need any, & if bad, They won't much mend It; yet One Thing I must precaution you of, I mean the little Time I had to finish It in (which, as I had almost swore to do ye HolyDays, I perform'd in little more y^n a Week) but that I believe I need not have mention'd, since the Hurry & ill Correction visible thro' the Whole, abundantly show It. However what It is, I humbly submit it to your Censure, & as It is something Odd for such a Boy as me to venture at a Peice of a Play, & lest more experienced Critics dam It on y^t very Account, I'le give ^them you a substantial Reason why I wrote It, first, because I cou'd not find any Thing for us to perform, & secondly to have an opportunity of telling you all together how much I am, Gentlemen, your most oblig'd, most obedient & humble Servant,   Rich^d. Farmer.

The Dramatis Personae and the actors are The Duke, Mr. New; Otto, his brother, Mr. Farmer; Rhynsault, the Duke's favorite, Mr. Palmer; Philip, his creature, Mr. Neal; Danselt, a merchant, Mr. Rogers; Saphira, his wife, Mr. Tilly; and Leiutenant [*sic*] of the Bastile, Mr. Von. Also, "Mob, a drunken Cobler, Guards, Attendants, &c." The scene was "Dola, at y^t Time the Metropolis of Burgundy." Thomas Neale preceded Farmer to Emmanuel College, admitted as a pensioner on 9 November 1752, taking his B.A. degree with Farmer in 1757 and then his M.A. in 1776. John Palmer was admitted a Fellow-Commoner to Emmanuel on 7 November 1752, but evidently did not proceed to a degree, succeeding his father as fifth baronet in 1765. None of the others entered Cambridge University.

The play, in blank verse, occupies twenty-seven and a half pages, and is loosely based on the life of Charles the Bold, Duke of Burgundy (1433–77). The names of the characters in the play are invented. I quote the opening speech of the play in which Otto addresses the Duke and the last six lines in which the moral is drawn.

> Take my Advice, my Liege, discard this Rhynsault,
> He's grown a Pestilence to all th' Court!
> Hug not this dang'rous Viper in your Bosom,
> But shake him off betimes, lest grown familiar
> He suck your Blood, I mean, your People's Love.

34 Early Years

Let Mortals hence, as in a Mirrour, see,
The dire Effects of smooth-tongued Flattery;
Nor let an honest Man be e're cast down,
Tho' for the Present, Fortune seems to frown:
Let him with Mind sincere in Patience wait,
And he shall surely find an happy Change of Fate.

I have found no other reference to the play or to its possible performance. Perhaps some slight significance attaches to the fact that Gerrard Andrewes, headmaster of the Leicester Free Grammar School, was praised because "by constantly attending Garrick, he read better than almost any man."[34] Possibly some of Andrewes's penchant for the dramatic rubbed off on young Farmer.

Farmer's Liber extends to another seventeen and a half pages, all still in his hand. Seriatim, they are devoted to A Prologue; Another Epilogue; An Invocation to the Muses; the Epistle of Dido to Æneas, burlesqued from Ovid (all in heroic couplets, the last running to six pages), a Poem in Imitation of Phillips beginning "Assist, Pierian Nine, a Bard who oft / With eager Lips has caught at Helicon, Celestial Spring" (two pages); Part of the 2^d Chapter of Proverbs, Imitated; A Soliloquy, spoke by M^r F——r on seeing Miss S—— (both blank verse), with four pages devoted to the Soliloquy); On the Fifth of November, A Poem ("Descend, O Muse with Pegasean Wing / Parnassus' Height, designing a while to leave," and for three pages); an Epigram; Another, in quendam Poetastrum; One from Owen, In Cornutum; Another, On One both Knave & Fool; Part of the first Chap: of Ecclesiasticus (with "School-Exercise" in square brackets and running to four pages, blank verse), a Pastoral, on the Return of Mr. Palmer (spoken by Thyrsis and Lycidas, names not hitherto unused, tipped in); The School-Boy's Day (three pages of blank verse); An Epilogue spoken by the Poet in Lethe, which was perform'd after the foregoing Play (actually *performed?*); Epigram from Baudasius; On the Return of a young Lady out of the Country; On two Beautiful Sisters. An Epigram; To my good Friends, the Criticks; and On the Prosecution of the Players, an Epigram. The young versifier did a bit of blotting, notably in the burlesque Epistle of Dido to Aeneas, searching for le mot juste. Here is one of the epigrams on page 42.

when
Old Jeptha's Daughter, ~~by~~ cross Fate assail'd,

(I've read)   Maidenhead
~~Full two~~ Months her ~~Virginity~~ bewail'd;

Early Years

Our Ladies too bewail Their's oft, yet None

Because   'tis safe   because
~~That it,~~ Like Her's ~~remains, but that~~ 'tis gone?

This small corpus of schoolboy verse is evidence of industry, not, certainly, of precocity.

Buried in a manuscript volume titled "Poems and Epigrams" in the Cambridge University Library (Add. 5805) is the one other extant piece of Farmer's versifying. The volume bears the words "James Plumptre Clare Hall 1793" and the statement that "Some of the things in this Collection were so abusive and gross that I cut them out, and did not continue it." In 1793 Plumptre was but twenty-two years old, having proceeded B.A. the previous year. In any event, and however he came to know of it, he copied these "Extempory Lines, by D.ʳ Farmer, at a Party where the names of all the Ladies toasted began with the letter B."

> Tis strange that Fortune should decree
> That all our favourites should begin with B
> But how to solve this paradox of ours?
> The Bee lights oftenest on the sweetest flowers.

These lines must have endeared him to all the ladies toasted.[35]

Farmer contributed but once more to a collection of occasional poems, this time on the occasion of the death of George II. The beautifully printed folio volume is titled *Academiae Cantabrigiensis Luctus in Obitum Augustissimi Regis Georgii II. Et Gratulationes in Serenissimi Regis Georgii III. Inaugurationem,* December 1760. All the Colleges were represented by one or more of their Fellows or Alumni. Besides Farmer, there were six other Emmanuel men, including the Master, Dr. William Richardson.[36] Poems in the volume were in Latin, Greek, Arabic, Hebrew, and, of course, English. Farmer's contribution was a Sonnet.

> Full little, blessed Spirit, need'st thou wear
>   The tinsel trappings of the Poets' train:
> Still be it their's to deck the Tyrant's bier,
>   And gild with lavish art the bloody reign.
> Ah, what th' avail? the Monarch's sung in vain,
>   Whose proper actions herald not his praise:
> But GEORGE will lustre through the colours plain
>   Of doubting Chroniclers in future days.
> Great King! be Thy foot guided by his rays;

36   Early Years

Inherit all the Honours of His mind:
Let soft-eyed Mercy wait Thy balanc'd ways;
    And laurel'd Peace shower olives on mankind.
Be Thy last Sun, in times far distant view'd,
Equally bright, and equally pursu'd.

All in all, given this small body of verse, admittedly by a schoolboy and then a young man—Farmer was twenty-five in 1760—one is grateful there is not more.

2

Master of Emmanuel College

On 21 March 1775, when Henry Hubbard declined the Mastership of the College because of his age—he was sixty-seven and was to die three years later—Farmer was elected Master, and served in that capacity until his death. On November 4 of this same year the new Master of Emmanuel was elected Vice-Chancellor of the University, prevailing over John Chevalier of St. John's College. And in the same year, probably the most eventful one of his life, he took the degree of Doctor of Divinity.

As Master of his College, Farmer came into his element. Despite strongly held political views, he was an essentially friendly and hospitable man, and despite the necessity for the formality of so many College and University ceremonies and events, he was informal by nature, often to the extent of sloppiness. William Cole, antiquary and friend of Farmer's, wrote of the friendship between Farmer and Thomas Gray,

it must have been about the Year 1770; as the first Time they ever met to be acquainted together, was about that Time, I met them at Mr Oldham's Chambers in Peter House to Dinner. Before, they had been shy of each other: and tho' Mr Farmer was then esteemed one of the most ingenious men in the University, yet Mr Gray's singular Niceness in the Choice of his Acquaintance made him appear fastidious to a great Degree to all who was not acquainted with his Manner. Indeed there did not seem to be any Probability of any great Intimacy, from the Style & Manner of each of them: the one a cheerful, companionable, hearty, open, downright Man, of no great Regard to Dress or common Forms of Behaviour: the other, of a most fastidious & recluse Distance of Carriage, rather averse to all Sociability, but of the graver Turn: nice & elegant in his Person, Dress & Behaviour, even to a Degree of Finicalness & Effeminacy. So that Nothing but their extensive Learning & Abilities could ever have coalesced two such different Men: & both of great Value in their own Line & Walk. They were ever after great Friends, & Dr Farmer & all of his Acquaintance had soon after too much Reason to lament his Loss, & the Shortness of their Acquaintance.[1]

38 Master of Emmanuel College

George Gleig, later to become Bishop of Brechin, wrote the biographical account of Farmer for volume one of the Supplement to the third edition of the *Encyclopedia Brittanica* (1797), 641–42. Gleig relied heavily on George Dyer's account of Farmer, his friend and former tutor, but was able to add a few personal reminiscences of Farmer as Prebendary of Canterbury Cathedral. Gleig wrote of Farmer's "want of attention to his external appearance, and to the usual forms of behaviour belonging to his station." In a somewhat exaggerated statement, he went on to add, "In the company of strangers, the eccentricity of his appearance and of his manners made him sometimes to be taken for a person half crazed." He claimed to have seen Farmer "one morning at Canterbury, dressed in stockings of unbleached thread, brown breeches, and a wig not worth a shilling." But, he concluded, "In his own College he was adored. In the University he had for many years, more influence than any other individual; and, with all his eccentricities, his death was a loss to that learned Body, which, in the opinion of some of its members, will not soon be made up." Reed, one of Farmer's closest friends, wrote of him, "As the Master of his College, he was easy and accessible, cultivating the friendship of the Fellows and inferior members by every mark of kindness and attention; and this conduct was rewarded in the manner he most wished, by the harmony which prevailed in the society, and by an entire exemption from those feuds and animosities which too often tore to pieces and disgraced other Colleges."[2]

Nichols, Reed, Dyer, and Gleig all left biographical sketches of Farmer. Gleig knew Farmer but slightly; Nichols and Reed were his contemporaries and much in his company. Dyer, a favored student under Farmer, both praised and condemned him. Joseph Cradock, nearly the same age as Farmer, a student at the Leicester Free Grammar School, had only good things to say about Farmer in his *Memoirs*. Henry Gunning, whose *Reminiscences* is one of the sources for anecdotes about Farmer, spoke well of him as dramatic critic at Sturbridge Fair, as Master of Emmanuel, as Vice-Chancellor, as a political animal, and as genial host in Amen House, Farmer's residence as Residentiary of St. Paul's. There are a few other scattered remarks about Farmer which should be recorded. Horace Walpole wrote to William Cole, Farmer's friend, on 9 March 1782, to tell him of Farmer's first visit to him: "Dr. Farmer has been with me, and though it was but a short visit, he pleased me so much with his easy simplicity and good sense that I wish for more acquaintance with him" (II.309). Although they met but once, and that in Cambridge, Samuel Johnson found a kindred soul in Farmer. Thomas Warton, writing to Richard Hurd in 1764, announced, "I have commenced a

Correspondence with a Mr Farmer of your College; who, though an Antiquarian, seems a very sensible and ingenious Man," an opinion he did not think necessary to change when he visited Farmer two years later.[3] Joseph Ritson, not the most charitable of men, visited Cambridge and met Farmer, finding him, as he wrote to a friend in 1782, "a most sensible, liberal, benevolent, and worthy man."[4] And in his *Remarks, Critical and Illustrative, on the Text and Notes of the Last Edition of Shakespeare,* published one year later, Ritson handled Farmer's notes gently, writing, of one of them, "The same ingenious and learned critic (whom every lover of Shakspeare, literature, and truth must always regard with the utmost gratitude and respect) observes" (100).

In his *Autobiography* Sir Samuel Egerton Brydges described Farmer as "complacent and indolent, surrounded by his cats and his books, and lost in his own bibliographical amusements: he was lax in his discipline and good-natured in his manners."[5] Brydges spent two years, 1780–82, at Queens' College, but as I have found no other possible connection with Farmer, the entire description, especially of the cats, which appears in no other account of Farmer, must be viewed with some suspicion. Dr. Samuel Parr, the so-called "Whig Dr. Johnson," wrote the Latin epitaph on Farmer for the College Cloisters and also the following, perhaps the finest tribute to Farmer.

> Of any undue partiality towards the Master of Emanuel College I shall not be suspected, by those persons who know how little his sentiments accord with my own upon some ecclesiastical and many political matters. From rooted principle and antient habit, he is a Tory—I am a Whig; and we have both of us too much confidence in each other, and too much respect for ourselves, to dissemble what we think upon any grounds, or to any extent: let me, then, do him the justice, which, amidst all our differences in opinion, I am sure that he will ever be ready to do to me. His knowledge is various, extensive, and recondite. With much seeming negligence, and perhaps in later years some real relaxation, he understands more, and remembers more, about common and uncommon subjects of Literature, than many of those who would be thought to read all the day, and meditate half the night. In quickness of apprehension, and acuteness of discrimination, I have not often seen his equal. Through many a convivial hour have I been charmed, by his vivacity; and upon his genius I have reflected in many a serious moment with pleasure, with admiration; but not without regret, that he has never concentrated and exerted all the great powers of his mind, in some great Work, upon some great subject. Of his liberality in patronizing learned men, I could point out numerous instances. Without the smallest propensities to avarice, he possesses a large income; and, without the mean submissions of dependance, he is risen to high station. His ambition, if he has any, is without insolence; his

40 Master of Emmanuel College

munificence is without ostentation; his wit is without acrimony; and his learning without pedantry. (*Lit. Anecd.*, II.647)

In a more restrained vein E. L. Shuckburgh, one-time librarian of Emmanuel, left a sober assessment of Farmer in two areas of the Master's duties or responsibilities. During his tenure as Master, Farmer, as might be expected, took thought for the health of the College library, for Shuckburgh states that "the increment of the library seems to have also accumulated in the hands of Farmer as Master. So that at the end of the century the library had £200 turnpike bonds, and a claim for £224. 14S. 5d. upon Farmer's executors, of which £60 was invested in more turnpike bonds" (198). Yet Farmer, as Master and, in fact, the bursar, did not do so well in other areas of College finances, for Shuckburgh bears evidence that the "increasing importance of the bursarship began with the closing years of Farmer's mastership, who was a poor man of business, and left the accounts between himself and the College in such confusion that the Bursar (Tyson) had the greatest difficulty in coming to a settlement with his heirs" (134). The latter statement accords well with accounts of Farmer's handling of his fees as tutor, for while the position of tutor was a fairly lucrative one, Farmer did not prosper therefrom. Gleig writes that Farmer's "accompts with some of his pupils, when Tutor of his College, were never settled to the day of his death; and the young gentlemen not infrequently took advantage of his unconquerable indolence to borrow of him considerable sums, well knowing that there was little chance of a demand being ever made on their parents" (641).

The everyday social life of a Master of a College might vary with the size, traditions, location, and other distinctive features of his College, but certain activities would be common in the lives of all. Visitors to the College, from those who enjoyed the hospitality of the College for a meal at high table to those who were put up in College for a period of days, had to be entertained in one fashion or another. One visitor to Emmanuel College in the years from 1782 to 1795, one who came virtually every year in that period, was Reed. Reed—bachelor, conveyancer, and anonymous editor of scholarly works—kept diaries. Most of his diaries are extant and have been edited. They throw considerable light on the activities of Farmer in those years, from some time in September to about mid-October, part of the period now known as the Long Vacation. This was also the period in which the famous Sturbridge Fair took place.

Farmer and Reed first met on 1 March 1782 while dining in London at the home of Dr. Richard Wright, physician, Fellow of

Emmanuel, and an avid book collector. One imagines that Reed and Farmer, bookish bachelors, took to one another immediately, their encounter leading to Reed's first visit to Emmanuel College. Both, incidentally, were sons of tradesmen: Farmer's father, a maltster; Reed's, a baker. Reed had met and become fast friends with George Steevens, another bookish bachelor and one who had been a Fellow-commoner at King's College, Cambridge. Indeed it was Steevens who rather engineered Reed's first visit to Emmanuel, for, writing to Farmer on 31 August 1782, he said "Reed is only desirous of hunting among your books for a day or two; and, with my usual freedom, I have promised him a lodging in old Bungay, which I hold to be the most black-lettered &c. archaeological part of your territories. He talks of being down on Monday night with nightcap &c. sheets" (Folger S.a.138). Steevens was already at Emmanuel when Reed arrived on 9 September 1782 at six o'clock. From the very first, after the obligatory visits to a number of Cambridge places of interest, largely the Colleges, Reed fell into a kind of routine, much of it in Farmer's company. Indeed, over the years when Reed visited Cambridge, there was hardly a day, except when Farmer was ill, or, more rarely, when Reed was himself indisposed, that the two did not spend some time together. And when Farmer was "confined with the Gout (1st time) of which he felt some symptoms in walking home last night" from Fen Ditton, Reed spent "the greatest part" of the next morning with him (149). When Reed went to take the Bath waters in 1796, Farmer wrote in commiseration, "I am truly sorry, that any *Disorder* would call you to *Bath*" (290). On his first full day at Emmanuel, Reed noted in his Diary that after breakfast "In Dr. Farmer's Library the best part of the Morning," after which he dined, walked about the Colleges, drank tea, all with Farmer, and spent the evening together with the Fellows of the College, Steevens, and guests. With some notable exceptions, this was the pattern of Reed's and Farmer's days. Much time was spent in libraries, that of Emmanuel, the Public Library (i.e., of the University, of which Farmer was Principal Librarian), the Pepysian library at Magdalene, and those of other Colleges. Much time was devoted to dining out as guests of various persons, both in and out of Cambridge. William Cole entertained them at Milton; Robert Masters, of Corpus Christi, at Landbeach; Sir John Cotton at Madingley. When the weather was good, they walked to some of these outlying villages; when bad, they went by coach. On a number of occasions, when they were to dine in Hall, the Emmanuel pond was dragged for a fish for the meal. On 4 October 1792 "The Pond was dragged for a Fish and one weighing 12¼ was taken from a vast number, some nearly of the same size" (195). On occasion, notably in 1795 when Farmer was

42 Master of Emmanuel College

sixty years old and Reed fifty-three, with nothing better to do, "The whole of this Morning after breakfast past in determining some bets about the possibility of a person going to sevl. parts of the College blindfold" (215).

These were not the only bets, although most were made in Hall. The Fellows of Emmanuel kept a Parlour Book, sometimes called a Wager Book, the first extant volume of which covers the period 1769–85; the second, 1786–90.[6] Herein were recorded the audits, fines for transgressing the rules of the Parlour, the acknowledgment of gratuities (i.e., bottles of wine given in honor or celebration of various occasions), other incidental information—and wagers. Much can be learned from these volumes, not least from the wagers recorded. Often, as noted in the matter of Farmer's birthday (above, page 15), the exact nature of the wager can only be guessed at since only the original betters knew the conditions of the wager. Thus, "Farmer versus Benson—no Brass" must remain a mystery, as will so many more, but "Farmer versus Mead—no war before commencement," recorded before the audit of 28 May 1771, lends itself to interpretation.[7] I give a few examples of various entries for Farmer, both before and after he became Master. It will be understood that with each new position or promotion he, as did the others, offered a gratuity of one or more bottles of wine. In 1771 he bet Blackall that "Ld North resigns before next Michaelmas" (36); in 1779 he bet Gage that "the 2^d Judge in the K: B: does not preceed the 3^d in the common pleas" (216), where "K: B:" is the King's Bench. In 1783 Reed bet him "that Lowth had not quoted or referred to the translations in the first book of B^p Warburton," Steevens also wagered on Farmer's side, the wagers "laid at Mr. Reed's Chambers" (274). And in 1784, two years after the publication of Reed's edition of the *Biographia Dramatica*, Farmer bet Oldershaw that "Havard's Play of K. Charles the first [is] in Mr. Reed's *Biographia Dramatica*" (294), as indeed it is (I.209).

Farmer paid his share of fines for a variety of reasons: appearing without buckles in Parlour; appearing in a morning gown; appearing in a new coat; "transgressing an [unspecified] order"; not preaching a Clerum; buying a horse; selling a mare.[8] He did not, as some others did in the Parlour, "talk nasty," nor was he guilty, as was Sir Stafford Northcote, of "putting the spitting-box upon the table" (190). Nor did he, either from forgetfulness or pedantry, quote Greek, as Askew did and was fined therefor (132). If one did not know from other sources the extent of Farmer's hospitality, one would learn that Homer recollected that "twenty dined at the Masters" on 27 December 1784 and bet Wilcox that his memory was good (312). This was on St. John's day and had become a tradition with Farmer by 1784.[9] Finally,

Master of Emmanuel College

although they remain a mystery, Farmer came into legacies on 14 September 1784, on 24 December 1786, and on 23 August 1790, the second of which was described as "Great" and the last as "little." On each occasion he gave a bottle.[10]

Both Farmer and Reed loved the theater, and they hardly missed a performance by the Norwich players during Sturbirdge Fair. The Fair also offered culinary treats. On 27 September 1782, during Reed's first visit, he and Farmer went to the theater and saw *The Clandestine Marriage* and *The Maid of the Oaks*. "After the Play the Master and myself went to a Booth and supped in company with some London Tradesmen" (121), and while the food was not mentioned on this occasion, at other times they feasted on oysters or pork at one of the booths. Two days later Reed "Lounged about the College with the Master, etc.; until 12 o'clock" (120), an admission too rarely encountered. Reed loved cards and he found a kindred soul in Farmer. On Reed's first visit, John Nichols, another of his friends, "came from London and he, Dr. Farmer, Dr. Pennington and myself played at Cards until 10 o'clock when we went home [Emmanuel] and supped in the Parlor" (121)—only one of many bouts of whist. Prior to Nichols's arrival, Reed and Farmer had been to the Fair, and when they returned, they "went first to the Castle Hill and then to Magdalene College," where Reed looked over some books.

Occasionally there were sightseeing excursions. Reed, Farmer, and two others agreed to go to Lord Howard's Audley End near Saffron Walden. Accordingly they went first to the village "and looked at the Church and Castle and from thence proceeded to the House and Gardens, where we were treated with fruit wine, etc." After exploring Lord Howard's home and estate, they returned to Cambridge, Reed adding as an afterthought, "At Saffron Walden Church we went into the family vaults where the bodies of the Howards repose" (147). This apparent interest in mortality coincides with Farmer's story, told him by the late Dr. Charles Collignon, that "the body of Mr. Sterne had been sent down to Cambridge and was anatomized. It was stolen from the burying ground beyond Tyburn where it was interred and was recognized by sevr. persons who knew him. I [Reed] remember Becket the Bookseller once told me that he, and I think another, were the only ones who attended the Funeral" (156).

The quiet of the 1789 Long Vacation was considerably disturbed by the suicide by hanging of Francis Dawes of Peterhouse, the Senior Bedell. Here is Reed's account:

He [Dawes] was to have dined yesterday at Mr. Bendish's but failed. It appears that at twelve o'clock he had ordered his hair dresser and his

44 Master of Emmanuel College

horse to be ready and had then walked out, After which he was not heard of for 30 hours untill he was found suspended in the turret where the bell is of the college. He had invited Lady Hatton and Mr. Vachell and their families to dine with him today and they came accordingly and were there when he was found. It was recollected by Mr. Steevens and Captn. Farmer that he had shewn some marks of absence of mind and derangement on Saturday and they accordingly went to give evidence before the Coroner's Inquest. After dinner I accompanied the Master to his room and communicated the melancholy account to him.

Dawes was "attended to the grave by Dr. Farmer, Mr. Steevens, Mr. Vezey, his Executor, Mr. Kendall, and the two beadles, Beverly and Mathew." Four days after the funeral "Dr. Farmer told me [Reed] he had just seen Dr. Plumptree the Professor, who in mentioning Dawes's Case said he had known instances wherein the stopping of the Piles [Dawes's condition] had occasioned a derangement of the Understanding" (171–73). Reed had met Dawes on his first visit to Emmanuel College; he and Farmer had dined in London at Dr. Wright's with Dawes; he and Farmer had dined twice at Peterhouse at Dawes's invitation; and in October 1788, one year before Dawes's suicide, he and Farmer and Dawes had dined in Landbeach at the home of Robert Masters.[11]

In 1794 Farmer and Reed and some others went to Robert Masters's home at Landbeach and dined there. Among the company was "Dr. Pearce, Master of Jesus" who "gave us this account of Mr. Coleridge who has just published a Drama called *The Fall of Robespierre*." The account continues,

He is one of three sons of a Devonshire Clergyman. His brother an Usher at Newcome's school Hackney. He has imbibed the wild democratic opinion floating about at present concerning religion and politicks. He is a disciple of Godwin, the Author of two 4^0 Volumes on the foundations of religion and politicks, and like him has entertained a foolish notion that the Life of man might be protracted to any length. He is an enemy to all establishments. or religion and conceives there should be no publick worship. He is also of opinion that every one should learn some mechanic art and has accordingly put himself an apprentice to a Carpenter. He is going to America. Dr. P. said that he (C.) was in town lately and having no money to carry him to Cambridge he wrote a poem, an elegy he thought, and sent it to Perry, the Editor of the *Morning Chronicle,* offering his correspondence to the paper and desiring the return of a guinea which he received. He asserts that his play was written in 8 hours. Dr. P speaks of him as a very ingenious young man, bating these extravagant and foolish notions which he entertains.

This is one of the earliest biographical sketches of Coleridge.[12]

Master of Emmanuel College 45

As has been noted, Farmer and Reed first met in London in 1782. Thirteen months later, and after Reed's visit to Emmanuel, they "Supped with Mr. Baynes," the other guests being "Mr. Ritson and Mr. Topham." The following day, April first, they dined "at Holyland's Coffee House with Dr. Colman" and later went to Covent Garden where they saw *A New Way to Pay Old Debts* and *Tom Thumb*. On April 4 they dined at Dr. Wright's; also present were "Mr. Henderson and Mr. Malone." This is the first time, according to Reed, that he and Malone and Farmer were together; thereafter they were together often. On 29 September 1787 Malone visited Emmanuel College while Reed was there. He stayed until October 13, spending virtually every day with Farmer and Reed, and left for London with Reed (154–57). Next year, on October 1, Reed recorded that he "went and sat with the Master, who was sitting for his picture for Mr. Malone to Mr. [Sylvester] Harding" (162). Two days later they dined at George Steevens's home; the three of them were alone (125). In the years from 1783 to 1793, Reed's diaries for 1794 and 1795–97, in which last year Farmer died, being either fragmentary or not extant, Reed and Farmer were together in London many days of Farmer's periods of residence in the city. Sometimes the two dined or went to the theater without other company. Steevens was an infrequent third—the necessity of walking back to Hampstead was probably the reason for the infrequency of his accompanying the other two. And in the course of the decade from 1783 to 1793 Farmer and Reed dined in the company of most of the prominent men in the scholarly, artistic, musical, and theatrical circles of London—Bishop Percy, Charles Burney, Arthur Murphy, Samuel Pegge, John Henderson, Alexander Pope (the actor), Edmond Malone, John Nichols, the two James Boswells, Sir Joshua Reynolds, George Romney, Michael Lort, Alderman Boydell, to name but a few. Often they were in the company of Oxford dons who were in London between terms. On Wednesday, 20 December 1786 Reed noted: "Dined at Sir Joseph Banks's. Present: Lady and Miss Banks, Sir Joshua Reynolds, Ald. Boydel, Dr. Blagden, Dr. Farmer, Mr. Steevens, Mr. Sayers, Mr. Boydel junr., Mr. Braithwte. and Mr. Nicol" (151). Farmer and Reed were increasingly, no matter what the rest of the company, invited out together or sought one another out, usually to go to the theater. In 1789, from February 4 to March 2 they were together, with others or alone, seven times; from February 5 to 19 March 1790, twelve times (165 and 175–76). On February 28 Reed "Dined at Dr. Farmer's with the Chapter. Afternoon at St. Paul's. Mr. Devie preached. Even. at Dr. F's," virtually the whole day spent together (175).

Farmer and Reed did not neglect some of the other attractions of

46   Master of Emmanuel College

London and its environs. They walked to Chelsea where they dined at
"Mr. Wynne's" who had inherited the estate of Little Chelsea, once
belonging to Narcissus Luttrell (133). In 1786 Farmer and Reed were
together on June 15, 16, 17, 19, and 20; on the seventeenth they,
Michael Lort, and Steevens went to John Palmer's New Theatre (144).
Next month Reed "Went to Osterly with Dr. Farmer, Romney, Irwin,
Long, Sharp, Green, and Nicol. Dined at Brentford. Even. at Vaux-
hall" (144). Osterley Park was and is famous for its Adam house and
fine furniture, and the friends had another full day there. When
Farmer and Reed had had enough of Holyland's Coffee House and the
Queen's Head, they, with Steevens, dined at Billingsgate (153), prob-
ably at the Three Tuns Tavern, the best-known eating place there. On
18 March 1791 the two, accompanied by Mr. Green, went "to see
Mme. D'Eon's Library" (188).

Farmer and Reed were both clubbable men. Dyer, again the authority, stated that "for many years he [Farmer] was a member of
different clubs, composed of men of letters, by whom he was much
esteemed," adding,

> Of this class was the Eumelean club, at Blenheim tavern, Bond-street, of
> which Dr. Ash was president; and of which Sir Joshua Reynolds, Mr.
> Boswell, Mr. Windham, M.P. Mr. Knight, M.P. Sir George Shuckburgh,
> Honourable Frederick North, Dr. Lawrence, M.P. Sir George Baker, Mr.
> Sharpe, Mr. Seward, Dr. Burney &c. were members: The Unincreasable
> club, Queen's head, Holborn, of which Mr. Romney, the painter, Mr.
> Long, Mr. Hayley, Mr. Braithwaite, Mr. Sharpe, Mr. Newbery,
> Mr. Topham, Dr. Beardmore &c. &c. were members. (401–2)

Dyer mistakenly thought Farmer was a member of Dr. Johnson's club
in Essex-street. Nichols supplied the corrective, i.e., that Farmer was
not a member of that club, but that he "was elected a member of the
Literary Club (founded by Dr. Johnson and sir Joshua Reynolds) Feb.
3, 1795." He also added that Reed was president of the Unincreasable
Club (*Lit. Anecd.*, II.638–39). Virtually all segments of the intellectual life of London were represented in the clubs to which Farmer
belonged: medical men, painters, politicians, authors, musicians (and
historians of music), publishers, lawyers, antiquaries, and churchmen.
Dr. Beardmore was Master of the Charter-house; Daniel Braithwaite,
a good friend of Reed's, was Comptroller of the Foreign Mails Department of the Post Office. A journalist, Edward Topham, was editor of
The World.[13]

Two occasions that lent themselves to special festivities in Emmanuel College were the annual observation of founder's day, cele-

Master of Emmanuel College 47

brated on September 29 unless that date fell on a Sunday, as it did in 1782 and 1793, and some Friday evening gatherings, almost invariably held at Emmanuel on alternate Fridays in September and October. These were called "The Family" or "Family night" and would seem to have persisted in some form until late in this century. Isaac Reed's entries in his diaries are the source for the Friday meetings, recording that they occurred when he was present in Cambridge in 1787, 1788, 1790, 1794, and 1795. He recorded four in 1790, two each in September and October (181, 183, 184, 186) and but two somewhere other than Emmanuel, one in October 1795 when, because he was wet and tired from walking back from Landbeach, he "declined an invitation to Mr. [James] Fawcett's (The Family) at St. John's" and went to bed (215). The first reference to the Family in the diaries is for 12 October 1787 when Reed "concluded the day with the Family Dr. [Busick] Harwood's invitation; President: Dr. Farmer, Mr. Masters, Mr. Barnes, Mr. Willcox, Mr. Malone, Dr. Harwood and myself" (156), evidence, incidentally, that the Family did not have a fixed membership and suggesting, what later entries bear out, that the Family met at one person's invitation. The following year Reed "Dined in the Hall and Spent the Evening at Dr. Barnes's, Peter House, with the Family" (163). Most of the Family nights, at least as recorded by Reed, whose stays were for a month, roughly from mid-September to about mid-October around the beginning of Michaelmas term, were held at Emmanuel, the two at St. John's and Peterhouse being the sole exceptions. From the scanty evidence of Reed's diaries, Family night seems to have been devoted, as were most nights in College, to a meal and conversation,[14] although the venue could be in the Fellows' rooms.

Reed records his first attendance on Founder's day in 1782 on the occasion of his first visit to Emmanuel when after breakfast at "Jude's and afterwds. lounged about the College untill eleven o'clock, then went to the Chapel, where Mr. Wilcox preached a Sermon in commemoration of the Benefactors to the Building. This was the Anniversary and an Entert. was provided to celebrate it. There were present 27 persons" (122). The succeeding entries confirm the pattern, a sermon in the Chapel by one of the Fellows of the College followed by a meal and entertainment in Hall rather than in the Parlour. While the sermon evidently did not attract great numbers—in 1786 those present were the preacher, Farmer, Reed, and Steevens, the last two being, of course, guests (149)—the following entertainment, including the festive meal, was well attended. Reed, a great one for detail, usually kept a tally, 26 in 1789, "only 27" in 1790, 22 in 1793, "The congregation [in Chapel] larger than usual, being at least 14 persons"

48 Master of Emmanuel College

in 1794 (208). Since there were only twelve Fellows of the College, the Founder's day feast included many guests, both from other Colleges and from outside the University. The grand occasion was the bicentenary celebration.

On 8 September 1784 Steevens wrote to Farmer:

My dear Friend & Master,
I shall trespass on your kindness for about ten or twelve days. A variety of circumstances deny me a longer absence from London. I wish I knew the number of your guests and the gage of their stomachs. Will no cunning mathematician, like Mr. Oldershaw, undertake this calculation? Two hundred weight of live turtle you will certainly receive; but how many people are necessary *to make nothing of it,* I am to seek. You had Wolsey in your eye when you employed this phrase.
—So looks the hungry feeder
Upon the savoury turtle that has nos'd him—
Then *makes him nothing*

Upon my word, if you will send me more circumstantial intelligence, turtles being as plenty as blackberries, you shall have enough of them.[15]

Not all academic occasions were as festive and enjoyable as others. Indeed, some were quite disagreeable, but Farmer, as Master of the College, had to attend. Cole records such occasions in a letter to Walpole dated 3 September 1778. Philip Yorke, second Earl of Hardwicke, was then High steward of the University, and gave annual official dinners. Cole wrote,

Lord Hardwicke's little enmities and meannesses are not unknown to this county. I heard a master of a college say in public company last year, and before some of his particular friends who endeavoured to defend him, that when he and his brethren paid their annual dining visit, they were always glad to get into their coach, for if he said nothing offensive, which was sometimes the case, his behaviour was so chilling and forbidding that, was it not for the disrespect, he would never go again. I heard Mr Lort say much to the same purpose two years ago. (Walpole, II.119)

The "master of a college" referred to is identified as Farmer; the "brethren" were the other heads of colleges.

Isaac Reed attended the celebration of the two hundredth foundation of Emmanuel, and while there is no mention of it in his diary for the year 1784, he did record "A List of those who dined at Emmanuel College 29 Septr 1784," broken down into the seating at the four tables.[16] Farmer, as Master, sat at the top of the first table; John

Master of Emmanuel College

Askew, as President, at the bottom. The honored guests, those at the first table, were the Earl of Westmorland, the Bishop of Peterborough, the Rt. Hon. William Pitt, ESQ., William Cockayne (Emmanuel M.A. 1775, as son of a nobleman), Lord Edmund Bacon, Lord John Cotton, Lord Edward Littleton, Lord John Borlase Warren, Lord Richard Chase (these last five were all Emmanuel men) George Pigott, ESQ. of Abington, Dr. Baker (Master of Christ's), Dr. Beadon (Master of Jesus), Mr. Torkington (Master of Clare and Vice-Chancellor), Soame Jenyns, ESQ., Dr. Cook (Provost of King's), and Dr. [John] Gooch (Prebendary of Ely). Farmer's close nonacademic friends—Reed, Steevens, and Malone—were seated at the third table in close proximity to Michael Lort, while John Nichols had a place at the fourth table. Reed's list of those at the celebration is on some of the blank end-pages of an anonymous fourteen-page pamphlet purporting to be *"An Account of the Festivation and Jubilee Holden at Emanuel College, Ynne Cambridge, September 29, 1684 . . . Nemo magis Rhombum stupuit."* Written in a crude attempt at seventeenth-century spelling, the pamphlet deals with the delivery and preparation of "Turtles fromme the Westerne Indies," those notables present and absent at the feast, the menu, and the music, and it concludes with a broad satire of Steevens as editor of Shakespeare. Reed wrote on the recto of the title-page, "The author of this Pamphlet is unknown. From the mistakes in it I should suspect he was not present at the Jubilee. This with three other copies directed for the Master—Mr. Askew & Mr. Wilcox—were dropt in the Hall of Emanuel College." John Askew was named the President of the College in Reed's list and sat at the bottom of the first table; Francis Wilcox, Fellow of the College, sat at the top of the second table.

In 1786 Farmer and the Fellows of Emmanuel came to the aid of one of their number, the Rev. Mr. James Devie. Devie was Vicar of Stanground cum Farcet. The Manor of Farcet belonged to Earl Brownlow who paid no tithe to the Vicar, according to long usage having to do with the tithe-free status of monastic lands. Despite the fact that no tithes had been paid on these lands for almost two hundred years, Devie claimed the tithe and set about to prove that the Farcet lands were not among the tithe-free lands. He brought suit against Earl Brownlow and won the case but had to pay costs of £2,600, and it was here that the College came to his aid. According to the College Order Book, under date of 18 May 1786, it was "Agreed That the Master be directed to give up to Mr. Devie his note for one hundred pounds, and to make him a present of fifty pounds toward the expense of his suit." Some four years later it was "Agreed That the Master be empower'd to put the College Seal, to an answer on the

50 Master of Emmanuel College

part of the College, in case depending between L.ᵈ Brownlow, and Mr. Devie." It was shortly thereafter that Devie triumphed.[17]

One would like to know a bit more about the County meeting, which took place on 6 July 1792 and in which Farmer played a prominent role. The meeting had been preceded by addresses to George III by the University on June 18 and by the Corporation of the town of Cambridge on June 30. The substance of the addresses, couched in similar language, was that both bodies reaffirmed their loyalty to his Majesty and expressed their approval of the measures adopted against "the wicked attempts of the enemies of our happy Constitution," in the words of the University address, and against "the pernicious attempts that have been made to unsettle the minds of your people, by specious arguments &. wild theories, tending to shake their attachment to that Constitution which for ages has been the admiration of the world," in the words of the Cambridge Corporation address. The proclamation, given on May 21 and delivered to both Houses of Parliament, was reprinted in *GM* for June 1792 (568) and was directed against the "wicked and seditious writings" being printed at the time with the admonition that all his Majesty's loving subjects contemn such writings and the command that all the Magistrates throughout the Kingdom be diligent to discover the authors and printers of those writings. Thomas Paine's *The Rights of Man* was one of the chief offenders. Cooper, in whose *Annals* the addresses are reprinted, reports the meeting in these words:

> On the 6th of July, a County meeting was held at which an address to the King, approving of the late proclamation, was agreed to. The address was proposed by the Earl of Hardwicke, seconded by Mr. Vachell, and supported by Mr. Yorke. A few words in opposition were said by Mr. Musgrave a reputable taylor and draper in the town, but the meeting did not seem much to acquiesce in his opinion. Mr. Hollick also, with great temper and propriety, "stated his reasons for not thinking the address necessary." [*Cambridge Chronicle,* 14 July 1792] Dr. Farmer created great merriment by illiberal allusions to Mr. Musgrave's trade, and concluded by a coarse jest having reference to an obsolete fashion in male attire.[18]

Henry Gunning, the chief source of anecdotal material about Farmer, reprints the University address to the king and the monarch's "most gracious answer" in his *Reminiscences,*[19] but seems not to have known, or remembered, the county meeting and the consequent notoriety, for notoriety there was. Soon after the confrontation between Musgrave and Farmer, an eighteen-page pamphlet was published in London with an elaborate title page, here reproduced.

Master of Emmanuel College

THE
BATTLE
BETWEEN
DOCTOR FARMER
AND
PETER MUSGRAVE,
THE
CAMBRIDGE TAYLOR;
IN HUDIBRASTIC VERSE;

With a Number of pleasant Quotations and admirable
EPIGRAMS this mighty Contest gave Birth to, particularly,
some happy Flights about the Doctor's celebrated

C*D-PIECE.
EMBELLISHED WITH
AN ETCHING OF THE BATTLE,
BY A CELEBRATED CARICATURIST.

What fashion shall I make your Breeches?
You must needs have them With a Cod-piece.

TWO GENTLEMEN OF VERONA.

Marry, here's grace and a Cod-piece.

LEAR.

LONDON:

———

PUBLISHED BY WILLIAM HOLLAND, NO. 50, OXFORD-
STREET.

———

1792.

52   Master of Emmanuel College

The etching shows Musgrave applying a pair of shears to Dr. Book-worm's codpiece and exclaiming, "D——n me I knew. twas right there's nothing in 'em," while a buxom female exclaims, "Bless me what a discovery." Dr. Bookworm, with a volume titled "Commen on Shakespr" bulging out of a pocket, is portrayed in a pugilistic stance, both fists at the ready, one eye asquint. Peter Taylor, the alleged author of the pamphlet, has this to say, among other things, in his prefatory remarks "To the Publisher,"

> Dr. FARMER'S elegant speech, as your Correspondent terms it, was *verbatim,* as follows:—"I should not have noticed what the learned gentle-man who last sat down, has said, if he had not made as free with ministers as with men upon his own shop-board. He reminds me of what my friend WILL. SHAKESPEARE says of *Jack Cade,* that *he wishes to put a new nap upon the Constitution.* What he has said, is as irrelevant to the subject before us, as a red cod-piece would be on a black pair of breeches."—He said not one word more, either good or bad, that I could hear; and yet he too is reported to have made an excellent speech in *favour of the Constitution!* To such ribaldry I would not *condescend* to reply, lest I should have sunk, in the esteem of sensible and worthy men, to a level with the Doctor: nor did I seek to revenge myself by any other means; the public suffi-ciently expressed their dislike, by attaching an epithet to his original name, which nothing is likely to obliterate. On the contrary, when I have seen inscriptions on the walls of public buildings, alluding to his conduct, I have ordered them to be rubbed out.
>
> Dr. *FARMER* is Master of a College, where he has nothing to do: he is Canon Residentiary of St. Paul's, where sometimes he reads prayers, for which he has One Thousand Pounds per annum. By the public confidence in my integrity I gain employ, which enables me to be superior to any meanness, and renders me independent of any body of men.

Dr. Farmer, in a second prefatory "To the Publisher," is supposed to be readying publication of his speech "delivered at the Town Hall," the title-page, already seen, "crammed with Mottos from his favourite Shakespeare," all having the word "cod-piece" in them. A doggerel-verse account of the events at the Town Hall is followed by six pages of "Epigrams by Peter Musgrave," virtually all having to do with Farmer's codpiece. One such epigram, the first, should suffice.

> In a public debate
> On affairs of state
>   The Doctor talks bold of the c*d-piece;
> But in private affairs
> The Doctor declares
>   The Ladies would think him an odd-piece.

Master of Emmanuel College   53

The other epigrams follow their leader faithfully. When one learns that Musgrave occupied premises on Emmanuel Street belonging to Emmanuel College, there is the arguable conclusion that he was biting the hand that housed him.

Musgraviana: or, Memoirs of a Cod-Piece, a twenty-three page pamphlet, has a dedication to Farmer signed by "Peter Taylor" and a statement by "The Editor to the Public." In the latter much play is made of the disappearance of Farmer's "Gentleman," i.e., the inhabitant of his codpiece. This broad attack is followed by the same doggerel-verse account of the meeting printed in the first pamphlet, but here attributed to J. Gooch. A James Wyard Gooch was admitted to St. John's College in 1781. Did he take his custom to Peter Taylor's establishment, or, more likely, was someone taking liberties with a contemporary name? A number of the epigrams are also reprinted. And while there is more broad satire, some on Farmer's supposed impotence, some on his sycophantic pursuit of preferment, some on his maniacal conduct at the town meeting, much on his death and will, there are some not unclever touches, as well as an accurate knowledge of Farmer's foibles and possessions, such as his horse Taffy being mentioned in his will.[20] The reputed author of those broad satires was John Twedell, elected Fellow of Trinity in 1792, the year of the pamphlets. "He had a considerable dislike to Dr. Farmer, on account of his persecution of Dissenters; and whenever he entered Christ's hall, (where he frequently dined in the long vacation,) he generally brought with him some witty epigrams" (*Reminiscences,* I.78).

Gunning has another story to tell about the happenings in 1792 and Farmer's reaction to them.

An attempt was made in the University and town to represent those who differed from Mr. Pitt as enemies to the constitution. Associations were formed against Republicans and Levellers, the resolutions against them were expressed in very offensive language, and all those who declined signing them were stigmatized as enemies to their King. The Dissenters (as a body) were included in that number. . . . A grocer named Gazam was reported to have uttered seditious expressions. The mob constructed a figure to represent him; a halter was put about his neck, and was affixed to a gallows; this was carried to the door of all good subjects, and those who did not subscribe were considered deficient in loyalty. I happened to be standing with some of the Fellows of Emmanuel at their college gate when the effigy was exhibited. We were joined by the Master, who laughed heartily: he gave the men who carried it five shillings, and desired them to shake it well, "opposite Master Gazam's house."

54 Master of Emmanuel College

Gazam's is a name otherwise unknown to fame, unless he made his mark in the new world, for he considered his safety and left Cambridge for America.

Perhaps it is not without relevance that Dyer somewhat grudgingly admitted that Farmer began "to think more favourably" of dissenters, and "to speak more respectfully; even of the ingenious Mr. Robert Robinson, preacher at Cambridge, of whom Farmer had been accustomed to talk contemptuously," although while later speaking of him with "admiration," and though he "continued to think him a disturber of academical repose, and a bold political innovator, yet he acknowledged him to be a superior genius, and a conscientious, sincere man" (402–3). According to the obituary notice of Dyer in *GM* for May 1841, after a brief period away from Cambridge he returned in 1779 and "entered the family of his friend Mr. Robinson the dissenting minister of St. Andrew's, not simply as a tutor to his family, but with a view of profiting by his doctrine and learned conversation" (545). Dyer wrote *Memoirs of the Life and Writings of Robert Robinson* (1796) and in his preface he acknowledged the assistance given to him, mentioning "P. Musgrave and others, in connection with the petition for the abolition of the slave trade" (x), thus establishing another link between Musgrave and Farmer. Of far greater importance is Dyer's account of the case of two young men of Emmanuel "who, during the time of worship, disturbed the congregation [Robinson's], obliging the people to disperse without concluding the services." As a result of this and other instances of "such improper behaviour" (69), Robinson's parishioners sent a letter to Farmer in his then capacity as tutor. The letter is dated "Dec. 69" and begins,

> The trustees for the meeting beg you would accept their warmest thanks for your impartial and generous help in regard to your two pupils. In consideration of the general character which you are pleased to give Mr. ———, they agree to omit his name in print, and persuade themselves, that you will think it as necessary to expose the other, when the following facts are attended to. (71)

The letter continues, after two paragraphs,

> A gentleman of Mr. Farmer's delicacy and piety will find it difficult to believe half of what we could tell him on this head. Would you imagine, sir, that we scarcely meet without interruptions from the under-graduates; that every agreeable female in the society is exposed to the same insults as in a bawdy-house; no pew privileged from a bold intrusion; no family, however considerable in fortune or credit, from insolent affronts? Is it

Master of Emmanuel College 55

credible, that prostitutes should parade our ailes in academic habits? An unforeseen accident discovered the sex of one but a fortnight ago. . . . Nothing induces us to mention them now but the desire to convincing Mr. Farmer, that our lenity has been infamously abused, and, consequently, that it is a duty we owe to the society under our management, vigorously to support prosecution. (72)

And after more in the same vein,

We are too well acquainted, sir, with your deserved character, to imagine any apology needful for this information Receive it, sir, as an apology for our exposing one of your pupils. . . . Allow us, good sir, to assure you, that we shall ever retain the liveliest gratitude for your extreme civility, and with profound respect are your obliged Servants. (74)

While Mr. M got off scot-free, his fellow disturber of parochial peace was fined fifty pounds. The case not only throws an unfavorable light upon the excesses of some undergraduates, but more importantly for present purposes shows Farmer in action as tutor as well as indicates the esteem in which he was held.

This esteem evidently was shared by Farmer's parishioners, although he does not seem to have gained a reputation as a preacher while serving as curate at Swavesy, and there is no record of his service in another curacy. Reed was a compulsive transcriber and note-taker, as well as a diarist, and much of a large body of his jottings is extant and housed in the Folger Shakespeare Library. In one memorandum book he noted,

D.r Hurd admitted of Emanuel 3 Oct.r 1733. He used to preach for sev[1] years in Sturbridge Fair, in a pulpit erected for that purpose &. was paid by the voluntary contributions of the People there by Shillings Six pences to the————amount D.r Farmer says in the whole 16 or 17 to each fair. He was succeeded by Hubbard who was followed by Farmer but neither of them preached in the Fair & the custom gradually declined &. is now lost. 19 Sept.r I saw the pulpit which was used on this occasion in Barnwell Church.[21]

Corroboration exists in Nichols's *Literary Anecdotes* where the date of Hurd's assuming the curacy is noted to be 1752. Nichols quotes Edmund Carte's *History of the County of Cambridge* (1753) to the effect that "The present curate [of St. Andrew the Less] is the Reverend Mr. Hurd, Fellow of Emanuel College, and is also the *Stirbridge Fair Preacher*," and that "on the two chief Sundays during the Fair, both morning and afternoon, divine Service is read, and a sermon

56 Master of Emmanuel College

preached from a pulpit placed in the open air, by the minister of Barnwell; who is very well paid for the same by the contributions of the Fair-keepers."

On Thursday, 19 September 1782, on his first visit to Emmanuel, Reed wrote in his diary, "went with Messrs. Steevens, Wilcox, Homer and Sisson to Sturbridge Fair. Met the Master there and in the way home viewed Barnwell Church and read the very extraordinary Epitaph of Jacob Butler [many years Church Warden]. In the church the iron-work remains on which near the pulpit the Hour Glass used to stand."[22] Richard Hurd was curate of St. Andrew the Less in Barnwell from 1753–56. In the "History and Antiquities of Sturbridge Fair" in the fifth volume of his *Bibliotheca Topographica Britannica* (1786), John Nichols reported that "The curate of St. Andrew's the Less, commonly called Barnwell, is also the Sturbridge Fair preacher, of which hereafter." In 1710, the Mayor of Cambridge, "contrary to law, ancient usage and custom, [tried to] set up an unlicensed preacher at Sturbridge Fair, in opposition to the present patron and minister, who claim the right of preaching there by immemorial prescription" (78–79). According to Reed, who probably was told by Farmer, by 1782 the curate of St. Andrew the Less no longer augmented his meager parochial income by preaching at the Fair. Thanks to Reed, however, one can add another ecclesiastical living to those already known to be held by Farmer.[23]

While it is known that Farmer held the curacy of Swavesey Church, some eight or nine miles from Cambridge, George Dyer, who is the authority, was unsure of the extent of that curacy, writing that "For many years, while tutor, he served the curacy of Swavesey" (393). Gunning, writing much later than Dyer, partially repeats him, i.e., "For many years before he was elected to the Mastership he had the Curacy of Swavesey" (*Reminiscences,* I.162). Farmer became tutor in 1760 and Master in 1775, so that he could have been curate for some fifteen years. In July 1769, and I quote Dyer again, Farmer "was appointed by Dr. Terrick, then Bishop of London, one of the Preachers at the Chapel Royal at Whitehall; an engagement that required him to be in London a certain number of months in the year" (394), a statement that would seem to preclude further parochial duties in Swavesey. However, the preachers at Whitehall, twenty-four chosen from Fellows of Colleges in Cambridge and Oxford, shared duties, two for every month, with a stipend of thirty pounds a year.[24] Dyer's statement about the duties requiring attendance in London "a certain number of months" is, therefore, inaccurate. Thomas Martyn pointed this out, stating that Farmer needed to be in London "only two Sundays, or at most two and a half. It was his

Master of Emmanuel College 57

Canonry of St. Paul's . . . that required three months residence" (*Lit. Anecd.*, VIII.420). In 1769 Farmer, with thirty pounds a year added to his income as a tutor and his stipend as a Fellow of his college, would not seem to have needed to ride to and from Swavesey the same day for the small sum his curacy would bring him, yet it is nevertheless true that in the years 1770 through 1773 he did exactly that. The parish register transcripts for Swavesey in the Cambridge University Library show Farmer's unmistakable signature on the transcripts for those years.[25] This does not, however, mean that he may not have officiated in other years and not signed the registers. Thomas Martyn, who claimed to have been "much oftener" a curate at Swavesey, only signed twice, in 1760 and 1766, in the years from 1760–80. Gunning refers to Dobson (actually Dodson) the church-warden during Farmer's curacy. Dodson's signature appears on the registers from 1750 through 1770 and then reappears in 1775 through 1778.

Dyer was the first to leave a description of Farmer as curate at Swavesey, writing that "he gained the respect of his congregation rather by his affability[26] and social manners, than by the solemnity of his carriage, or the rigour of his doctrines." Dyer, who is quoted verbatim by Nichols, then further characterizes Farmer as a priest.

> Swavesey was at this time frequented by methodists; occasionally by the reverend Mr. Venn, the rector of Yelling, in Huntingdonshire, formerly fellow of Jesus college, and by the reverend Mr. Berridge, then vicar of Everten, Bedfordshire, formerly fellow of Clare-hall. Between these gentlemen and Farmer there existed no great cordiality; for Farmer was no friend to their doctrines, which appeared to him irrational and gloomy: he classed them with Presbyterians, and both Presbyterians and Methodists he consideredd as Puritans and Roundheads. Farmer was a greater adept in cracking a joke, than in unhinging a Calvinist's creed, or in quieting a gloomy conscience. He, however, possessed a spirit of benevolence, and knew how to perform a generous action to a distressed family: there are men who can read over a person's grave, "He was a kind man," with greater satisfaction, than "He was a great Preacher." (*Lit. Anecd.*, II.621n.)

Thomas Martyn, also a curate at Swavesey, took exception or simply wished to correct Dyer's account as repeated in Nichols's *Literary Anecdotes,* for in the "additions" to the second volume of the *Anecdotes* he wrote, "I was much oftener Curate of Swavesey than Dr. Farmer. Mr. Allenson, the Vicar, went every other year to see his relations in Yorkshire, and was absent 12 months. At these times Dr. Farmer or I were his substitutes. I never recollect there being any Methodists in the parish" (VIII.420). Dyer's account is suspect because Henry Venn did not move to Yelling until 1771 (DNB), later

58 Master of Emmanuel College

than the time at which, as I have suggested, Farmer relinquished his curacy.

Dyer says nothing about Farmer as a preacher. Thomas Martyn wrote that Farmer "was not famous as a Preacher. His Sermons were florid, and composed in haste; his enunciation was loud and hurried; his setting-off was so violent as to make nervous people start. As a proof of his hurrying, I heard him relate, that, having been to preach at Huntingdon, and on his return riding over a bridge, he heard a man say to his companion, 'Ay, there he goes; if he rides as fast as he preaches; he will soon be at Cambridge' " (*Lit. Anecd.*, VIII.420).

Farmer died on 8 September 1797. Fifty-five years later Henry Gunning wrote his *Reminiscences of the University, Town, and County of Cambridge from the Year 1780;* he was twelve years old in 1780. On 13 October 1789, the same day Farmer was elected to the Caput, Gunning was elected one of the Esquire Bedells. The two knew one another; indeed Gunning wrote, "To me he was ever particularly kind, and never failed inviting me to the college feasts, which were numerous, and most strictly observed" (I.162). Gunning also records another instance of Farmer's kindness toward him, and this at the time of the election of the Esquire Bedells: "At Emanuel I had the votes of all the Fellows: and the Master fixed the audit the day before the election, that the Fellows might not have the trouble of a second journey" (I.130). In any event, given that Gunning, who became Master of Arts in 1788, only knew Farmer for a few years, his circumstantial account of Farmer as curate of Swavesey, as other of his reminiscences, must be taken with the slightest grain of salt. But as he is the sole source for so much anecdotal material about Farmer, albeit of necessity having derived that material at secondhand (or from Farmer himself), he certainly cannot be dismissed out of hand.

> For many years before he was elected to the Mastership he had the Curacy of Swavesey, (about nine miles distant,) where he made a point of attending in all weathers. He began the service punctually at the appointed time, and gave a plain practical sermon, strongly enforcing some moral duty. After service he chatted most affably with his congregation, and never failed to send some small present to such of his poor parishioners as had been kept from church through illness. (I.163)

In 1778, a more specific example of his thought for the poor is an entry in Farmer's hand in one of the records in the Emmanuel College archives which reads, "To the Mother of *Chatterton,* alias Rowley the Poet, 1.1.0."[27] On another and much later occasion he, as a member of the Vice-Chancellor's court in 1795, signed a document assuring "the poor Inhabitants of the Town of Cambridge" that "we will take every legal measure to reduce the price of meat, by preventing the butchers buying and selling in the same Market, and all forestalling, ingrossing, and regrating."[28] Farmer's small presents to the poor accord well with other tributes to his unobtrusive generosity. Dyer called him a "kind-hearted man" and wrote that his was "a character that had in it much of the milk of human kindness" (399, 403). He could, however, be acidulous in his comments, as witness his remark as applied to William Hales, recorded by William Bennet, Bishop of Cloyne, in a letter to Richard Gough dated 5 June 1800. "Dr. Hales, who is the author of the Inspector, and lives retired in a College Rectory is an exception [to the absence of literary work], and yet he is one of those men of whom our friend Dr. Farmer used to say, that they had a great deal of knowledge in their heads, but it always presented itself with the wrong end foremost" (*Lit. Illustr.*, IV.712). He could be equally and adversely witty at the expense of Gough, Edward Capell, and David Hume, among others.

One other anecdote about Farmer's preaching exists, recorded by William Cole and quoted in Nichols's *Literary Anecdotes*. Cole wrote, "His voice was strong and his manner of speaking rapid and quick. So, that one day a lady hearing him preach at St. Mary's and end his Sermon abruptly, turned to an officer of dragoons who was with her, and said that Dr. Farmer knew how to stop short in full gallop as anyone of the men in his company" (II.637 and note). In Swavesey, with its largely rustic parishioners, as well as in Great St. Mary's in Cambridge, with its fashionable ladies and its officers of dragoons in their pews, Farmer rode post through his sermons.

Twice in his academic career Farmer was a member of the very powerful Caput, a body of five members of the University elected from among fifteen, the Vice-Chancellor nominating five and each of the Proctors also nominating five. Only the Heads of the Colleges, or their representatives, Doctors, and the two Scrutators, who were the tellers in the nonregent house, could vote. Winstanley notes that in the eighteenth century the Vice-Chancellor's nominees were usually voted in and that he chose those who "were likely to be agreeable to his successor in office." The Caput consisted of the Vice-Chancellor ex officio and a doctor from each of the three faculties of divinity, law, and medicine as well as a nonregent and regent master of arts, a regent being a Master of Arts of no more than five years' standing.[29] No grace could be submitted to the Senate without the unanimous approval of the Caput, although the number of times any member of that body exercised his right to a negative vote was very small. In any event, the Graces passed during Farmer's two periods as member of

60   Master of Emmanuel College

the Caput did not allow of much controversy. Since he had been a Conservator of the Cam in 1786 and 1787, i.e., a person "having charge of a river, its embankments, weirs, creeks, etc., and supervision of the fisheries, navigation, watermills, etc. thereon" (OED), he enthusiastically endorsed a petition of the University to the House of Commons on 13 March 1790 against a "Bill for Extension of the Navigation from Stortford in Herts to the River Brand in Norfolk," claiming that such a Bill would be "prejudicial, if not entirely destructive to the Navigation of the River Cam" and asking that "their Agent or Counsel" be allowed to appear before them.[30]

3

Later Academic Career

On 4 November 1775, the traditional date set for the election of the Vice-Chancellor of the University, the new Master of Emmanuel College was elected to that office. Some idea of the demands of that office can be had from this partial quotation from *Observations on the Statutes of the University*, by George Peacock, Bishop of Ely, published some sixty-five years after Farmer became Vice-Chancellor.

> He is the chief and almost the sole administrative officer of the University, all others being placed under his immediate direction and control: he summons and presides at all congregations of the senate, and gives admission to all degrees; he presides at the meetings of every syndicate, however numerous and laborious they may be; he proposes and decides nearly every academical prize, and assists at all examinations for University scholarship and medals; he is the judge, either by himself or with the other heads of houses as his assessors, in all complaints brought before him by the Proctors and other officers, whether relating to members of the University or others, in cases which are subject to his jurisdiction: he examines and grants every licence, including the lodging-houses of students and the public houses of the town, and for every public proceeding in the University; he is the public host and gives public dinners in succession to all the resident graduates in the University; he manages the public and trust estates and finances of the University, ordering and superintending every repair, making every payment, and keeping, verifying, and balancing the entire account of receipt and expenditure during his year of office.

Bishop Peacock suggested the instituion of two pro-Vice-Chancellors, nominated "from those heads of houses who have already served the office," with well-defined duties. The financial part of the Vice-Chancellor's duties might also be given over to a new academic officer, a university bursar (137). Only seven years after Farmer was elected Vice-Chancellor, a former Vice-Chancellor, Robert Plumptre, Master of Queens' College, wrote a pamphlet titled *Hints Respecting Some of the University Officers, Its Jurisdiction, Its Revenues* &c. (1782), addressed to the members of the Senate. Plumptre had been Vice-

Later Academic Career

Chancellor in 1761–62 and was elected to the same office in 1777 to fill out the term of Hugh Thomas who was seventy years old and ill. Plumptre knew whereof he wrote when he suggested, more modestly than Bishop Peacock was to more than half a century later, that the Vice-Chancellor should have an assistant, especially for the paying of quarterly and annual bills and the writing of official letters. And the Vice-Chancellor should not be, as in 1782 and for years later he was, a member of every Syndicate, nor should his presence be necessary at every meeting of each Syndicate. Nor should he be the head of the Press Syndicate, that position more properly to be held by a member conversant with Press business. Nothing had changed when Farmer was elected Vice-Chancellor again in 1787.

While one can get some general idea of what Farmer had to be responsible for in his two tenures as Vice-Chancellor, some more specific information from Cambridge University archives will serve to bring the whole matter into bold relief. To take the matter of University finances as a first example: the Vice-Chancellor had to see to the payment of salaries to the Principal Librarian and the Librarian, and to the Bedells and Lecturers, and also the wages of all who performed various services for the University (sweeping, weeding, care of the market, bookbinding, tuning the organ at Great St. Mary's, building library shelves, etc.). He paid out the rents to the town of Cambridge, paid the salaries of the Vicars of Barton and Burwell, and gave sums to charities in various parishes of the town. He was responsible for the payment of legal and travel expenses for members of the University on University business, for monies to the clerics of Ely, for the transcribing of letters, for support of Addenbrooke's Hospital and the payment of apothecaries' bills as well as all repairs to University buildings. He paid the winner of the Seatonian Prize poem and those who gave speeches on November 5 (Guy Fawkes day). He was present at the assizes, both Lent and Summer, and on those occasions made a present of twelve pairs of gloves to the Judges. On occasion he had discretionary powers, so that when the tutor of Edmund Garwood, Sizar of Magdalene College, certified that he "is a person of very indigent circumstances; and that he hath been put to considerable expense on account of a violent strain which he received in walking down a steep descent on Friday the 27th March 1776," Farmer allowed three guineas for Garwood's use. These were but some of his financial responsibilities.[1]

The Vice-Chancellor quite naturally presided over the Vice-Chancellor's Court, the other members being the heads of houses, their jurisdiction extending to all members of the University. The com-

Later Academic Career

plaints and crimes and misdemeanors that came before the Vice-Chancellor's court were varied and, except in a very few instances (one being duelling), what one would expect in a university town. Prominent among these were drunkenness, assault, and maintaining or frequenting "disorderly" houses. Abuse of horses, "blasphemous libels," and "scandalous and indecent words" were not unusual. Here is a partial table of contents of one archival manuscript.

Royle (Schol. of Joh.) rusticated for *assault* on Mrs. Morden.	18 February, 1782
Proctor v. Cleaver for *rescuing a prostitute.*	1785
Applethwaite (Pemb.) expelled for *killing R. Ricroft in a duel,* and J. Holland Expelled for *being his second.*	1791
Proceedings v. Sherard (Pet.) for a *row* at Magdalene.	1791
Proctors v. Dayrell (F.C. of Chr.) for *disorderly behaviour, contumacy, insolence and disobedience,* (expelled).	1792
Proctors v. Halliday (F.C. of Trin.) and Bunbury, (Schol. of Trin.) for *riotous, disorderly and disobedient behaviour.* (Rusticated for six months).	1792[2]

Not all cases were solved out of hand and at one sitting, as witness the sixty pages, covering the period from June 12 to 29 June 1781, given over to the case of six students who were punished in various degrees of severity for Assault and Affray. Farmer, as Master of Emmanuel, was one of the signatories to the sentencing.[3]

Here, too, is a typical entry in the records of the Vice-Chancellor's Court at a time when Farmer held that position. "At a meeting of the Vice Chancellor and the Heads at the Lodge in Emanuel College on the twelfth Day of June, 1788." "Present D.ʳ Farmer Vice chancellor" and the heads of houses, "M.ʳ Myddelton Junior Proctor" complained that "Dodd Scholer of St. John's College" on Wednesday, June 4, at 10:00 A.M. was in a house of ill fame in Barnwell (the red-light district of eighteenth-century Cambridge) and was there found by the Proctor "in the company of several women of ill fame, without his gown." Dodd, sober, offered no resistance to the Junior Proctor. In Dodd's defense, his tutor, Mr. Whitmore, said there had been no previous "public censure" of Dodd in St. John's and that except for the present complaint he "would have been mentioned with credit at

64   Later Academic Career

the late public examinations." Despite this, or possibly because of this, depending on whether the sentence seems harsh or light, Dodd was rusticated from the University until 10 October 1789.[4]

Some of those appearing before the Vice-Chancellor's court were tried for complaints a cut above those of the undergraduates. One such person who attracted much attention was Dr. William Howell Ewin of St. John's, M.A. 1756 and LL.D. 1766, who lent large sums of money to students at enormous rates of interest, in one instance lending £300 to William Bird, of Trinity College, a scholar and a minor. Later loans to young Bird brought the total to £750. In 1778 Ewin's degrees were suspended, and he was ordered to be expelled from the University. Upon appeal his degrees were restored and he was readmitted. Again Farmer, as head of a house, was one of the signatories to the sentencing. Affairs such as Ewin's and others were quite protracted and made demands upon all involved.[5]

Not all the Vice-Chancellor's duties and responsibilities were so onerous. On June 23 of each year he and other dignitaries of the University met "in the Senate-House at eleven in the forenoon," discussed the cakes and wine provided by the "School-keeper," and then proceeded by coaches to proclaim "Barnwell Fair, commonly called Midsummer Fair." The biggest occasion was the proclamation of and attendance at Sturbridge Fair, one of the biggest fairs in all Europe. On September 18 the Vice-Chancellor and other dignitaries follow the formula for Barnwell Fair and then proceed by carriages to Sturbridge common where, after the proclamation of the opening of the Fair, "the Proctors treat the Company with Oysters, at the tiled booth," while "the Taxors find the bread, beer, and butter for the oysters."[6] There was, however, much more gormandizing to come, and Gunning is again the authority, for he, as Esquire Bedell and Senior Esquire Bedell, attended yearly. Here is what Gunning wrote:

> The scene which presented itself on entering the room I can describe most accurately, for the dishes and their arrangement never varied. Before the Vice-Chancellor was placed a large dish of herrings; then followed in order a neck of pork roasted, an enormous plum-pudding, a leg of pork boiled, a pease-pudding, a goose, a huge apple-pie, and a round of beef in the centre. On the other half of the table the same dishes were placed in similar order (the herrings before the Senior Proctor, who sat at the bottom). From thirty to forty persons dined there; and although the wine was execrable, a number of toasts were given, and mirth and good humour prevailed, to such an extent as is seldom to be met with at more modern and more refined entertainments. At about half-past six the dinner party broke up, and, with scarcely an exception, adjourned to the theatre. Previously to this, however, a day (usually the 24th) was fixed for holding

Later Academic Career
65

the Commissary's Court, and for repeating the oyster-eating and dining I have just described.[7]

For Farmer and his friends the chief attraction was the performances by a company of players from Norwich. Gunning has left a delightful picture of Farmer and his friends at these performances, writing that Farmer was present virtually every day of the three weeks of perform-ances, "except on Michaelmasday, which was the anniversary of the foundation of Emmanuel, and which was always celebrated by a splendid dinner in the College Hall." Farmer, with Steevens and Reed and a few others, was "accustomed to occupy that part of the pit which is usually called 'The Critics' Row,' and which was scru-pulously reserved for them. They seemed to enjoy the play as much as the youngest persons present." They never expressed disapproval at any part of the performances, "but when they approved, the whole house applauded most rapturously. Farmer's "hearty and peculiar laugh" could "easily be distinguished. At play's end they returned on foot and adjourned to *Emmanuel Parlour*, where half-a-score persons were either waiting for them, or accompanied them home."[8] And while it may have been looked upon as an additional chore, the Vice-Chancellor often entertained eminent visitors to Cambridge.[9]

Other perquisites of the Vice-Chancellor's office existed. "On Mid-lent Sunday the Vice-Chancellor, or a Preacher of his appointment, preaches a Sermon at Burwell," said Gunning in his *Ceremonies* (87). It is Gunning again, this time in his *Reminiscences*, who gives an intimate picture (he was there in his capacity as Esquire Bedell) of the hospitality afforded the Vice-Chancellor on one of these annual visits to Burwell where the University owned "a considerable estate." After the sermon the Burwell estate tenant gave the Vice-Chancellor and those who accompanied him dinner. On this occasion, in 1795, dinner consisted of "three huge fowls," "an enormous sirloin of beef," "a huge ham of excellent flavour," as well as a "pigeon-pie" and "an unusually large plum-pudding"—all this for the tenant and his three guests. "The beer was excellent. After dinner, wine was introduced; the port was as good as ever tasted, and the tenant circulated the bottle very briskly" (I.11). Given such hospitality, it is little wonder that the Vice-Chancellors often exercised their prerogative, and it is little wonder, too, that Farmer in his dual capacity of Master of a College and Vice-Chancellor of the University should feel the effects of such excesses.

Probably the best-known story about Farmer, at least in an official capacity, is one which occurred during his first tenure as Vice-Chan-cellor. The story has been told a number of times, but with some

66   Later Academic Career

variations. John Nichols wrote the obituary account of Farmer in the 1797 *GM,* and if he knew anything about the affair, he did not so much as mention it. Reed, a close friend of Farmer's, wrote a general account of his character and of some of his achievements for William Seward's *Biographiana* (1799), but also said nothing. George Dyer, whom Farmer had taught and befriended, wrote a strange account of his one-time mentor in the *Annual Necrology* for 1797–98, strange because he both praised and condemned him. Dyer only glanced at the story in these words,

> it may be proper to observe that the two parties of Whig and Tory, at Cambridge, had for some time carried their contention rather high, till, on the 17th of March 1769, an address was presented to the King by the Tories, containing nothing short of a reprobation of the principles and conduct of the popular party. A few years after happened the American war, replete with nothing but dishonour to its adherents in this country, and terminating, at length, in the emancipation of the Americans. An address [in 1775], no less sycophantic than the former, was again presented by the Tories, justifying the cruel measures then pursued and the men who adopted them. (400).[10]

Dyer's sympathies are immediately apparent. It remained, however, for someone not close to Farmer to give public utterance to the story. George Gleig, later Bishop of Brechin, wrote the account of Farmer for the first volume of the Supplement to the third edition of the *Encyclopedia Britannica,* published in 1797, later than Dyer's account in the *Annual Necrology.* Here is the first printed version of the story:

> The disturbances in America having by this time become serious, the university of Cambridge, with numberless other loyal bodies, voted an address to the king, approving the measures adopted by government to reduce the factious colonists to their duty. The address, however, was not carried unanimously. It was, of course, opposed by JEBB, so well known for his free opinions in politics and religion, and by some others, of whom one man, a member of the CAPUT, carried his opposition so far, as actually to refuse the key of the place which contained the seal necessary on such occasions. In this emergency, Dr. Farmer, who was then vice-chancellor, is said to have forced open the door with a sledge-hammer; an exploit which his democratical biographers affect to ridicule, by calling it *his courtly zeal,* and the occasion of all his subsequent preferments.
> If it be indeed true, that he broke the door in pieces with his own hands, his conduct must be acknowledged to have been not very decorous; but if the office which he filled be taken into consideration, we apprehend it would be as difficult to prove that conduct essentially wrong, as to vindicate the obstinate arrogance of him who occasioned it. The seal was

Later Academic Career 67

the property of the university, of which this outrageous supporter of the bill of rights was but an individual member. The university had resolved that it should be employed for a certain purpose, which it was the duty of the vice-chancellor to carry into effect; and since the seal was refused to him, he had no alternative but to get possession of it by force. We hope, however, that he employed a servant to break the door; and, indeed, as vice-chancellor, he must have had so many servants at his command, that it is not conceivable he would wield the sledge hammer himself.

Gleig writes that "it was at Canterbury that the writer of this sketch [himself] had the happiness to be introduced to him [Farmer], and witnessing his hospitality" (641). The introduction to Farmer took place in 1786 when Gleig came from Scotland to London and Canterbury *(DNB);* his association with Farmer was slight. This is the first account of the affair, although his reference to Farmer's "democratical biographers" who accuse Farmer of "courtly zeal" poses a problem, in that the words "courtly zeal" do not occur in Nichols, Reed, or Dyer. Only Dyer, of the three "biographers," accused Farmer of courting preferment, "his good friend at court, Dr. Hurd" not harming him "on his way to preferment" (399). Dyer also accused Farmer of ploughing "in a soil whence sprung the prebend of Canterbury and residentiary of St. Paul's" (401). Nichols quoted Gleig's account of the affair both in his *History* of Leicestershire in 1811 and in his *Literary Anecdotes* in 1812.

William Cole, at whose home in Milton Farmer was often a guest, included an account of the affair in his "Collectanea for Athenae Cantabrigienses," reprinted by Sir Egerton Brydges from Cole's sketch of Robert Tyrwhitt, Fellow of Jesus College.

> In the autumn of 1775, when an address to the King was voted by the University against the factious Americans, and their more blameable *Fautors* in the mother country, this person, who was one of the scrutators, and kept the key of the University chest, in which their seal was kept, refused to deliver it: the ostensible pretence was, that the Caput was not legally constituted, as Dr. Halifax, who was LL.D. had lately also procured a Mandamus for a D.D. degree, in order to qualify himself for the Headship of Catharine Hall, when it should fall, and therefore he was not properly the senior of the law faculty: yet the real motive was their inveterate hatred to order, and submission to Government. The Vice Chancellor, on his obstinacy, was forced to go with proper assistance and break the chest open to get at the key.[11]

According to Cole, who died in 1782 and hence left the most contemporary account of the story, Farmer did have some unspecified assistance and did in some unspecified way "break open the chest."

68 Later Academic Career

Tyrwhitt, who obviously was anathema to Cole, was a most troublesome member of the Senate, offering Graces for excusing "gentlemen, who were candidates for the degree of Bachelor of Arts, from subscribing the 39 articles" and for abolishing "the sermons at St. Mary's at certain Saints' days, and for the appointment of a Syndicate to consider plans for inforcing a proper attendance at the University Sermons." All were rejected by the Caput.[12] Farmer's disapproval of Tyrwhitt's efforts at what must have seemed subversion must surely have added to his anger at the refusal to surrender the key. Three years after Farmer's death "H.M.," i.e., Henry Meen, wrote to the editor of the *European Magazine* in February 1800 to correct inaccuracies in the *Encyclopedia Britannica* account of Farmer (115–17). Among other matters he stated that opening the University chest was not an act of intemperate zeal but sanctioned by the Senate: "before the Vice chancellor exerted his authority, and gave his servant his official order to break open the chest."

Henry Gunning recalled the story in his *Reminiscences,* printing the address in full and writing that "A dispute arose after the address was voted about affixing the University seal. One of the Scrutators (Mr. Tyrwhitt of Jesus) refused to furnish his key of the common chest to enable the Vice-Chancellor to obtain the seal. . . . The Vice-Chancellor, with the aid of the blacksmith, obtained the University seal by a summary process" (I.175–76). Gleig has Farmer forcing the door with a "sledge-hammer," although he conceded that the actual operation must have been done by one of the Vice-Chancellor's many servants.[13] Gunning introduces the blacksmith but specifies no instrument. E. S. Shuckburgh, one-time librarian of Emmanuel College, writing about this, has Farmer "using a crow-bar with his own hands."[14] Sir Sidney Castle Roberts reports Gleig's original statements, but is not convinced that Farmer delegated the work to another.[15] Sledgehammer or crowbar, blacksmith or other servant—or Farmer himself with one or the other of the tools—the story still stands as evidence of the strength of Farmer's beliefs, if not of his arms.[16] At least one of Farmer's friends took a light view of the whole affair. Michael Tyson wrote to Richard Gough on 15 November 1775 and gave this account of the Address: "The Heads met on Sunday, to hear the proposal for an Address from Dr. Farmer—but few were present, and the determination was postponed till Tuesday 1st, when a hasty-pudding was produced; and, if the chancellor can digest it, the pot is to be sent up as soon as possible.—I call it a hasty-pudding, because I hear the ingredients are all very mild, and fit for a weak stomach" (*Lit. Anecd.,* VIII.617).

Farmer, this time not alone in his firmly taken stand, had had

Later Academic Career

occasion to make his voice heard in a matter of considerable importance to the University in the preceding year, 1774. John Jebb, who had been a fellow of Peterhouse College until his marriage in 1764, continued his association with the University as a lecturer in mathematics. In 1773 he offered a grace, the first provision of which was that all noblemen and fellow-commoners were "to be subjected to public examinations in the senate-house" upon admission, to take effect after the first Monday in May 1774. In a letter to a friend, Jebb wrote, "You cannot imagine how greatly, certain spirits are alarmed with the disposition there appears, to do something effectual. Dr. Powell, and the Emmanuel men, and Dr. Halifax, labour to spoil, what the friends of literature and good morals, are mediating to establish." On 28 March 1774 the syndics agreed to have the grace submitted to the senate, and Jebb wrote praising "the vice-chancellor and his associates, i.e., the major part of them: for Halifax and Farmer did all in their power to obstruct and distress their brethren. . . . Farmer declares it will be the ruin of the university, and shake the foundations of the constitution both in church and state."[17] The grace was rejected, and Farmer and his associates prevailed, although his reaction to the proposal seems extreme.

Dyer, writing soon after Farmer's death, was unequivocal in his condemnation of Farmer's part in the Jebb affair.

> It would have afforded the biographer great pleasure to have found Farmer, in many respects a very amiable man, in these several contests among the friends to humanity and public liberty; but he acted the other way; and, while he was tutor of Emanuel College, when, afterwards, he became master, and vice chancellor of the university; towards the reforming party, Jebb and Tyrwhitt, he carried himself with bigotry and violence. He lived, then, at a favourable era; he had adopted *lucky* principles; and ploughed in a soil whence sprung the prebend of Canterbury and residentiaryship of St. Paul's. (401)

Robert Tyrwhitt of Jesus College had, in Dyer's words, "attempted to restore religious liberty to the members of the university of Cambridge, by proposing a grace for removal of subscription to the thirty-nine articles at the time of taking degrees," (400) a grace that Farmer vigorously opposed. Dyer was, of course, a prejudiced observer.

Farmer's political convictions, evidently shared by most of the Fellows of Emmanuel, came to the fore again a few years later. Admiral Augustus Keppel, later Viscount Keppel, was charged by Vice-Admiral Sir Hugh Palliser with various capital offenses arising from his conduct in action against the French navy in 1777. Keppel

70   Later Academic Career

was tried by a court-martial and was acquitted on 1 February 1778. Cooper records that on February 13, two days later, while most of the windows in the Cambridge Colleges were illuminated to celebrate the acquittal, those of Emmanuel were stoned by the mob because they were not illuminated. Palliser, Cooper adds, was hung in effigy (*Annals,* IV.388).

During Farmer's second tenure as Vice-Chancellor, from 4 November 1787 through the following year, some major decisions were made and important matters were discussed, largely having to do with affairs of state as well as with more local matters. On 26 January 1788 the Chancellor, Masters, and Scholars of the University petitioned the House of Commons, "understanding that an Application will soon be made to your Honourable House for the Suppression of the Slave Trade, desire to express our hearty approbation of so benevolent a design."[18] On the same date, although not the first such petition from the members of the University, joined by the Mayor, Bailiffs, and Burgesses of the Town of Cambridge, another petition stated that "if proper powers were given to pave, cleanse, light, watch, and otherwise improve the said Streets, Lanes, Courts, and other Publick Passages and to remove all annoyances, obstructions and encroachments *that* it would tend greatly to the Health, Convenience, Safety, and Emolument of the said University and Town and would also be of publick Utility."[19] The petitions bore fruit, for on May 8 an act was passed which resulted in the improvements asked for, and on September 18 the lamps were lit for the first time, and in the next month the first street was paved. Among others who were to see that the act was carried out was "the Vice chancellor or his deputy."[20] On the occasion of the amendment, in 1794, of the Act of 1788, Henry Gunning described "the wretched state of the streets," where the "gutters were in the middle of the streets, in several of which it was impossible for two carriages to pass each other, on account of the encroachments that had been made;" the front of Pembroke College was thought of as a particular hazard (*Reminiscences,* I.293). It was Gunning, still on the deplorable conditions of the streets of Cambridge, who stated that it was "Owing to the joint efforts of Mr. [John] Mortlock [Deputy Mayor of Cambridge] and Dr. Farmer (who most cordially cooperated with him, and who, on that account, was termed the self-elected Aedile), every obstacle was surmounted, and from that time to the present the town has been gradually improving" (I.295). Dyer wrote that the "Uncomfortable state of the town, previously to its being lighted and paved, is in every one's recollection: and to the honour of Farmer it should be mentioned, that he was the author of its improvement; and as he was the principal mover in

Later Academic Career 71

getting the town lighted and paved, so was he also, in his office of justice of the peace, the means of having many inconveniences removed" (403). The following year, 1789, mobs in Cambridge rioted over the high price of provisions, especially meat, and a handbill was circulated promising a reduction in the price of meat. The handbill bore the signatures of Lowther Yates, in his capacity as Vice-Chancellor, John Mortlock, Richard Farmer, and Thomas Bond, an alderman (*Reminiscences,* II.5). It may have been this that Isaac Reed had in mind when he wroter of Farmer as magistrate that "he was active and diligent; and, on more than one occasion of riots, displayed great firmness of mind in dangerous conjunctures."[21]

One other notable occurrence during Farmer's second tenure as Vice-Chancellor took place on 19 February 1788, and has gone unremarked, since the account of it was printed in the *GM* of that date (173) under the heading of Country News.

> On the 19th instant a great riot took place at Cambridge, occasioned by a man of genteel appearance going from shop to shop, pretendedly in great haste, and purchasing articles liable to the stamp-duties. Having thus canvassed the town, he went before a magistrate, and lodged informations against all who had been tardy in producing the stamps according to Act of Parliament. When this was known, the populace were so exasperated that they were determined to find him; and being informed that he was at the Rose Inn concealed, they assaulted the house, broke the windows, and were proceeding to commit other outrages; when Dr. Farmer, the Vice Chancellor, interposed, and by his presence dispersed the rioters, but not without reading the Riot Act thrice. The informer is said to have made his escape in the disguise of a Cambridge student.

One instance where a cap and gown stood someone in good stead.

Of lesser moment, but of some interest as indicative of other duties or decisions incumbent upon the Vice-Chancellor and on Farmer in his first tenure, in particular, were grants of £50 "Towards rebuilding the Episcopal Church in Edinburgh" given on 19 January 1776 and one of £100 "to the Clergy of the English Church in America" to relieve their impoverished condition. Four Colleges also contributed, among them Emmanuel.[22]

It may be recalled that Robert Plumptre suggested in 1782 that, among other demands upon the Vice-Chancellor of the University, his membership in all the syndicates and his heading the Press syndicate were among the duties that should be changed, especially since very few Vice-Chancellors would be sufficiently knowledgeable to conduct affairs of the Press and their one-year tenure was too short for them to learn very much. Indeed, it is recorded that in 1783 a syndic of the

72   Later Academic Career

Press did not know the difference between "collating" and "collecting" manuscripts.[23] Given Farmer's bibliophilic instincts, one would imagine that he did not find the affairs of the Press too difficult to comprehend and manage. However, the Press was a business, and the Vice-Chancellor and the members of the syndicate had to cope with financial matters. Here is an entry in Orders for the Press, 1770–83 in the University archives (Pr. v.2) for 4 July 1778.

> At a meeting of the Syndics for the Press, the different and opposition Opinions of M[r] Wedderburn respecting the enforcing the payment of £500 p[r] ann. which the Stationers Company are bound by Articles to pay to the University, but which they refuse to pay, having been read and considered; agreed that the said Gentlemen be desired to meet and confer on the Subject, & to give us their thoughts upon it after such conference: and also that the Vice-chancellor do take the Opinion of some third Lawyer of Eminence on the Case, together with that of the two University Counsel.

This is signed by R. Plumptre as Vice-Chancellor and R. Farmer as member of the syndicate. Plumptre knew whereof he wrote in 1782. On 21 December 1786 Messrs. Dunning and Wedderburn were again asked to confer, but there are no further entries on the affair. The one entry for 1788 (May 1), when Farmer was Vice-chancellor, is an agreement on the part of the Syndics "to print a new edition of the Brevier bible without notes N° 9000" and that "a new font of brevier types be ordered, weight 1000.[lbs.]" The entries show, however, that Farmer was fairly regular in his attendance as a Syndic, at least until the 1790s. Twice Vice-Chancellor, Master of Emmanuel from 1775 to his death, and holder of various ecclesiastical positions, Farmer had little time for scholarship or antiquarian studies.

David McKitterick's exhaustive study of Farmer as Principal Librarian of the University Library[24] has left very little for others to do. I add a few gleanings that will tend to corroborate or emphasize points already made by him rather than to add anything markedly new. Although Farmer sometimes sent scholars, notably Thomas Percy, books from the University Library, he did not always accede to requests for the use of books elsewhere than in Cambridge. Evidence of his polite hints at the dangers of such a practice exists in a letter from a medical man, Walter Caddell, to Farmer.

Sat.
25 Feb. '87

Later Academic Career 73

D.r Farmer

I rec.d y.r L.r just now & could not but attribute y.r Silence, to its right Cause, the Want of Leisure————why did not You mention before, the Risk you w.d be exposed to, in sending the Books? By no Means think of it—I w.d not subject You to any Danger that may arise from their Miscarriage or the common accidents of this Town, not for a Hospital full of rich Patients. I can do very well without them till I come to Camb.————Tis likely that I shall not be a bit the wiser after the Perusal: it has proved so w.th a Multitude of the Fraternity. I have been sadly deceived by Authorities, & am very much at a Stand in Conseq.ce; my own slight Exp.ts having run directly Contre to what has been delivered ex Cathedra. I don't know whether I can go to Camb. this Term; but I will endeavour: otherwise I shall be found there early in April. I will send my Question next Week.

> Yrs sincerely,
> Walt.r Caddell (Folger, C.b.10, #25)

Farmer's implied reluctance to send books to London for Caddell's use cannot be put down to his distrust of him, for Dyer is witness to Farmer's liberality toward those with whom he differed in political or ecclesiastical matters. Dyer wrote,

> This was particularly manifest in his conduct towards Mr. Sharpe, a well-informed gentleman, but, on a variety of subjects, more particularly political, widely differing from Farmer: towards him and towards others in these societies [clubs to which Farmer belonged], he behaved with modest deference; and when Mr. Sharpe was engaged in a literary work, that required him to consult scarce books, Dr. Farmer was ever ready to furnish him from the public library at Cambridge.

He added that

> even when the university had evinced public marks of their disapprobation, by depriving him [Gilbert Wakefield] the liberty of printing his Silva Critica at the University press, out of the funds appropriated to the publication of learned works . . . Dr. Farmer always showed a willingness to entrust to him books from the public library, of which acknowledgments are made by Mr. Wakefield (p. 402).

One such acknowledgment is in Wakefield's edition of Lucretius's *De Rerum Natura* (1796, I.10). Richard Sharpe, although a member of both the Unincreasable and Eumelean clubs and a friend of Reed's, among other things which would make him anathema to Farmer, "cooperated [in 1792] with the leading members of the whig party in

74   Later Academic Career

forming a society for obtaining a reform of parliament, which was
known as 'Friends of the People' " *(DNB)*. Farmer and Sharpe were
together in London in Reed's company in 1785, 1786, and 1789
(Diaries, 138, 145, 165). Wakefield's religious views would hardly
have endeared him to Farmer. In the Honours lists, after the name of
the Senior Wrangler, "*four* additional names used to be inserted at the
discretion of the Vice-Chancellor, the two Proctors, and the Senior
Regent . . . in 1776 four names were placed between the senior
wrangler and Gil. Wakefield of Jesus. Wakefield thought this was an
artifice of the V.C., Ri. Farmer, and the senior proctor, W. Bennet,
both Emmanuel men, to make the interval seem greater between him
and their senior wrangler (Archdeacon) John Oldershaw" of Emmanuel.[25] George Dyer states that William Frend lent the dissenting
minister Robert Robinson a manuscript he "had taken out of the
public library."[26] Frend, a unitarian who wanted to abolish subscription to the Thirty-Nine Articles as a condition of obtaining a Master's
degree, was no ally of Farmer's. And Farmer, as Master of Emmanuel,
was one of the signatories to the sentence of banishment meted out to
Frend in 1793 for a pamphlet he wrote.[27] Farmer would seem to have
acceded more often to requests for loan of books from the Library
than to have refused.

Farmer was equally generous with the loan of scarce works from
his personal library. Horace Walpole wrote to William Cole to tell
him that "a gentleman abroad" was collecting books and manuscripts
about the "Order of Malta" and could he, Cole, help. Cole was able
to help, as was Farmer, who was solicited by Cole. On 21 June 1772
Cole wrote from Milton, near Cambridge

> my friend Mr Farmer of Emmanuel, who wrote an ingenious book on *The
> Learning of Shakespeare,* has sent me to this place a most curious and
> scarce book, being *Statuta Hospitalis Hierusalem.* It is in folio, printed at
> Rome in 1588, full of fine prints, containing the heads of all the masters to
> Cardinal Hugh de Loubenz Verdala, whose head is twice elegantly en-
> graved, and various prints of him in different situations throughout the
> book, representing the functions of the knights: the first is a representa-
> tion of Hugh de Loubenx on his knees before Pope Sixtus V, who is
> putting the Cardinal's hat on his head. There is a neat map of the island
> and a plan of the city of Valetta. As Mr Farmer has written the following
> notes on a blank leaf, I will transcribe them, especially as it is possible
> from the scarcity of the book that it may not readily be met with.
> (Walpole, I.257)

Farmer's notes are of bibliographical interest only.

One episode that occurred in the same year Farmer became Prin-

Later Academic Career 75

cipal Librarian deserves to be resurrected from Nichols's *Literary Anecdotes*. According to Nichols, as late as 1778 Cole "was perplexed as to the disposal of his MSS." Cole wrote, "I have long wavered how to dispose all of my many MS volumes; to give them to *King's College,* would be to throw them into *a horse-pond;* and I had as lieve do one as the other; they are generally *so conceited of their Latin and Greek, that all other studies are barbarism.* Nichols added,

> He once thought of Eton College; but, the MSS. relating principally to Cambridge University and County, he inclined to deposit them in one of the libraries there; not in the Public Library, because too public, but in Emanuel, with the then Master of which, Dr. Farmer, he was very intimate. Dr. Farmer, however, happening to suggest that he might find a better place for them, Mr. Cole, who was become peevish and wanted to be courted, thought proper to think this "coolness and indifference" as a refusal. In this dilemma he at length resolved to bequeath them to the British Museum, with this condition, that they should not be opened for twenty years after his death. (VIII.387)

Farmer therefore must take the blame, or the credit, for the Cole manuscripts coming to rest in the British Museum.

Nichols, writing under one of his pseudonyms, M. Green, in the *GM* for November 1793, stated that "Mr. [William] Hayley, the congenial writer of CRASHAW'S life in the *Biographia Britannica,* has told us, that, by the liberality of Dr. Farmer, he had been indulged with sight of a literary curiosity, a 'Collection of Sacred Epigrams, printed at Cambridge, 1734'" (1001). The work in question is Crashaw's *Epigrammatum Sacrorum Liber,* his first published volume. One wonders if this "literary curiosity" was sent to London for Hayley's inspection, for otherwise would it be so strange that a visitor to the University Library should be allowed a sight, on the premises, of a scarce work? Hayley's acknowledgment comes in a footnote in volume IV (431).

The architect James Essex wrote to Richard Gough on 14 October 1781 to inform him that he had found "the two volumes of tracts that you mentioned in the Royal Library." After describing the two volumes of tracts, Essex concluded his letter by stating that "nobody can have a book out of this class except the Vice-Chancellor, or Dr. Farmer, librarian; but, if you want an account of the contents of each tract, Mr. Cole can have the perusal of both volumes by means of Dr. Farmer, and I dare say will make any extracts you desire" (*Lit. Illustr.,* VI.292). One should know that this was only four years after Charles Burney, the younger, had stolen eighty-eight books from the Royal Library. And yet Farmer, some ten years later than the thefts, could

76 Later Academic Career

lend Burney some manuscripts from the University Library.[28] Farmer, the elder Burney, Reed, and others dined at Sir Joseph Banks's on 26 November 1790, the only time Farmer and Burney met in Reed's company (*Diaries,* 187), so that Farmer's leniency toward the younger Burney can hardly be put down to partiality.

Henry Hubbard, whose declining the mastership of Emmanuel led to Farmer's election to that position, kept a journal which he evidently left to Farmer or to the College. In any event, Hubbard's Journal is now in the University Library (Misc. Collect. 36), thanks to Farmer. The Journal has a manuscript headnote by William Cole, transcribed from the British Library's Add. Ms. 5852, p. 109, which reads,

> Feb. 10, 1780. The following Quarto MS, with other things was lent me by Dr Farmer in January 1780. The Master said nothing about it, when he sent it, & having no Title, or Explanation at the Head of it, I can only guess it to have been the original Bedle's Book of my late esteemed & worthy Friend, Sir James Borrough, Master of Caius College.

Cole finished his transcription of the Journal on 6 March 1780. During the course of his work, he realized that Hubbard was the author. Farmer must have thought that there would be greater access to the Journal in the University Library than at Emmanuel. What is described as "the fine twelfth-century Greek manuscript of S. Gregory" was acquired by the University Library as a result of an exchange between Farmer and Lord Shelburne of an unnamed manuscript which the former gave up "on Lord Shelburne's earnest request," and which Farmer had purchased at the sale of Dr. Askew's manuscripts in 1785.[29]

John Bagford, bookseller and historian of printing, left a number of manuscripts which eventually came to rest in the British Museum. Nichols reported that

> It has been said that there are more of this man's curious collections for the same purpose in the Public Library at Cambridge; and that they have never been opened since they came there. But we have the authority of the late worthy master of Emanuel College, to assert, that this is not a fact. It would, indeed, have been a reproach to so curious and inquisitive a man as Dr. Farmer, to have had such papers in his custody, without the curiosity to inspect them. (*Lit. Anecd.,* II.464)

Nichols was, of course, quite right. Farmer was far from a model librarian,[30] but he knew what the University Library possessed.

Not only was Farmer kept from scholarship by his duties, he was

Later Academic Career 77

often ill. From all accounts it is very evident that with the exception of those years when he served as one of the curates of Swavesay Church, a curacy which necessitated riding some eight or nine miles each way on horseback, and with the possible exception of a period in the early 1780s when he was fined by his colleagues at Emmanuel for buying a horse (1781) and for selling a mare (1783),[31] Farmer led a sedentary life. A certain amount of walking in Cambridge was, of course, necessary; indeed, given the condition of the streets, mandatory. There were the occasional longer walks: Farmer and Steevens and Reed walking to Milton to dine with William Cole in 1782, for example (*Diaries*, 118). Farmer, with Reed and others, also walked to Landbeach, Fen Ditton, Grantchester, and Madingley as a matter of course. Indeed, given his love of his pipe[32] and his bottle, and the hospitality for which he was noted, a hospitality that necessitated even more than the usual parlor consumption of wine, it is little wonder that he suffered from that common eighteenth-century complaint, gout. Gunning, it will be recalled, was invited by Farmer to the College feasts, "which were numerous, and most strictly observed," and he is the authority for the anecdote corroborative of Farmer's returning to Cambridge to be present at these feasts when he was doing his ecclesiastical stint in London. "I well remember," Gunning writes in his *Reminiscences,* "his exclaiming, on entering the vestry at Great St. Mary's on Ascension-Day, 'I have had hard work to be with you in time, Mr. Vice-Chancellor, for at three o-clock this morning I was blowing my pipe with the worshipful Company of Pewterers' " (I.162, 169). And again, "consistently with his love of good fellowship, he gave excellent dinners to the Minor Canons [of St. Paul's] on a Sunday, at one o'clock. In the evening a hot supper was always ready at nine" for Cambridge friends (I.185). With Reed and others he often dined out, when in London, at the homes of various friends, or he went to the Queen's Head or to some other well-known eating place. One gets the impression that they did themselves very well at table. Indeed, according to the Parlour, or Wager Book, in Emmanuel College Library, wagers on the comparative weights of the Fellows were fairly common. In 1769 Meen and Farmer wagered something about "13 stone," which *may* mean that one or the other weighed 13 stone (11). Four years later Askew bet Alpe "Farmer heavier than Wilcox" (80), and it is not without significance that Wilcox was also later to be afflicted by the gout (*Diaries,* 196). In his portraits Farmer is depicted as a man of some portliness. Unfortunately, gout was not only extremely painful, it was also extremely dangerous. Reed recorded, for example, that Farmer informed him that "the Porter of the College who had waited at table yesterday in apparent health had

Later Academic Career

died suddenly in the night. He had lately been troubled by some Gouty disorders" (*Diaries*, 184). Gout could, of course, have been only a contributing factor.

On 2 October 1786, Reed reorded "The Master was this morning confined with the Gout (1st time) of which he felt some symptoms in walking home last night" from Fen Ditton (149). Dr. Johnson defined "gout" in his *Dictionary* (1755) as "The arthritis; a periodical disease attended with great pain," bolstering the definition by quotation of "Arbuthnot on Diet," i.e., "The *gout* is a disease which may affect any membranous part, but commonly those which are at the greatest distance from the heart or the brain, where the motion of the fluids is the slowest, the resistance, friction, and stricture of the solid parts the greatest, and the sensation of pain, by the dilaceration of the nervous fibres, extreme." Dr. Arbuthnot listed among the common causes of gout "a too rich and high Diet, and too copious use of Wine and other spirituous Liquers, especially at Supper; . . . a full gross Habit of Body; . . . a Sedentary Life, with a plentiful Diet, and intense Study, and Application of the Mind." The cure: There "are no better Rules than Abstinence from those things which occasion it."[33] Farmer did not (probably could not because of his position as Master of his College) abstain, so that further attacks of gout were sure to occur. The next attack came about three months later. Farmer wrote to Reed in London on 30 December 1786 apologizing to him and Steevens for not being able to join them in London because of an attack of gout.[34]

In May of 1762 Farmer, with most of academic Cambridge, was ill with influenza to the point that he wrote to Percy that he thought he had "more Spirits than Body."[35] Many years later, on 27 July 1778 Farmer wrote to Richard Gough apologizing for not replying sooner to a letter. Among other reasons for the delay, he wrote, "When I received your Letter, I was confined by the rheumatism; and, as soon as possible, carried into the country to get rid of it" (*Lit. Anecd.*, II.631).

Farmer was near death from influenza in the winter of 1779. Michael Tyson wrote Richard Gough on November 29 to tell him that "Dr. Farmer, being given over by the Professor [Isaac Pennington, M.D. Professor of Chemistry], was advised to take Dr. James's Powders; and, if he is now alive, it is owing to their efficacy" (*Lit. Anecd.*, VIII. 655). A month later Farmer had just recovered, so William Cole wrote to Horace Walpole, from "death's door" from influenza and was well enough to invite Cole to "play a game at whist, and eat a piece of brawn only for supper" (Walpole, II.179–80). Steevens "sincerely rejoiced" at his friend's recovery, enclosing a printed copy of his transcript of Edward Capell's Catalogue of Shakespeare materials in a letter of 4 January 1780, adding that "at night" the Catalogue might "prove serviceable in the Parlour" (Folger MS C.b.10 item 161). Farmer seems to have been free of any serious indisposition until October 1792, some six years after an attack of gout, but on that date the gout struck again, although he was able to take the coach to London ten days after the onset of the attack (*Diaries*, 195, 197).

On 20 September 1793 Farmer had a cold (*Diaries*, 199), and while he soon recovered from it, he was again "not well" on October 8, although "wonderfully recovered" the next day (*Diaries*, 202). Reed left Cambridge on the fourteenth of the month; on the twentieth Busick Harwood, Professor of Anatomy and a regular participant in the Emmanuel evening activities, wrote to George Steevens in London,

> The Master has mended but slowly since you left us—I did not like his *Visnomy* for some days—He was feverish too &c. his bottom-belly far too large. I gave him two or three trimming doses of castor oil; &. these last two days he is (as he terms it) hugely mended—his belly is reduced &. his appetite returned, he has rode out, &. will I trust be quite himself again by the end of the week. The most difficult task will be to keep him within due bonds in future, &. I assure you he shall not want a Remembrancer. (Folger MS. C.b.10, item 83)

Farmer's lifelong conviviality was taking its toll, but he adhered to old practices, as witness Francis Barnes to George Steevens in a letter of 3 September 1794, writing of his own pork: "Dr Farmer delivered a fine Oration in praise of it," doubtless having done justice to it himself (Folger MS. C.b.10, item 7).

Henry Meen, Fellow of Emmanuel, was one of Bishop Percy's correspondents. Percy, who had ties with Emmanuel, having proceeded Doctor of Divinity of Emmanuel in 1770, had had much correspondence with Farmer on scholarly matters and was therefore interested in his health. Meen wrote to Percy on 26 July 1796 and added a postscript to his letter to the effect that "Dr. Farmer, we hear, intends to spend some part of the summer at Bath or Buxton. We are sorry to hear he is not better in health than when he was in town" (*Lit. Illustr.*, VII.39). Farmer wrote to Steevens from Bath on September 11, saying that he thought his stay in Bath had been of some "service" to him and that he hoped to be back in Cambridge on the twenty-fourth, intending to go to Leicester before the end of the week (Folger MS. C.b.10, item 71). On October 3 Meen assured Percy that Farmer had "certainly been benefited by his excursion to Bath," but that he had not heard from him or Farmer's nephew since their return to Cambridge. He hoped to see Farmer in London at the end of October (*Lit.Illustr.*, VII.41), but Meen was mistaken. Steevens wrote to Percy on October 24 with an entirely different and authentic account of the results, or nonresults, of Farmer's trip to Bath:

> On the 24th of last month, when our excellent friend Dr. Farmer returned from Bath to college, he was the mere shadow of what he had been. He assured me, he had neither the benefit of appetite, sleep, or spirits. In the course of the next three weeks, however, he eat as much as he ought[!], slept with few interruptions, and enlivened his companions as much as ever. But in these circumstances, I must confess, I have little confidence. He still wants flesh and the genuine color of health. His disorder, I am afraid, is referable to the state of his liver. I should add, that this supposition is merely my own, and has not been authorised by our London or Cambridge physicians.

Meen, "prebendary of Twyford, in the Cathedral Church of St. Paul, in which Cathedral he held also the office of Lecturer" (*Lit. Illustr.*, VII.36) and one hence who would see much of Farmer in London, wrote to Percy on December 15, explaining his delay in sending a packet to him, among other matters having to attend twice every day at "St. Paul's, in the absence of the Residentiary [Farmer]. Next February I hope once more to see our friend Dr. Farmer in town, and to see him in better health than when he last attended here." By December 26, when Steevens next wrote to Percy, Farmer was continuing in "a state of convalescence. The last reports of him were sufficiently favourable. Tomorrow (being St. John's day) he feasts his whole college" (*Lit. Illustr.*, VII.9–10). In a letter to Malone dated 31 January 1797 Farmer wrote, "I flatter'd myself, that I might possibly get to *London* for some part of my *February—Residence,* but I now think it more likely that I shall never get thither again" (Bodleian MS Montagu. d. 13 f. 12).

In this same month both Meen, on 23 January 1797, and Steevens, on January 30, wrote to Percy. Both letters contain anticipatory and detailed accounts of Farmer's declining health. Meen wrote,

> The state of Dr. Farmer's health will not permit him to return to town in February, which is his month of residence; I therefore took the first opportunity that offered to pay my respects to him in college, and spend a few days with my college-friends. It will, I am certain, be satisfactory to your Lordship, to know how Dr. Farmer does. I wish it were in my power to give you, my Lord, a more favourable account of our worthy friend's health. But he is very far from well. There is a visible change in his person and appearance. He looks enfeebled and emaciated. Occasionally his spirits revive, and he recovers for a time his usual cheerfulness. He

complains much of the cramp, which frequently disturbs his rest; and he is apprehensive that it will finally seize some vital part, and prove fatal. No arguments will prevail upon him to alter his habits. He takes but little exercise, and sees but little company, except that of his own society, with whom he spends his most comfortable hours. But I am happy to hear him say that he intends to be with us in June. I sincerely wish that he would exert himself a little; and not sink under his infirmities with a langour bordering upon despondency. Much, it is thought, might yet be done by a change of air, diet, and exercise: and nothing surely should be omitted, that can prolong a life valuable as his. (*Lit. Illustr.,* VII.42–43)

Steevens's account, at secondhand, is much the same as Meen's,

> I am sorry to add, that I can send you no good account of our friend Dr. Farmer. I am taught to believe he is in a confirmed decline; that he is quite unmanageable; and both eats and drinks in direct opposition to such advice as has been offered by the most experienced of his medical neighbours. I have likewise been told that there is an appearance of swelling in his legs. Should this last circumstance prove true, a dropsy may be at no great distance. I cannot conclude without a hope that my apprehensions are groundless. (*Lit. Illustr.,* VII.13)

Samuel Johnson took his definition of "dropsy" from John Quincy's *Lexicon Physico-Medicum* (1719): "A collection of water in the body from too lax a tone of the solids, whereby digestion is weakened, and all the parts stuffed." It may be remembered that Johnson, "imagining that the dropsical collection of water which oppressed him might be drawn off by making incisions in his body, he, with his usual resolute defiance of pain, cut deep, when he thought his surgeon had done it too tenderly" (*Life,* IV.399). One thing is clear—despite all advice to the contrary, Farmer was clinging to his old ways; in a real sense, he was eating and drinking himself to death.

The chronology of the last year of Farmer's life comes largely from the letters of Steevens and Meen to Percy. Steevens, again secondhand, hearing unfavorable reports of Farmer's health, wrote to Percy on February 6 that he feared his "last autumnal visit to our University has been paid." When he next wrote to Percy on March 10 he had learned from Farmer's nephew that his uncle was "sinking very fast. His legs swell; as often as he sleeps he is attacked by the cramp; and, contrary to his former practice, he sees every thing through a gloomy medium." Next month, on April 12, another letter to Percy and another bulletin on Farmer,

But as I find Dr. Farmer is so languid that he cannot bear company, and

82   Later Academic Career

even avoids the parlour at Emmanuel, I begin to fear that my last visit to our university has been paid. He has almost determined on a tour to Leicester; but his nephew (who came to town on Saturday last) assures me he is utterly irresolute, and seems to have given his case up as a lost one. What is still more discouraging, I learn that our physical professors are of the same opinion.

On May 1 he hoped Farmer was "breathing his native air at Leicester," and on the next day Meen was able to add substantially,

Dr. Farmer, I am sorry to say, is very unwell; weaker and worse than in January. He has been much solicited, and, I believe, is come to a resolution, to spend some time with his friends and relations of Leicester. The change of air, of diet, of company, and the kind attention of friends constantly about him, will certainly be of service, and contribute, I hope to prolong his valuable life.

Farmer was hoping to take his farewell of his native city and his friends and relatives there.[36]

On June 10 Steevens wrote to Percy that "Our friend at Emmanuel is growing weaker and weaker, and was unable to attend the annual meeting of his college at the Crown and Anchor on Tuesday last." Five days later Meen informed Percy that Farmer continued "in very indifferent health, and is unwilling to quit his college residence for Leicester, to which place his relations and friends are desirous to bring him." August 30, Meen quoted Farmer's nephew in a letter to him: "The Master seems to be no worse now than when you last saw, some months ago; though in the interim he has been very bad indeed. Professor Harwood thinks Dr. Farmer might in some measure reinstate his health, if he would get into the air. But he has not been down stairs these two months and upward." Steevens provided another report a few days later, on September 3. "The Master still continues in the same melancholy situation, nor can any hope of his recovery be entertained. He has taken to a milk diet; is said to be as pale as the fluid he lives upon; and is quite reduced to a skeleton. He will see none but his own family."[37] At some indecipherable date in September, Dr. Francis Barnes, Master of Peterhouse College, wrote to Steevens. Barnes had often made one of the party in the Emmanuel parlor or when Steevens and Reed made their autumnal visit. Barnes wrote,

I was told on Sunday last by M.ʳ T. Farmer that his Uncle was something better—but to be better satisfied I called myself, yesterday—after 1.ˢᵗ comp.ᵗˢ I inquired what good News he had—"Nay that I expect from you, as I never stir out"—I have received a Haunch of Venison from M.ʳ Steevens—"Very well, I hope he will not send me any—nay it would be an

Later Academic Career

83

insult if he did—for I can eat nothing." I send you this short Conversation, to satisfy you that there is no Defect in ye mental Powers. He lives now on Milk Diet entirely—&c. and so I should conclude from his Countenance—for his colour has forsaken it—yet Prof.^r Harwood says he wishes to have it thought that he eats nothing, &c. yet that in ye Day he picks up his Crumbs tolerably well—In my Judgement, I fear there is nothing that can give us Hope that he will get ye better of his Complaint. I made him laugh heartily when I told him that you &. he had been proclaimed to ye World the supreme Judges of the Works of Shakespeare. that the Author of ye Pursuits of L-[iterature] had ventured to quote from one of Shak.^s
(he says)
own Plays, "for so *now* seems (as Dr F. & G.S. Esq, give to him & take away just as they please.") He seemed very much delighted with ye Pleasantry of y.^t (Folger MS C.b.10, item 9)

The end came on September 8. Farmer's nephew wrote to Steevens that same day from Emmanuel.

When I left Cambridge we were in hopes the Master was getting much better; he however on Wednesday last was surprised by the continual throwing up of Bile, under the severe exertions of which he died this morning at seven o clock—Melancholy Event for all his Friends; but scarcely supportable by me who have attended him very strictly for some Time—He fell as if asleep & left this World without the least Struggle. (Folger MS. C.b. 10, item 74)

Four months later Francis Barnes wrote to Steevens on 8 January 1798, telling him that "As to Eman. C as far as recording his Sayings & Pleasantry we are able to preserve his Memory, the late Ma^r. may be said to live amongst us" (Folger MS. C.b. 10, item 10). Steevens wrote to Percy on the fourteenth, repeating Thomas Farmer's account of his uncle's last moments, but prefacing it with his observation that he "foretold, that the first effort of nature to relieve poor Farmer would be the last moment of his existence" (*Lit. Illustr.*, VII.33). A little more than two years later Meen wrote to Percy to inform him of Steevens's death, adding that Steevens had left Dr. Farmer one hundred pounds in his will "with benefit of survivorship" (*Lit. Illustr.*, VII.50), the last, albeit posthumous, record of a friendship of many years.

4

The Abortive History of Leicester

On 15 May 1766 the Cambridge University Press printed "Proposals for printing, by Subscription, The History and Antiquities of the Town of Leicester; originally collected by William Staveley, Esq. Barrister at Law, and formerly of Peter-house in that University. Now first offered to the Publick from the Author's Manuscripts, with very large Additions and Improvements; and an Appendix of Papers relative to the Subject. By Richard Farmer, M.A. Fellow of Emanuel College in Cambridge, and of the Society of Antiquaries, London." Nichols, from whose *Literary Anecdotes*[1] I quote the title of the Proposals, gave the date of the Proposals as May 13 in his obituary notice for Farmer in the *GM* in 1797 (II.888). His corrected date is that of Farmer's "birthday," a bit of sentimentality on Farmer's part. Farmer had been elected to the Society of Antiquaries on 19 May 1763, a near miss of his birthday. In any event, the Proposals attracted much notice, although a few scholars and antiquaries had known for some time that Farmer was collecting materials for such a history. The Rev. John Simmonds, Vicar of St. Mary's, Leicester, already mentioned as a book collector whose library was open to young Farmer, wrote to Farmer soon after the Proposals were issued, telling him that several subscriptions had already been received by John Gregory, printer and bookseller of Leicester, and that Samuel Heyrick had called in to tell him that the William Stavely of the Proposals should be Thomas Stavely.[2] Accordingly, the next year, when Farmer received the imprimatur for the History, the name was correctly given.

Sir Thomas Cave, who, in Nichols's words, had "undertaken the pleasing though arduous, task of a new History of the County of Leicester," wrote a series of seven letters to Farmer, from 20 October 1766 to 13 August 1767, which Nichols reprints in his history of Leicestershire (III.i.vi–viii). Farmer wrote to Joseph Cradock on 16 June 1766, partly about the printing of the *Essay* on Shakespeare's learning, but more urgently to enlist Cradock's aid in approaching Sir Thomas: "I am informed that he has in his possession some papers of Mr. Carte, formerly Vicar of St. Martin's, which may be of service to

The Abortive History of Leicester

85

me: and, as he has been long a collector, in all probability other MSS. or extracts. I hope, from a love of literature in general, and his county-town in particular, he will not refuse his assistance; and I will return him all the honour in my power."[3] I suppose Cradock's efforts on Farmer's behalf bore fruit in the form of these seven letters.

Sir Thomas had already accumulated much material about the county but also had "a MS History of Leicester, wrote by a very excellent author, which I believe you never saw; and it is highly necessary you should see and peruse it." He offered to let Farmer peruse it, either in Leicester or London (III.i.vi). In subsequent letters Cave gave a lot of information to Farmer and acknowledged Farmer's help. When the antiquary "Honest Tom Martin of Palgrave" wrote to Farmer on 31 December 1766 to subscribe to Farmer's projected History and to offer to transcribe Peter Le Neve's marginal comments on William Burton's "Leicestershire," i.e., *Description of Leicester Shire* (1622) (III.i.7), Farmer told Sir Thomas of the offer. The latter replied in a letter dated 14 March 1767 entreating Farmer to use his interest with Martin to get him the use of the volume. There is no evidence that Sir Thomas and Farmer ever met. Their mutual friend Dr. Anthony Askew acted as liaison for them in London. In Sir Thomas's last letter to Farmer, he wrote, "I am glad so much grist comes to your mill, where I am confident it will be made to produce the finest flour. If you visit Leicestershire this year, I indulge myself in thinking you will not pass me unregarded, as I am Mr. Farmer's most obedient, T. Cave" (III.i.ix). The letter was written 13 August 1767. Sir Thomas died in 1778, and his papers were given to Nichols in 1790. If Sir Thomas and Farmer continued to correspond, their letters are not extant.

When Farmer originally conceived the idea of a history of Leicester is not known, but it is not the kind of project that would ordinarily stir the imagination of a schoolboy. Farmer must, however, have started collecting materials and information some time before 1760, for Nichols records in his *Leicestershire* (I.ii.452), that "The following royal mandate was copied by Dr. Farmer, in the year 1760, from the original." The mandate, having to do with officials of the "Borough of Leicester," includes no members of the Farmer family. Nichols also prints "A Catalogue of some of the more Rare Plants found in the Neighbourhood of Leicester, Loughborough, and in Chatley Forest," by an anonymous botanist. "It was compiled," writes Nichols, "many years ago, nearly in the state in which the reader now sees it, at the request of the Rev. Dr. *Farmer,* at the time that gentleman had some intention of publishing a History of the Town of Leicester, with a view to have been inserted in that work" (I.i.clxxvi and clxxvii). Thomas

Martyn, Farmer's school fellow at Leicester and then his senior by one year at Emmanuel College, comes to mind. The *DNB* account styles him as a "student of botany from his childhood," one of the "earliest English exponents" of the Linnean system which is used in the nomenclature in the *Catalogue*. It is not unlikely that "many years ago" Farmer asked his friend Martyn to undertake a task the latter was sure to find congenial. While there are a number of references to books, and to pages of most of these books having to do with Leicester in a manuscript book of Farmer's jottings in the Emmanuel College Library, there are no dates, although they are certainly later than his undergraduate days.[4] Two references, however, are to "Harleian Catalogue, 2 vols. Fol. 1759," which gives at least a terminus à quo. On 14 July 1763 Thomas Percy, writing from Easton Maudit to Thomas Astle, an antiquary who had made an index of the Harleian MSS. in the British Museum, published in 1759, came to "the Petition of my friend, the Rev. Mr. Farmer . . . fellow of your Society of Antiquaries," In short, Farmer had asked Percy to ask Astle if he could have "a Copy, with the arms blazoned in colours" of "The Descent and Arms of Farmer of Radcliffe in Comitat. Leicester, dat. A.D. 1640" to be found in "fol. 996" of Harl. MS. No. 11764 (art. 180)." Farmer would, of course, pay the expenses, "and in return will procure you anything out of their Libraries at Cambridge," a generous return for the favor requested.[5] The manuscript is mentioned in Nichols's *Leicestershire* as being among "the late Dr. Farmer's papers" (IV.ii.950). Not only did Astle provide the copy but on 11 December 1766, he wrote to Farmer to tell him "two fine drawings of tessellated pavements have exhibited at the Society of Antiquaries; they were found at Mr. Reading's, near Leicester; are very curious, and different from any I have yet seen. They will be great ornaments to your work."[6] The penultimate item in the sale catalog of Farmer's library is "A piece of tessellated Pavement, and Roman Chimney." Astle wrote again on 8 January 1767, sending "a transcript of a charter relating to the earldom of Leicester, from the original in my collection" and offering further information (III.i.7).

Many scholars and antiquaries offered Farmer help of one kind or another. Thomas Warton wrote from Oxford on 19 June 1766, shortly after the Proposals, to say that he was extremely glad that "the Antiquities of Leicester are fallen into your hands" and sent certain entries from his "Collectanea from the Rolls Chapter" relating to Farmer's subject.[7] Farmer reciprocated Warton's kindness in a letter of 29 December 1766, in which, after providing Warton with the manuscripts and information he had asked for, he asked that someone at Oxford "look at Dugdale in the Ashmolean, 6502, 12F2. p. 327," adding, "Can I ask likewise, at somebody's leisure, for a peep at the said Dugdale MSS. Angl. 292. No. 6491?," a query to which Nichols, who quotes part of the letter in the *Literary Ancedotes* (II.622–623–5), adds, "He had then his 'History of Leicester' very much at heart." Some time before his death on 22 December 1768 Charles Lyttleton, Bishop of Carlisle and President of the Society of Antiquaries, wrote to Farmer about "the old work in St. Nicholas's churchyard at Leicester, now called the Jewry-wall."[8] George Ashby, "learned antiquary and sometime president of St. Johns's College Cambridge" *(DNB)*, held the rectories of Hingerton and Twyford in Leicestershire until 1767. He wrote an "Essay on the Roman Military" in 1772, which was printed in 1793 and reprinted by Nichols in his *Leicestershire* (I.i.clv–clvii). The essay is largely concerned with the Latin inscription on a stone found near Thurmaston in Leicestershire, two copies of which inscription Farmer "laid" before Ashby in November 1771, and then a third. All of the copies had been variously and incorrectly interpreted. Ashby supplied missing letters to the abbreviations and made sense of the inscription; he gave a copy of his completed transcription to Farmer (clv). Farmer was not only receiving help from others, at the same time he was sharing his knowledge and material with others. William Cole of Milton was also among those who provided materials, writing to Farmer on Easter Sunday, 19 April 1767, "with some MS. notes by Mr Willis, & Mr Baker relating to the Religious Houses in Leicester" as Farmer was "being about to print an History of that Town."[9] Farmer and Cole were to become fast friends.

Farmer would seem to have been very sanguine about the composition and publication of his History. Although the Proposals were printed on 15 May 1766, he could end his *Essay on the Learning of Shakespeare,* published in January 1767 with this sentence: "And when I am fairly rid of the Dust of topographical Antiquity, which hath continued much longer about me than I expected, you may very probably be troubled again with this ever faithful Subject of SHAKESPEARE and his Commentators." Now while there can be no doubt that Farmer was soliciting information and accumulating materials for the projected work at least as early as 1760, apparently very little actually reached print. If George Dyer can be trusted, and there would appear to be little reason why he should lie about this, Farmer undertook the work "rather from local partiality, than a well principled love for the employment" and "though he had actually printed three pages of the history, yet the materials collected were not considerable."[10] Nichols, in his obituary notice in the *GM*, 1797, ii.806, gives four as the number of pages printed while George Gleig, the

88   The Abortive History of Leicester

least authoritative of Farmer's early biographers, writes that "so great, indeed, was his [Farmer's] love of ease, that, after having announced for subscriptions a History of Leicestershire, and actually began to print it, rather than submit to the fatigue of carrying it through the press, he returned the subscriptions," implying that it was actually finished.[11] Jonathan Darker, F.S.A., F.R.S., and MP for Leicester, wrote to "Honest Tom Martin" on 13 December 1766 and ended his letter by supposing that "Mr. Farmer's 'History of Leicester' will soon be published, and I dare say will give satisfaction, by the accounts I hear of it" (*Lit. Anecd.*, V.700). Darker's supposition was, of course, wrong. Indeed, in an Advertisement to his *Essay* on Shakespeare's learning, Farmer took the opportunity to notify his subscribers "that many of the Plates are already finished; and the whole Work is prosecuted with all the Expedition consistent with the Nature of the undertaking. But the important Communications he has been favoured with, which greatly enlarge his Book, must necessarily defer its publication somewhat longer than he expected. Subscriptions will be received till Lady-day next," i.e., 25 March 1767, presumably when the work would be completed. Thomas Percy wrote to Farmer on 7 June 1766 and said, among other things, "Last night I saw M[r] Johnson, and mentioned to him your new proposed History of Leicester: which he much appro[ved] of and has promised to assist me in getting Subscriptions: So send me up 20 Receipts at least" (II.109). In December Percy was glad that the History "advances so fast" and asked for "more Receipts by the first Post: Dodsley had none left, when I came out of London." As an afterthought he adds, "M[r] Johnson desired me to tell you that he formerly saw a Curious MS Account of your Town of Leicester in the hands of the then Minister of Great Cch: if not the same with Staveley's (of which he is now uncertain,) He desires you will inquire after it" (*Letters,* II, 118, 119–20). Johnson would seem to have been much interested in the projected History. In April 1767 Percy undertook a chore for Farmer about "the draught of Leicester" (II.134), and in March 1768 Dr. Ducarrel promised Percy "a Transcript of a small paper about *Leicester*" (II.142).

Needless to say, "Lady-day next" came and went without the completion of the History, despite Richard Gough's belief that it would be "published about Lady-day," which he expressed in a letter dated 16 February 1767. Gough knew that a "very particular account of the Earls of Leicester will be included in this quarto volume" (*Lit. Illustr.*, V.308). He wrote to the Rev. Michael Tyson, Fellow of Corpus Christi College, Cambridge, on 29 September 1771 to tell him that "The History of Leicester is promised in the Leicester newspaper to

The Abortive History of Leicester 89

appear next winter. I wish to have some Proposals for it." And again on December 27 of the same year he reminded Tyson, "This is the season wherein I look for Farmer's Leicester. Do you take care I am not forgotten as a subscriber." And then, less optimistically, a month later on 30 January 1772 he wrote to Tyson, "Once more! When is the *Leicester* to come out?"[12] Percy wrote to Farmer on 4 December 1771, and told him he had been "not long since down at Leicester where I saw the old Roman Mile Stone which was found in making the Turnpike Road between Leicester and Thurmaston. I have copied the Inscription. . . . I shall therefore send it you in a future Letter" (II.156). And on January 21, 1773, still expecting Farmer to proceed with the History, Percy asked if Farmer knew of a copy of "Burton's Leicestershire 'interleaved with Rich[d] Gascoyne's Notes transcribed from a Copy of this Book in Jesus College Library Cambridge'" (II.161–62). Others were becoming impatient, as witness Gough to Tyson on 16 March 1772, "Do you see how Farmer's knuckles are rapt in the last St. James's [Chronicle]?," a query which occasioned Tyson's reply two days later: "There is not a more honest and generous man than my friend Farmer; and his delay in publication is owing to extreme ill usage from the *Corporation of Leicester*. I saw at his room, the other day, Steevens's proof sheets of the new edition of Shakespeare. Farmer is making additions," (*Lit. Anecd.*, VIII.587). Percy had brought Farmer and Steevens together, and, after much importuning on Steevens's part, Farmer, his heart evidently not in the History of Leicester, made very considerable additions to the 1773 Johnson-Steevens *Shakespeare*.[13] Somebody evidently felt that Farmer was being mistreated, for Gough wrote to Tyson on 28 March 1772, shortly after the knuckle-rapping, that an "apology for Farmer has already appeared in the St. James's Evening. If you tell me who was the Champion, I will tell you who was *not* the Challenger" (*Lit. Anecd.*, VIII.587–88). Gough seems to be implying that Tyson was Farmer's "Champion" and that he, Gough, was not the "Challenger."

Farmer did not remain indifferent to the knuckle-rapping in the *St. James's Chronicle*, especially since it had evidently been repeated, for he wrote to Henry Baldwin, the proprietor of that periodical, on 12 November 1772. His letter was occasioned by a subscriber's complaint, at the delay in publication of the History, which was in the *Chronicle* for November 7. As the letter is Farmer's fullest explanation of the reasons for that delay, I quote it in full from Nichols's reprinting of it.

> Sir; A Correspondent of yours, in the Chronicle of Saturday, informs you that he is a Subscriber to some Book, which he has long wished to

90 The Abortive History of Leicester

receive; and complains, with seeming justice, of the delay of publication. He must, however, be candid enough to own, that there may be causes which do not originate in the Author, and those unforeseen ones; such, at least, he will soon find, in the Preface to the *Description of Leicester Shire* has been the case with that Work. The matter is too long for a Newspaper disquisition; but it will appear, that Mr. Farmer has been the person must deceived in his reasonable expectations; and that not his Time only, but his Money, has been sacrificed to the Honour of his Town, and the Interest of his Subscribers. When the delay proved inevitable, it was repeatedly advertized in the Country Journals, that the Subscription-money would be returned by the Booksellers to all those who should please to accept it; and the same notice was given to Mr. Beecroft, in London, from whom almost all the Town Receipts were taken. This is again offered; and Mr. Farmer flatters himself that no room is left for complaint.

Some time ago Mr. Farmer, on the authority of some persons whom he supposed to be better acquainted than himself with the business of Plates and Printing, was induced to tell his friends in the country, that the Work would be finished in the course of the Winter. He is very sorry to find himself unavoidably deceived and must necessarily beg a little further indulgence; he hopes only *to* the Summer; certainly not *beyond* it. (*Lit. Anecd.*, II.627–28)

It must not go unnoted that Farmer still hoped for publication by the summer of 1773, "certainly not *beyond* it."

The fact that the history was not published in the summer of 1773 or even in the early months of 1774 did not go entirely unremarked. The Rev. Mr. Tobias Heyrick, M.A. of Trinity College, Cambridge, "and for some years one of the two Curates of Church Langton in Leicestershire," wrote to a friend on 29 May 1774 to complain of the delay in publication of more of the long delayed volumes of a projected edition of a history of Northamptonshire. He ended his letter with an unmistakable reference to Farmer, "Another fellow, *an historical cheat,* has played the same trick with regard to the 'Antiquities of Leicester'; has pocketed the money, turned Critic, and writes Notes on Shakespeare" (*Lit. Anecd.*, VIII.347 and 348). Next year, 1775, Farmer was elected Master of Emmanuel, and in the 1789 edition of his *Essay on the Learning of Shakespeare,* he wrote, "This Work [the History] was just begun at the press, when the Writer was called to the tuition of a large College, and was obliged to decline the undertaking," adding that the plates and materials had long ago (i.e., 1775) been "put into the hands of a gentleman who is every way qualified to make a proper use of them" (95). The gentleman who was to make a proper use of the plates and materials was, of course John Nichols. Farmer helped Nichols in 1781 when Nichols was working on his history of Hinckley. Indeed Farmer would seem to have been quite

The Abortive History of Leicester

91

involved, as witness Cole's letter to Nichols, 27 September 1782, in which he writes, "Your last two books of Mr. Bowyer, and the proof-sheets of Hinckley, greatly please me: Dr. Farmer sent me the last," leading to the justifiable conclusion that Nichols asked Farmer to read the proofsheets for him.[14] In his eighth volume of his *Bibliotheca Topographica Britannica* (1790), devoted to "Antiquities in Leicestershire," Nichols acknowledged two manuscripts given to him, which he had been "delicate" in his "extracting from them" as they were to be of "singular service" in his larger work, the history of Leicestershire. "These articles, with several engraved plates, were in the most liberal manner contributed by a Dignitary of the first eminence in literature, from whose pen there was once reasons to have hoped for 'The Antiquities of Leicester.' The manner in which this circumstance has been mentioned by himself in print [in the 1789 *Essay*] will be an additional inducement to the Editor to use his best exertions in endeavouring to deserve the compliment which DR. FARMER has condescended to bestow on him" (viii). Farmer was especially helpful to Nichols in the latter's account of the "History and Antiquities of Barnwell Abbey and Sturbridge Fair," giving him access to a manuscript of the thirty-first year of Queen Elizabeth's reign, which granted the mayor and commonality of Cambridge the power of building and disposing booths in the Fair (V.77). Another of Farmer's manuscripts, dealing with various rules for the booths, was quoted in toto (V.90–96). The acknowledgment was repeated in volume one, part one (1795) in the *History* of Leicestershire, with some slight changes in the wording, particularly in the new description of Farmer as a "learned Dignitary of the Church." Farmer helped Nichols in other ways, especially by interesting others in Nichols's great work. Thus, the Rev. Mr. Thomas Leman, who took the B.A. degree at Emmanuel College in 1775, wrote to Nichols to tell him that Leman's friend "Dr. Farmer spoke to me about it [the History] when I was last in Cambridge" and offered to give him information about "the Roman Roads or Stations in that county" (*Lit. Illustr.*, VI.443). The offer bore fruit in Leman's essay on the "Roman Roads and Stations in Leicestershire" printed in volume one, part one of the history.[15]

Quite ironically, less than a year before Farmer's death, some correspondent, in a communication in the December 1796 number of an unnamed periodical, asked if Farmer had published his History and whether "he received subscriptions" to his work. Nichols answered in the July 1797 *GM*.

Without entering into the motives for such a question, I will answer, that Dr. Farmer did receive such subscriptions, and that the book is not yet

The Abortive History of Leicester

published. But let me add, that the very respectable Dignitary here called in question, more than 20 years ago, advertized in the St. James's Chronicle that he had declined the undertaking, and that the subscription-money was ready to be returned. Should any one doubt this assertion, I am ready to give the best proof of it, by repeating the same offer in the Doctor's name. You may, therefore, Sir, assure your readers, that, if by chance there should be still any one or more subscriptions outstanding, the money will, on demand, be returned by

J NICHOLS.

Thus ended the saga of the ill-fated history of the town and antiquities of Leicester.

Although Farmer abandoned his history of Leicester, he never turned his back on his native city. On 21 September 1774 a new organ "was opened at the anniversary of the Leicester infirmary . . . to a brilliant and respectable assembly." The musicians "were honoured with the assistance of the Earl of Sandwich, upon the kettle-drums. Besides most of the nobility and gentry of these parts, who were of the auditory, was Omiah, the famed native of Otaheite." The church wardens of St. Martins' Church thanked Farmer's friend, Joseph Cradock, for making much of the affair and the occasion possible. Farmer was among those present.[16] Some four years later, writing to Richard Gough on 27 July 1778, Farmer excused himself for not writing earlier for a number of reasons, including "a Sermon to make for our Infirmary business."[17]

There were other ties to Leicester, for Farmer was, after all, one of its most famous native sons. When there was the possibility of his using his influence with others to help old friends or acquaintances, he was not forgotten. On 10 August 1786 William Bickerstaffe wrote to Edward Lord Thurlow, High Chancellor of Great Britain, asking to be considered for the soon to be vacated living of St. Nicholas in Leicester. Bickerstaffe had been, from 1750 on, Usher at the Free Grammar School, where Farmer had been a student; he was also seven years a Curate of St. Mary's, his and Farmer's native parish, and six years curate at St. Martin's with All Saints. Bickerstaffe enlisted Farmer's aid by letter:

I think, if Dr. Farmer would undertake my course, through means usually at hand with men of eminence, I might, by Divine Providence, find the Lord Chancellor disposed to serve me. . . . I presume Mr. Secretary Pitt, the Representative of Cambridge University, and even the Chancellor of the same, with a crowd of other great personages, have eyes, ears, and hearts, at the service of its late Vice-chancellor, and yet Master of Emanuel.

The Abortive History of Leicester

To another friend Bickerstaffe wrote:

> At 58 years of age, having more inclination to a church-living than a wife, I applied to my old neighbour and playfellow, Dr. Farmer, to procure me St. Nicholas parish here; and my application was so well-timed, as to get the business into the hands of Mt. Pitt, their University-representative, by the kind service of the Vice-Chancellor. . . . Dr. Farmer informed me, that this Chancellor was his particular friend; and that, if St. Nicholas's was pre-engaged. I was put in the way of church-preferment. (*Lit. Anecd.*, II.635, 636)

Cradock, incidentally, remarked that "Farmer, at the latter part of his life, kept very high company, and no man ever more profited by polite and refined society" (*Memoirs*, I.37). As for Bickstaffe, whatever "church-preferment" he may have received was short-lived; he died on 26 January 1789.

5

The Essay on the Learning of Shakespeare

One of the first notices of Farmer's scholarly interest in Shakespeare comes from Thomas Percy in a letter to Farmer dated 9 October 1763, in which Percy writes, "And now we are upon the subject of Shakespear, I cannot but express my approbation of the scheme you hint at in your Post-Script: . . . I am charmed with your plan: *A series of Letters on the subject of Shakespear and his commentators,* will from your hands be an interesting work" (*Letters,* II.50). Percy may be referring to the last sentence of Farmer's *Essay on the Learning of Shakespeare* where one reads that "you [Joseph Cradock, to whom the *Essay* was addressed] may very probably be troubled again with the ever fruitful Subject of SHAKESPEARE and his COMMEN-TATORS." The "series of letters" phrase was almost surely used by Farmer in a letter no longer extant. Strange that Percy, in October 1763, should be quoting the last sentence of a manuscript *Essay* that was not to be published until January 1767. The reason for the delay is not known. Percy, in October 1762, had written to Farmer to tell him that Samuel Johnson "intends to add an appendix to his Shakespear, wherein he will give all such notes &c as shall be communicated to him by his friends, (with their Authors names) at full length. . . . *Have you any inclination to become a contributor? If so now's your time*" (*Letters,* II.13–14). By this time Percy and Farmer had corresponded about the former's work on his *Reliques of Ancient English Poetry,* Farmer being Percy's chief helper, his arbiter in all questions of scholarship (*Letters,* II.ix). Over two and a half years later Farmer wrote to Percy on 25 February 1765: "Since I last heard from you, I have had the unexpected pleasure of Mr JOHNSON'S Company at *Cambridge* . . . I had little opportunity to speak to him about *Shakespeare:* he ask'd my assistance, and refused my Subscription. I told him, that my time just now is too much employ'd—but I suspect I shall have enough before his Publication" (*Letters,* II.84, 85). Johnson's *Shakespeare* was published on 10 October 1765; Farmer was too sanguine or too lazy—or actually too busy—to contribute to Johnson's Appendix, for it contains no notes by him. His time was no doubt "too much employ'd" with his *Essay* on Shakespeare's learning which appeared some fourteen to fifteen months later. Johnson was so impressed with Farmer's *Essay* he told Percy that he wished Farmer "would throw together all [his] Knowledge about Shakespeare and old English writers in general and give us a large Volume," a sentiment in which Percy concurred (II.133).

Soon after the appearance of his *Shakespeare,* Johnson joined forces with George Steevens in a revision of the edition. He wrote to Farmer on 21 March 1770 again to solicit his aid.

> As no Man ought to keep wholly to himself any possession that may be useful to the publick, I hope you will not think me unreasonably intrusive, if I have recourse to you for such information as you are more able to give me, than any other Man.
>
> In support of an opinion which you have already placed above the need of any more support, Mr Steevens a very ingenious Gentleman lately of King's College, has collected an account of all the translations which Shakespeare might have seen and used. He wishes his catalogue to be perfect, and therefore entreats that you will favour him by the insertion of such additions, as the accuracy of your enquiries has enabled you to make. To this request I take the liberty of adding my own solicitation.
>
> We have no immediate use for this catalogue, and therefore do not desire that it should interrupt or hinder your more important employments, but it will be kind to let us know that you receive it.[1]

Evidently Farmer had not been forthcoming, for Johnson wrote about a year later, on 18 February 1771, to say that Steevens "begins to fancy that he wants" the catalog of translations. He added, of the yet-to-be published 1773 *Shakespeare,* "I have done very little to the book, but by the plunder of your pamphlet, and the authorities which Mr Steevens has very diligently collected, I think it will be somewhat improved. If you could spare us any thing we should think your communication a great favour."[2] Farmer evidently bestirred himself, for his help with the catalog of ancient authors was properly acknowledged in an advertisement in the 1773 edition to the effect that "the list has received the advantage of being corrected and amplified by the Reverend Mr. Farmer, the substance of whose very decisive pamphlet is interspersed through the notes which are in this revisal of Dr. Johnson's Shakespeare" (E6ᵛ). Farmer's contributions to the 1773 Johnson–Steevens *Shakespeare* were, then, the correction and amplification of the catalog, the use of the *Essay* in the notes to the text, and a very considerable *Letter to Mr. Steevens,* covering forty pages of small type with notes on every one of the thirty-six plays of the accepted canon.

96   The Essay on the Learning of Shakespeare

Professor T. W. Baldwin has traced in great detail the various stages in the controversy concerning the extent of Shakespeare's learning, especially his knowledge of classical literature at firsthand.[3] The eighteenth-century editors of Shakespeare up to the time of Farmer's *Essay* were Nicholas Rowe, Alexander Pope, Lewis Theobald, Sir Thomas Hanmer, William Warburton, and Samuel Johnson, and all but Hanmer and Warburton had something to say on the matter of Shakespeare's learning. Rowe conceded that Shakespeare had some Latin as did Pope. Theobald would not completely commit himself: "And therefore the Passages, that I occasionally quote from the *Classics,* shall not be urged as Proofs that he knowingly imitated those Originals; but brought to shew how happily he has express'd himself upon the same Topicks" (Baldwin, I.60). Johnson noted that some had seen Shakespeare as deeply learned in "many imitations of old writers; but the examples which I have known urged, were drawn from books translated in his time." He, too, conceded that Shakespeare "had learned *Latin* sufficiently to make him acquainted with construction, but . . . he never advanced to an easy perusal of the *Roman* authours" (Baldwin, I.61, 62). Johnson, as Smith points out, was almost surely influenced, both in his general comment and in those examples he adduced, by Farmer whom he had recently visited (xxvi, nn. 1 and 2). But it was Peter Whalley, a sometime Fellow of St. John's College, Cambridge, who took it upon himself to settle the matter in his *Enquiry into the Learning of Shakespeare, with Remarks on Several Passages in his Plays in a Conversation between Eugenius and Neander,* published in 1748. Whalley quite obviously took Dryden's *Of Dramatic Poesy, an Essay* as his model, even to the extent of employing two of the names of Dryden's amateur critics. Whalley's Preface begins, "The Learning of the Poet having been long made a Question, I recollected many parallel Places which I had taken notice of in the Study of the Classics. Upon bringing them together I perceived a very manifest Conformity between them, sufficient in some Measure to persuade one that *Shakespeare* was more indebted to the Ancients than is commonly imagined." He gave as parallels, or sources, among others, Saxo Grammaticus for *Hamlet,* whom Shakespeare must "certainly" have read "in the Original" Latin; Virgil's *Aeneid* for a passage in *The Tempest* in which Juno is recognizable by her "gait"; and another passage in the *Aeneid* for that in *Measure for Measure* in which Claudio describes the "fiery floods" and "thrilling regions of thick-ribbed ice" in an intermediate state after death. Farmer was to address these and other examples set forth. Whalley knew that others had claimed that "*Shakespeare* took his Hints from the Translations, which were made in the Reigns of Queen *Elizabeth*

The Essay on the Learning of Shakespeare 97

and King *James*." But as Shakespeare's "own Translations" from his "favourite Author," Ovid, "prove him to be a Master of his Works, I think it may be concluded he was a competent Judge of other Authors who wrote in the same Language" (79). Whalley refers to Shakespeare's supposed authorship of Ovid's Epistles of Paris and Helen, claimed for him by George Sewell (Smith, 323). While Farmer would answer other proponents of the theory that Shakespeare knew and imitated Latin authors, and possibly some Greek writers, Whalley's *Enquiry* and its arguments were both nearest in time to his own efforts and the lengthiest summary of the position he was to oppose. Farmer seems to have been unaware of Christopher Smart's "Brief Enquiry into the Learning of Shakespeare," printed in the *Universal Visiter and Monthly Memorialist* in January 1756. Virtually all Smart's parallels are commonplaces, except for his pointing out that the passage on the kingdom of the bees in the first act of *Henry V* is almost a translation of a passage in Virgil's fourth Georgic. T. W. Baldwin, not mentioning Smart anywhere in his two volumes, concludes, "Apparently, the passage from Virgil was under Shakespeare's eye as he wrote, else he had memorized it, for he uses it in sequence and in detail" (II.478). Smart's aperçu went unnoticed for many years, Malone quoting Lyly's *Euphues and his England* as Shakespeare's probable source in the 1821 Boswell-Malone *Shakespeare* (XVI.279–80). It was Whalley's *Enquiry* largely, and the scattered remarks of the various editors and critics of Shakespeare's plays, to which Farmer addressed himself in the first edition of his *Essay*.

John Nichols gives 1766 as the date of publication of Farmer's *Essay on the Learning of Shakespeare,* but the first edition bears the date 1767. Farmer had written to Joseph Cradock on 16 June 1766 saying "I have deferred an answer to your very friendly letter for a day or two, that I might be able to guess whether I could print the Essay (to which I begged the honour of prefixing your name) before the Commencement [usually in early July]; but I fear my many necessary avocations will make it impossible."[4] Edmond Malone's presentation copy of the second edition of the *Essay* has a note in his hand: "The first edition was published at London in Jany 1767. It was written in the preceding year, and printed at Cambridge in *Octr 1766*, as the Author told me."[5] On Dec. [29, 1766] Farmer wrote to William Huddesford, "Pray tell Mr Warton, Y^t I am printing ye little Essay on ye Learning of Shakespeare, & shall send some copies to Trinity."[6] Percy had received a copy, probably before publication, for his letter of thanks is dated 15 January 1767, while the editor of his letters gives the date of publication of the *Essay* as January 22 (*Letters*, II.120, n.1). Since the *Essay* was reviewed in the *Critical Review* for January

98   The Essay on the Learning of Shakespeare

1767, it must have appeared at least early in that month, since the *Critical Review* for January was published in February. On the same page of the *Literary Anecdotes,* where he gives the 1766 date, Nichols appends a footnote to the effect that a "second edition . . . was called for in 1767, in which are only a few corrections of style, but no additional information" (II.623–25, so numbered). This is a gross misstatement, for the second edition, as will be seen, is a greatly expanded version of the first. Very little is known about the composition of the *Essay,* some evidence being provided by Thomas Martyn, who wrote that Farmer "was occasionally writing Remarks on Shakespeare from the very first of his residing at Cambridge. I perfectly recollect his little *porte-feuille,* filled with scraps of paper of all sizes, in no order, which I occasionally attempted to arrange; and sometimes he would bring me some of his own writing to decypher, when he could not make it out himself" (*Lit. Anecd.,* VIII. 420). If Martyn, writing after a period of sixty years, is correct, Farmer, at age seventeen or eighteen, had begun to take notes on Shakespeare and did so for some thirteen years, as he had entered Emmanuel in 1753. Any one who has had to "decypher" Farmer's hand will sympathize with Martyn. At one juncture in the *Essay* Farmer, addressing Cradock, writes, "You have long known my opinion concerning the literary acquisitions of our immortal Dramatist" (2). Cradock was admitted to Emmanuel in November 1761, but as one who went to school in Leicester and was but seven years younger than Farmer, he may have known Farmer's opinion before 1761.

Very few voices were raised in condemnation of the *Essay* upon its publication. David Garrick wrote to George Colman early in 1767 and asked, "have You read Farmer's Learning of Shakes[r]?—some good things in it, but he's a conceited University Man, pert, & fantastical with a dash of the Nonsensical." On December 30 of the following year Garrick wrote to Joseph Cradock and asked, "pray have you heard of any new intended publication by Your friend M[r] Farmer? It would give me great pleasure to hear that he has such a design—I heard a hint of such an intention, but . . . I suppose there is nothing in it." Evidently Garrick had had second thoughts about Farmer and his *Essay,* for in another letter to Cradock, dated 2 October 1769, he asked, "Is Y[r] Friend M[r] Farmer asleep? Such Men ought to be Wak'd pro bono publico." Some years later, writing again to Cradock, Garrick added a postscript to his letter: "I sh[d] have been proud of seeing M[r] Farmer—a charming writer." Cradock, the editors of Garrick's letters write, "always avoided introducing Richard Farmer to Garrick. 'I knew,' he writes, 'that Garrick duly estimated his "Essay on the Learning of Shakespeare," and I feared that his

The Essay on the Learning of Shakespeare

coarse manners would sink him in the estimation of the great actor'."[7] What is more, Cradock had written that "Farmer, to speak plainly, absolutely mouthed a sentence, as dogs mouth a bone, and he was not always adverse from freely reciting passages of poetry in a mixed company" (*Memoirs,* I.36–37). Garrick's opinion was expressed privately, but Farmer's *Essay* had to face the reviewers. The editors of the *Monthly Review* virtually ignored it, relegating it to its Monthly Catalogue and giving it a page and a half (XXXVI, 153–54). The reviewer for the *GM* wrote that the "question, whether Shakespeare had any considerable knowledge of the learned languages, has been long agitated among the critics. Mr. *Farmer* is of opinion with those, who imagine that he had not" (1767, 120–21). He then devoted the rest of his review to quotation from the *Essay.* The reviewer for the *Critical Review,* almost surely William Guthrie, was not so noncommittal. His review ran to some six and a half pages (XXIII., 47–53), and he was avowedly of the opposite school of thought, although he promised "to lay before our readers, not only a candid, but a favourable view of this author's arguments." By quotation from the *Essay* and by expression of his own counterarguments, Guthrie was yet able to conclude that Farmer had "brought to light many curious circumstances relating to Shakespeare, of which we believe the public were ignorant before this publication," without giving up his own position. On 18 April 1767 Farmer wrote to William Huddesford, keeper of the Ashmolean Museum, saying, "I am plagued for another Edit. of ye Pamphlet, which when I have a little time, I will make somewhat *fatter,* & send you Copies."[8] When the second edition of the *Essay* appeared some months after the first, Guthrie reviewed it in the November 1767 *Critical Review* (400), stating that "we only thought it probable that he [Shakespeare] was not unacquainted with the Latin" language. Farmer did not know the identity of the *Critical's* reviewer, but he responded to Guthrie's earlier review in the second and third paragraphs of the preface to the second edition in language that angered Guthrie. As a consequence, Guthrie protested that he had been "illiberally and ungenteely attacked by Mr. Farmer, in this edition of his Essay." He concluded, "We are vain enough to believe that our Review has resolved some difficulties in Shakespeare, and corrected many blunders in his editors and commentators; but nothing advanced by Mr. Farmer against us in his edition has in the least varied, but rather confirmed our already declared opinion on the subject." Guthrie had further reason to take umbrage, for in this second edition of the *Essay* Farmer had taken him to task by name for having claimed in his *Essay upon English Tragedy* (1747) that Lady Macbeth's portrait was copied from

100   The Essay on the Learning of Shakespeare

Buchanan. Guthrie's was one discordant note in the almost universal chorus of praise that greeted the *Essay* upon its publication, and one wonders, with Garrick, why Farmer never published another work.

Percy wrote to Farmer from London on 15 January 1767, having received four copies of the *Essay* from James Dodsley, one of which he sent to Johnson. Percy wrote,

> I must now tell you what M[r] Johnson says of it: for I sent him his Copy yesterday and went to him to-day, to hear his Opinion.—I never saw him so pleased with any literary production of modern date, before in my life. He speaks of it with the most unreserved applause, as a most excellent performance; as a compleat and finished piece that leaves nothing to be desired in point of Argument: For That the question is now forever decided. (*Letters,* II.120–21)

Johnson's praise of the *Essay,* relayed by Percy, not only resulted in an addition to the preface of the second edition of the *Essay* in which Johnson's praise is quoted, but almost surely put Farmer sufficiently into Johnson's debt so that he could not refuse to help in the 1773 Johnson–Steevens *Shakespeare.*

In the first edition of the *Essay,* Farmer had taken issue with "Mr [George] Colman, in the Preface to his Elegant Translation of Terence" (1765) who had claimed Shakespeare's knowledge of the Latin of Terence's plays, including the flat statement, "But a character in the *Taming of the Shrew* is borrowed from the *Trinummus* [of Plautus], and no translation of *that* was extant." Farmer countered, "Mr. Colman indeed hath been better employ'd: but if he had met with an old Comedy, called *Supposes,* translated from Ariosto by George Gascoigne, he certainly would not have appealed to Plautus." In 1768, after the publication of Farmer's second edition, Colman took occasion to respond most politely to Farmer's remarks, acknowledging how far he "coincided" with Farmer. He raised some more questions about the probability of Shakespeare's knowing Ovid in the original as a result of quotation of two lines from the *Heroides* in *The Taming of a Shrew,* although he acknowledged that Farmer had questioned Shakespeare's authorship of the whole play. He also asked if the word "thrasonical" in the canonical *Love's Labour's Lost* did not prove that Shakespeare got it from Terence. Colman concluded by repeating Ben Jonson's remark that Shakespeare had "small Latin, and less Greek," adding that this charge "seems absolutely to decide that he had *some* knowledge of both; and if we may judge by our own time a man who had any Greek is seldom without a very competent share of Latin; and yet such a man is very likely to study Plutarch in English, and to read translations of Ovid." Five years later, in a note in the second Appendix to the 1773 *Shakespeare,* Farmer wrote of the

The Essay on the Learning of Shakespeare 101

word "thrasonical," "It was introduced to our language long before *Shakespeare's* time. *Stanyhurst* writes, in a translation of one of Sir *Tho. More's* epigrams, 'Lynct was in wedlocke a loftye *thrasonical* hufsnuffe.' " After a few more rather less than amiable comments on Colman's ignorance of older literature, Farmer concluded, "Let me however take this opportunity of acknowledging the very genteel language which he has been pleased to use on this occasion." If Colman and Farmer ever met, it was not in Reed's company, for while Reed dined once in Colman's company, Farmer was not present.[9] Colman was to have the last word in this controversy, for in his collected *Prose on Several Occasions,* three volumes, 1787, he added a postscript to his appendix, taking up the argument about "thrasonical" and related matters in the note on *Love's Labour's Lost* (II.179–88). Among other things, he wrote, "I flatter myself that my remarks on the subject of the Learning of Shakespeare, and my idea of the extent of his literature, were not extravagant; and that I expressed myself in such terms as were not calculated to provoke censure, or ridicule. . . . I must own too that I was rather surprised to see the Reverend Essayist, whose remarks I had treated so respectfully, making his reply as a flippant Annotator on another publication, and rising from the bottom of the page of Love's Labour's Lost" (183). Farmer is seen in a poor light; Colman emerges as the more temperate antagonist and, on the whole, on the right side of the entire question of the extent of Shakespeare's learning. It is of no little significance that George Steevens, writing to Percy on 1 January 1788, could report, "I have been told that Mr. Colman also threatens us with a new edition" of Shakespeare (*Lit. Illustr.,* VII.2). Praise for the second edition was expressed by Charles Godwyn, Fellow of Balliol College, Oxford in a letter to a friend dated 30 October 1767: "There is a Cambridge Antiquary whose name is Farmer. He published some time ago a very good pamphlet upon the 'Learning of Shakespeare.' He has now reprinted it with great additions, and you will be highly pleased with it. By dealing in black-lettered books, of which he has purchased a very great number, he is in possession of Shakespear's study" (*Lit. Anecd.,* VIII, 249). Farmer's fame as scholar and book collector was growing. Nor should it go unremarked that Godwyn, unlike some, was aware of the "great additions" made in the second edition of the *Essay.*

On 8 March 1768 Farmer wrote to William Huddesford, seeking information,

> You were so kind as to promise me some time ago a Transcript from the *Bodleian* relative to a *Monkish* Library at *Leicester:* I should be glad of it at your Leisure, as I want to get that *Jobb* [?] out of hand. There is likewise

102   The Essay on the Learning of Shakespeare

in the *Bodleian Shakespeare's Venus & Adonis*, 1602—may I beg for a Copy of the Title-page & the *Latin Motto*, which I allude to in the Essay, p. 35. *Literatim*, & if convenient in a *Post or two*. Mess. *Colman* and *Warner* have given me, I find, some good Words & bad Arguments—but I suspect I shall quarrell not with my old Friend *Capell* tho' I have not yet seen his book. His obstinacy is intollerable & I fear I must be obliged to hold [him] up to be laughed at. Comp.ⁿ to Mʳ Warton—I should be glad to know whether he has met with any thing more relative to the Plot of the Tempest.—when shall I see you?—your's affectionately. [The signature is cropped.]

Huddesford complied, and his transcript of the title-page of the 1602 *Venus and Adonis* is kept with Farmer's letter (Bodleian MS Ashm 1822 f. 200). Farmer had written in the *Essay* that Dr. Sewel (actually Charles Gildon) had stated that "Shakespeare hath somewhere a *Latin Motto*," and that he, having noted that Gildon had held up the motto to *Venus and Adonis* as proof of Shakespeare's knowledge of Latin, wished to see the motto himself. The passage, on page 35, was left unrevised, however.

When the third edition of the *Essay* was published in 1789 it bore an advertisement,

It may be necessary to apologize for the republication of this pamphlet. The fact is, it has been for a good while extremely scarce, and some mercenary publishers were induced by the extravagant price, which it has occasionally borne, to project a new edition without the consent of the author.

A few corrections might probably be made, and many additional proofs of the arguments have necessarily occurred in more than twenty years: some of which may be found in the late admirable edition of our POET, by Mr. *STEEVENS* and Mr. *REED*.

But, perhaps, enough is already said on so slight a subject:—A subject, however, which had for a long time pretty warmly divided the criticks upon *Shakespeare*.

Michael Lort, writing to Percy on 11 July 1789, told him that Farmer was "threatened" with a pirated edition of the *Essay* and "has been prevailed on at last to put out a third edition, with few or no alterations" (*Lit. Illustr.*, VII.502). In 1789 the reference to the late edition of Shakespeare by Steevens and Reed would be to the 1778 Johnson–Steevens edition and the 1785 edition by Reed. No notice was taken of the reprinted *Essay*. Guthrie, who might have relished another chance to review the *Essay,* had died in 1770.[10]

The first piece in the second volume of Steevens's 1793 *Shakespeare,* nominally edited by Reed, is Farmer's essay; the verso of the title-page

The Essay on the Learning of Shakespeare 103

bears the words, "Though our commentaries on the following Plays have been enriched by numerous extracts from this celebrated Essay, the whole of it is here reprinted. I shall hazard no contradiction relative to the value of its contents, when I add—*prosunt, singula, juncta juvant.* Steevens." Steevens, or Reed, in a note on the *Essay,* identifies Farmer's reference to "our Greek Professor" as "Mr. afterwards Dr. Lort" (41)—Michael Lort being well known to both men. Steevens and Malone add notes to the effect that *Hamlet* was best known for its ghost scenes (67–68), and Malone adds "See the *Essay on the Order of Shakespeare's Plays,* Article, *King John*" (68) to Farmer's discussion of Shakespeare's early "essays in dramatick poetry." Reed retained these notes in his 1803 *Shakespeare* and added three more. The first (14) is corroboration of Farmer's note on John Dennis's expulsion from college for "attempting to stab a man in the dark." Reed adds "See this fact established against the doubts and objections of Dr. Kippis in the Biographia Britannica, in Dr. Farmer's Letter to me, printed in the European Magazine, June 1794, p. 412." The second note is an addition by Reed (31) to Farmer's discussion of the pronunciation of "aspect." Reed writes "See also a wrong accentuation of the word *aspect* in Mr. Ireland's unmetrical, ungrammatical, harum-scarum Vortigern, which was damned at Drury Lane theatre, April—1796—the performance of a madman without a lucid interval." Reed may have seen the play, but his extant diary for 1796 begins on April 29 and the single performance was on April 2. *Vortigern* is roundly criticized in the 1812 *Biographia Dramatica* (III.387), either by Reed or Stephen Jones. The most interesting of the added notes is on Farmer's stated belief that *The Optick Glasse of Humors* was by T. Wombwell. Reed was able to quote from "Dr. Farmer's MSS" the correction, "So I imagined from a note of Baker's, but I have since seen a copy in the library of Canterbury Cathedral, printed 1607, and ascribed to T. Walkington, of St. John's Cambridge" (47).

Since Farmer's *Essay* is his major contribution to Shakespeare studies in a publication bearing his name as author, it is of intrinsic interest whatever its received value. There is every evidence that he approached this work con amore. Thomas Martyn remembered that Farmer was writing notes on Shakespeare in 1753 in his first year at Emmanuel; the *Essay* was published in January 1767; reviewed by Guthrie in that same month; extensively revised and added to that same year; and reviewed by Guthrie in November of the same year. A third edition was published in 1789. The first edition of the *Essay,* it is well to repeat, ran to fifty pages of text; the second, ninety-five. Where the first edition contains only seven notes,[11] the second has

104   The Essay on the Learning of Shakespeare

seventy. To reprint the *Essay*, as D. Nichol Smith does (see note 3), without the notes at the foot of the page, or with some omitted and some shortened, is to do Farmer a disservice. The difference in length between the two editions resulted from Farmer's response to Guthrie's review of the first edition, questions and suggestions by Thomas Percy, and a number of afterthoughts. Much of the added material was, then, in the notes, many of them occupying a half-page, others a full page, and one taking up two pages.[12] Percy's questions and suggestions led Farmer to add twelve notes, expand one passage in the text, and clear up some ambiguities in his text.[13] The matter of the relationship between Percy and Farmer has been explored by Cleanth Brooks, editor of the Percy–Farmer letters, but the latter's role in Shakespeare studies, as influenced by that correspondence, requires fuller analysis.

While the extensive additions to the first edition of the *Essay* are, of course, of overriding importance, it must not go unremarked that Farmer polished the *Essay,* making it both more readable and, in many instances, more specific. And he corrected a few errors in the process. Take, for one example, a discussion of the play *Double Falshood* where the first edition has "Mr. *Pope* himself, in a Letter to *Aaron Hill,* supposes it of that [Shakespeare's] age; but a mistaken accent determines it to be modern." The second edition adds "after all the strictures of *Scriblerus*" and revises "to be modern" to "to have been written since the middle of the last century." Farmer had stated of *A Yorkshire Tragedy* that "it was not written by our Poet at all," adding in the second edition "nor indeed was it printed in his life-time." Mentioning a performance of *Pericles,* he added "which *Ben Jonson* calls *stale* and *mouldy*." Although Farmer was at pains to specify a book size, a page number, or a specific as opposed to a general reference ("in *Macbeth*" becomes "where *Banquo* addresses the Weird-Sisters") where the first edition was silent, one example must suffice for many more. Farmer had said that the story of *All's Well That Ends Well* was "originally indeed the property of *Boccace*" and added a note citing Dryden's opinion that "the Epic performance *Palamon and Arcite*" was of unknown authorship. Farmer wrote, "But he is mistaken: this too was the work of *Boccace,* and printed at *Ferrara* in Folio," adding in the second edition, "con il commento di *Andrea Bassi,* 1745." In the first edition he had written that he had seen a copy of it; in the second, he added, "and a Translation into modern *Greek*." Not satisfied with this, he added a final sentence: "It is likewise to be met with in old *French,* under the Title of *La Theside* de *Jean Boccace,* contenant les belles &. chastes amours de deux jeunes Chevaliers Thebains, *Arcite & Palemon*."

The Essay on the Learning of Shakespeare 105

While Farmer's *Essay* is far from a classic of English prose, Farmer revised the first edition with an eye to a more readable version. "Granted" took the place of "this is certainly true"; "protracted," queried by Percy, who suggested "extended" (*Letters*, II.122), became "enlarged"; "a word" gave way to the emphatic "a single word" in the discussion of the word "suggestion." Possibly suspecting himself of an unintentional discourtesy, Farmer dignified the bare "Menage" by adding a polite "M.[onsieur]" to the name of the dead author. Mention of Garrick's note on "swearing on the sword" in *Hamlet* prompted Farmer to add "a *Gentleman, who will be always allowed the First commentator of Shakespeare,* when he does not carry us beyond *himself.*" Garrick left the stage in 1776, and while there is no evidence that Farmer saw him perform, an avid playgoer, and Farmer was, would almost surely have seen Garrick during one of his stays in London. Having had occasion to find some errors in *Biographia Britannica,* he modified his praise of that work by adding "tho' very unequal" to his original unqualified "excellent work." The "celebrated Mr. Warton" becomes additionally "an Associate in the question" of Shakespeare's learning. As he came to his summing up, Farmer, addressing Cradock, wrote "I hope, my good Friend, you have by this time acquitted our great Poet of all piratical depredations on the Ancients. He [Shakespeare] remembered perhaps enough of his *school-boy* learning. . . ." Feeling the transition between the two sentences was too abrupt, he added "and are ready to receive my Conclusion" to the first sentence.

Incidentally, Farmer paid Johnson a compliment in his revised *Essay.* George Colman had pointed to Shakespeare's having quoted a line from the *Eunuch* of Terence in a purposely altered form as proof of his Latinity; Johnson had written in the Preface to his edition of Shakespeare, "Our Author had this line from *Lilly;* which I mention that it may not be brought as an argument of his learning." Farmer had written "I could cut the knot by saying somewhat against Shakespeare's property in this part of the Play [*Taming*]; but at present be contented with Mr. Johnson's observation" (32), which he changed in the second edition to "This remark [Colman's] was previous to Mr. *Johnson's;* or indisputably it would not have been made at all" (65).

The *Essay on the Learning of Shakespeare* did not solve the question of Shakespeare's learning, but left no doubt as to the extent of Farmer's learning. Thomas Percy, immersed as he was and had been in his *Reliques of Ancient English Poetry,* and erudite as he was, found a number of references in the *Essay* beyond him. "Query, in what Piece of *Drayton's* is Shakespeare's Excellence determined to the *naturall Braine?* . . . Who is Digges? and whence have You those Lines?", he wrote upon receipt of his copy of the *Essay*, and followed these two queries with a number of others. Which of Lilly's pieces? What is "the *Genevra* of Turberville"? Where is the story of "the Yorkshire Tragedy recorded?" "The name of Flemming I am not acquainted with, neither do I know what he translated." "I do not understand this about the gates of Troy." "Whence have you those curious passages about the hot and cold Hell?" And so on. As I have mentioned, Farmer obliged Percy by providing the answers to most of the queries in his revised *Essay*, doubtless answering some of the more obvious questions in lost correspondence. For example, Percy had asked "Where in Johnson's Appendix, am I to look for Holt's Arguments &c? I have turned to the Book but cannot readily find it." He had not looked hard enough, and Farmer could not dignify the query by adding an unnecessary note.[14] Farmer, incidentally, is handsomely thanked by Percy for his help in the first edition of the *Reliques*, as well as for "many corrections and improvements" in the second and third editions of that work.[15]

Farmer was able to suggest that Percy examine works by Drayton, Digges, Fleming, and others because he owned many of these works. On Monday, 7 May 1798 and for "Thirty-five following Days (Sundays excepted)," his library was sold by auction. The verso of the title-page of the sale catalog printed, from a "Paper in the hand-writing of Dr. Farmer," what he had once proposed would act as an Advertisement to a "Catalogue taken at his Library." Farmer had written,

> This Collection of Books is by no means to be considered as an *Essay* towards a *perfect Library;* the *Circumstances* and the *Situation* of the *Collector* made such an attempt both *unnecessary* and *impracticable.* Here are few Publications of *great price,* which were already to be found in the excellent *Library* of *Emanuel* College: but it is believed that *not many private* Collections contain a greater Number of really *curious* and *scarce* Books; and perhaps *no one* so rich in the ancient *Philological English* Literature.

There were 8,267 lots, including prints and portraits, which fetched £2216.18s.6d. The number of lots only indicates the number of titles, some lots containing as many as twenty.[16] Dyer wrote that Farmer "was as often seen at the end of an old book stall, as in the splendid shops of more respectable booksellers, and the *sixpence apiece* books were to him sometimes of more value than a Baskerville classic, or a volume printed at Strawberry Hill" (395). Farmer had many books; what is more, he read them and remembered their contents. Most of the works quoted or cited in the *Essay* formed part of his personal

The Essay on the Learning of Shakespeare   107

library; others are to be found in the extant records of his borrowings from the Emmanuel College library.[17]

The first addition to the revised *Essay* was the Preface, in which Farmer answered the "very Few [critics], who have been pleased to controvert any part of his Doctrine, have favoured him with better manners than arguments and claim his thanks for a further opportunity of demonstrating the futility of *Theoretick* reasoning against *Matter of Fact*." After several somewhat facetious remarks, he concluded, "I hope I may assume with some confidence, what one of the first Criticks of the Age was pleased to declare on reading the former Edition, that "The Question is *now* forever decided." The critic was Samuel Johnson, but, as is already evident, Johnson's opinion was based on an edition that was soon expanded to almost twice its original size. What Johnson and readers of the first edition could not have foreseen is the wealth of additional information that Farmer was able to add in only a few months.

I shall proceed seriatim, giving page references to the second edition of the *Essay* and to D. N. Smith's edition for the additions to the text of at least sentence length, having already mentioned that the footnotes had been increased tenfold, from seven to seventy: the paragraph on Hales of Eton's on Shakespeare's learning (4–5, 156); Pope's assertion that Shakespeare copied from Plutarch in *Coriolanus,* and Farmer's destruction of that argument; an alleged plagiarism from Anacreon and Farmer's answer.[18] There is the extended discussion on the accenting of "aspect," on the authorship of *Double Falshood,* and on some of Milton's imitations of earlier poets (26–31, 168–71) as well as Shakespeare's knowledge of mythology, whether taken from the ancients or from earlier English literature and the paragraph on Richard Hurd's statement on Shakespeare's learning (36–41, 173–76). Shakespeare's dependence on the chronicle histories for his portrayal of Cardinal Wolsey and the quotation from Skelton were added.[19] Included were refutation of John Upton's assertion that Shakespeare knew "Cicero's *Offices*, . . . even more critically than many of the Editors," more on Shakespeare's use of Holinshed, and refutation of Guthrie's statement that the portrait of Lady Macbeth was taken from Buchanan.[20] Farmer added the sources of *Hamlet*, beginning "It hath indeed been said," with Shakespeare's dependence on novels for sources and the variety of these early novels (57–61), 185–87), and information on the authorship of *The Taming of a Shrew* and of *Locrine* (66–69, 189–90). He found a word in *Love's Labour's Lost* was not evidence of Shakespeare's knowledge of Italian (89, 196), and then included one sentence in the

108   The Essay on the Learning of Shakespeare

courting scene in *Henry V:* "Indeed, every friend to his [Shakespeare's] memory will not easily believe that he was acquainted with the Scene between Catherine and the old Gentlewoman; or surely he would not have admitted such obscenity and nonsense" and the possibility of collaboration in that play beginning "Connections of this kind" and ending with the reference to Capell's *Prolusions.*"[21]

Reference to these additions to the text and to those added footnotes further reveals the extent of Farmer's learning and the readiness of his remarkable memory. Indeed, one is tempted to challenge Adam Smith's statement that Samuel Johnson "knew more books than any man alive," with any one of the trio of friends, Farmer, Reed, and Steevens, competing for that distinction. In any event, in the Preface to the second edition of the *Essay,* Farmer ranged from Robert Dodsley's *The Toy-Shop* to "a fragment of Euripides preserved by Stobaeus," with the "Arabian Tales" and John Taylor, the water poet, thrown in for good measure. In text and footnotes the more prominent additions include Hales of Eton, Ronsard, Alexander Barclay, Samuel Daniel, Gawin Douglas, Kuster on Sophocles, Bentley on Milton, Manwaring's *Treatise of Harmony and Numbers,* Green's specimen for a new version of *Paradise Lost* in blank verse, Shelton's translation of *Don Quixote,* Dunbar, Newton on Milton, Harington's *Ariosto,* Stephen Bateman's *Golden booke of the leaden Goddes* (1577), "*Edm. Howes'* Continuation of *John Stowe*'s Summarie (8vo. 1607)," Robert Whytinton, Nicholas Grimald, *Rex Platonicus, Annales d'Acquytayne* (Par. 1537), Gosson's *School of Abuse,* Gascoigne's *Certayne notes of Instruction concerning the making of Verse,*" the *French Alphabet* of De La Mothe and the *Orthoepia Gallica* of John Eliot," Tarleton's *Jests, The Optick Glasse of Humors,* Churchyard's poems, Mr. Baker's MSS., "*Recherches* sur les *Poetes couronnez,* par M. l'Abbe *du Resnel,* in the *Memoires de Litterature,* Vol. 10. *Paris.* 4to. 1736," the *Romaunt of the Rose,* Petrarch, Leland's *Itinery,* Whately's *Gazetteer,* Anthony Copley, long notes on John Taylor, the water poet, and on Holinshed, and Ascham's *Toxophilus.* The mere listing of these works gives no idea of the offhand way in which they are introduced, a compliment to the reader who is expected to recognize most, if not all, of the works and authors referred to so familiarly. But for those who want precise references and bibliographical details, the footnotes are provided.

Something more of the nature of these additions can be had from quotation of one footnote and two examples from the text. Farmer had mentioned the editor of Shakespeare's poems, "the well-known Mr. Gildon," who was "One of the first and most vehement assertors of

The Essay on the Learning of Shakespeare 109

the learning of *Shakespeare,*" to which statement he added a footnote in the second edition.

> Hence perhaps the *ill-starr'd rage* between this Critick and his elder Brother, *John Dennis,* so pathetically lamented in the *Dunciad.* Whilst the former was persuaded, that "the man who doubts of the Learning of *Shakespeare,* hath none of his own:" the latter, above regarding the attack in his *private* capacity, declares with great patriotick vehemence, that "he allows *Shakespeare* had Learning, and a familiar acquaintance with the Ancients, ought to be looked upon as a detractor from the Glory of *Great Britain.*" *Dennis* was expelled his College for attempting to stab a man in the dark: *Pope* would have been glad of this anecdote. (6)

The matter of Dennis was to come up again.

One addition to the text is useful both for the further information given and as an example of how Farmer revised his *Essay.* In the first edition he wrote, "Our excellent friend Mr. *Hurd* hath endeavoured to *fasten* only one imitation on Shakespeare: which hath been insisted upon likewise by Mr. *Upton* and Mr. *Whalley.* You remember it in the famous speech of *Claudio* in *Measure for Measure:* Ay, but to die and go we know not where! &c." (23). The revision reads,

> Our excellent friend Mr. *Hurd* hath borne a noble testimony on our side of the question. "*Shakespeare,*" says this true Critick, "owed the felicity of freedom from the bondage of classical superstition to the *want* of what is called the *advantage* of a learned Education. This, as well as a vast superiority to Genius, hath contributed to lift this astonishing man to the glory of being esteemed the most original *thinker* and *speaker,* since the times of Homer." And hence indisputably the amazing Variety of Style and Manner, unknown to all other Writers: an argument of *itself* sufficient to emancipate *Shakespeare* from the supposition of a *Classical training.* Yet, to be honest, *one* Imitation is *fastened* on our Poet: which hath been insisted upon likewise by Mr. *Upton* and Mr. *Whalley.* You remember it in the famous Speech of *Claudio* in *Measure for Measure:*
> Ay, but to die and go we know not where! &c. (40–41)

Richard Hurd remains Farmer's "excellent friend" and is done the further honor of quotation from his notes to Horace's *Epistolae ad Pisones et Augustum,* 1757, and to his *Marks of Imitation* added to the edition of Horace. Both because of its length and the controversy caused by its inclusion in the second edition, one should note the addition to Farmer's remarks on the *The Taming of the Shrew.*[22]

There are only four omissions from the first edition. The first occurs in the discussion of the word "suggestion," which William

110   The Essay on the Learning of Shakespeare

Warburton had noted as being glossed by "the late Roman writers" as *"SUGGESTIO est cum magistratus quilibet principi salubre consilium suggerit"* in his note on *Henry VIII*, IV.ii.33. Farmer's eye for parallels played him false, for he wrote "And it was one of the articles of his [Cardinal Wolsey's] Impeachment in Dr. Fiddes' Collections, 'That the said Lord Cardinal got a Bull for suppressing certain Houses of Religion, by his untrue *Suggestion* to the Pope' " (28) and later realized that this was not a true parallel, as an untrue suggestion in the sense of the Latin gloss was a contradiction in terms. There may be some doubt as to the reason for the next major omission. Farmer had adduced parallels from *"Hieronymo"* and from *"Dekker's* Satiro-Mastix, or the *Untrussing of the humourous Poet"* for the matter of swearing upon a sword. He had written that Sir Rees ap Vaughan had sworn "in the same manner" (as Hamlet) in Dekker's play (29). Sir Rees says "by the crosse a this sword and dagger, Capten you shall take it." To which Tucca replies, "Dost sweare by daggers" (IV.ii.142–43), and Farmer saw, again, that he did not have a true parallel, since Sir Rees swore on the cross made by a dagger and a sword rather than on the hilt of a sword. Accordingly, he substituted the parallel from *Piers Plowman* where David's knights swore on their swords (51; 182 in Smith). A third omission came at the request of Percy. Farmer had made a passing reference to "the Works of *Surrey*, of which you will have a beautiful Edition from the able hand of my Friend Mr. *Percy"* (25). Percy, in the letter of 15 January 1767 in which he asked questions about the first edition of the *Essay*, concluded by expressing the wish that he had not been named "as Editor of the proposed publication of SURREY. It is a work to which I never intended to affix my name" (*Letters*, II.128–29). The last omission is of a rather trifling nature but demonstrates again Farmer's scrupulous attention to detail. Aubrey had written that Shakespeare took the "humour of the *Constable* in the *Midsummer Night's Dream"* at *"Crendon in Bucks,"* to which Farmer objected, "not such a place as *Crendon* in *Bucks*, if we may believe *Spelman* and the *Index Villaris"* (pp. 38–39). Percy had written, "No such place as *Crendon* occurs in Adams's Index Villaris folio: which is more full than Spelman—I have purposely looked" (II.125–26). Farmer omitted his original remark and substituted a footnote in which he added that Crendon was also not in "*Speed's Tables* and *Whately's Gazetteer:* perhaps, however, it may be meant under the name of *Crandon;*—but the inquiry is of no importance. It should, I think, be written *Credendon;* tho' better Antiquaries than *Aubrey* have acquiesced in the vulgar corruption" (74). These early antiquaries, Farmer included, might have considered

The Essay on the Learning of Shakespeare   111

what D. N. Smith points out, that Crendon was a misprint for Grendon (324).

Farmer had done the necessary reading for the task he had set himself. He had studied the commentary in the editions of Pope, Theobald, Hanmer, Warburton, and Johnson and the critical studies by Zachary Grey, John Upton, Benjamin Heath, John Holt, Charlotte Lennox, and Elizabeth Griffith. He knew and quoted or cited William Dodd's *Beauties of Shakespeare,* Rowe's *Account* of the life of Shakespeare, William Guthrie's *Essay upon English Tragedy,* Gerard Langbaine's *English Dramatick Poets,* and, of course, Peter Whalley's *Enquiry into the Learning of Shakespeare.* He quoted, without naming the author, Daniel Webb's *Remarks on the Beauties of Poetry,* and Thomas Tyrwhitt's *Observations and Conjectures upon Some Passages of Shakespeare* (1766), a work Farmer described as "sensible" in an addition to the revised *Essay* (89), evidence that he was keeping abreast of the literature on Shakespeare. And he refers more than once to Edward Capell, the first time being a reference to "a very curious and intelligent Gentleman, to whom the lovers of *Shakespeare* will some time or other owe great obligations," who had "favoured" him with the "fragment" of the "Hystorie of Hamblet" (57). Capell is identified two pages later as "my communicative Friend above-mentioned, Mr. *Capell* (for why should I not give myself the credit of his name?)" and complimented on the same page as one "most able" to show how Shakespeare only appeared to be "beholden to some *Novels,* which he hath yet only seen in *French* or *Italian*" (59). The complimentary references to Capell are of no little interest as Capell took the opposite position from Farmer in the preface to his 1768 *Shakespeare.* Farmer wrote to Percy about the middle of March 1768 and said "as to my old *Friend* [Capell], I believe, I shall bring him to his senses by a little *castigation.* I find after all his tirade, he is totally ignorant of the Language of the time, as I can already demonstrate in 40 or 50 very notorious instances" (*Letters,* I.141). Percy wrote to Farmer that Capell complained to Garrick that he had written him a letter *"so full of Disrespect to the Old Quartos and of Acrimony against him and his labours that he did not doubt but you would attack him in print"* (*Letters,* I.144). Some time after Farmer's death Steevens wrote to Percy to the effect that "Dr. Farmer, who scarcely spoke with severity of any man, has left a string of bitter Philippicks against Capell. In one place, he says of him— 'The little he ever knew, he stole from me when I was a boy' " (Folger C.b.10. item 163). Capell was briefly at St. Catharine's College, Cambridge in 1730 and spent most of his life in London. He

112   The Essay on the Learning of Shakespeare

was forty years Farmer's senior, and the two must have achieved their early friendship mainly by correspondence.

The *Essay* is, it should be quite apparent, a personal document. The tone is conversational; Cradock is addressed directly. Farmer's friends and acquaintances are praised for their scholarly efforts or are referred to with esteem. I have already mentioned the praise of Hurd, Johnson, Thomas Warton, and Garrick. Indeed, most of the scholars and men of letters quoted, cited, or alluded to are almost invariably treated courteously. A reference to "a very learned and inquisitive Brother—Antiquary, our *Greek* Professor, hath observed to me" (42) is to Dr. Michael Lort, who is named later on as Farmer's "generous Friend, Mr. *Lort*" who had favored him with a copy of a very rare work (61). Thomas Percy is described as "My good friend, the very ingenious Editor of the *Reliques of ancient English Poetry*" (p. 22). Occasionally Farmer waxed sarcastic, but often the provocation was great. Charles Gildon is attacked to the extent of a full page for his "sagacious remarks," a heavily ironic description of his contention that Shakespeare knew the Latin classics because there were no trans-lations of them (naming Ovid and Virgil) as old as Shakespeare's time (32). Lewis Theobald, recently unfairly castigated by Johnson in the Preface to the 1765 *Shakespeare* ("a man of narrow comprehension and small acquisitions") is spared much opprobrium. Farmer accused him of making "a deal of learned dust" in setting something right (38–39). Warburton is mentioned, cited, or quoted eight times, usu-ally with respectful acknowledgment of his learning even when he is wrong. But it was John Upton, author of *Critical Observations on Shakespeare* (1746), with a revised edition in 1748, who came in for the sharpest criticism and the most notice as his name appeared sixteen times. At one point Farmer compared Upton to Hudibras: "He, like the learned Knight, at every anomaly in grammar or metre, 'Hath hard words ready to shew why, / And tell what *Rule* he did it by' " (7). Upton, having come a cropper on a passage in the last act of *The Merry Wives of Windsor,* earned this gentle rebuke: "Surely poor Mr. *Upton* was very little acquainted with *Fairies,* notwithstanding his laborious study of *Spenser,*" a reference to Upton's two-volume edition of the *Faerie Queene* published in 1758 (21). And fast on the heels of this last, the rhetorical question was asked, "What . . . could induce this man, by no means a bad scholar, to doubt whether *Truepenny* might not be derived from τρύπανον and quote upon us with much parade an old scholiast on *Aristophanes*?" (22). Compare Johnson on Upton in the Preface to the 1765 *Shakespeare,* "Every cold empirick, when his heart is expanded by a successful experi-

The Essay on the Learning of Shakespeare 113

ment, swells into a theorist, and the laborious collator at some unlucky moment frolicks in conjecture."

A few remaining aspects of the *Essay* deserve notice. Farmer was firmly convinced that Shakespeare had had no hand in *Pericles*, even though it was published with his name on the title-page (25), and he was equally convinced that *The Taming of the Shrew* was "not *originally* the work of *Shakespeare*, but restored by him to the Stage, with the whole *Induction* of the *Tinker*, and some other occasional improvements; especially in the Character of *Petruchio*" (66). He wrote of *Titus Andronicus*, "Indeed, from every internal mark, I have not the least doubt but this *horrible* Piece was originally written by the Author of the *Lines* thrown into the mouth of the *Player* in *Hamlet*, and of the *Tragedy of Locrine:* which likewise from some assistance perhaps given to his Friend, hath been unjustly and ignorantly charged upon *Shakespeare*" (69). Farmer was not alone. Johnson wrote in his General Observation on the play that "All the editors and criticks agree with Mr. Theobald in supposing this play spurious. I see no reason for differing from them." Farmer asserted that "the *French* ribaldry" of the courting scene in *Henry V* "was at first inserted by a different hand" (85), and had "no doubt but *Henry the sixth* had the same Author with *Edward the third*, which hath been recovered to the world in Mr. *Capells Prolusions*" (88). In his *Prolusions, or Select Pieces of Ancient Poetry*, published in 1760, Capell reprinted the anonymous play *Edward III* with a tentative attribution to Shakespeare. Farmer was later to revise his opinion of the authorship of *Pericles*, discussing Shakespeare's hand in "the latter part of the play" (see below, p. 126). Two lengthy footnotes, one on Skelton's laureateship (49–50) and on Peele (77) are of biographical interest. In the latter he refers to and quotes two sentences from a supposed letter of George Peele published in *The Theatrical Review*. "This is pretended to be printed from the original MS. dated 1600; which agrees well with Wood's *Claruit:* but unluckily, *Peele* was dead at least two years before. 'As *Anacreon* died by the *Pot*, says *Meres*, so *George Peele* by the *Pox*.' *Wit's Treasury*, 1598, p. 286." What Farmer did not know was that the Peele letter was one of Steevens's earliest fabrications, the 1600 date being a deliberately planted clue to the hoax. One wonders if Steevens ever confessed his authorship to Farmer.

Farmer's assessment and statements of his accomplishment, voiced in the Preface to the second edition of the *Essay* and at the end, are modest ones. In the Preface he states, "Upon the whole, I may consider myself, as the *Pioneer* of the *Commentators*: I have removed a

114   The Essay on the Learning of Shakespeare

deal of *learned Rubbish,* and pointed out to them *Shakespeare's* track in the ever-pleasing *Paths of nature*" ([4]). Farmer uses the word "pioneer" in the military sense: "one of a body of foot-soldiers who march with or in advance of an army or regiment, having spades, pickaxes, etc. to dig trenches, repair roads, and perform other labours in clearing and preparing the way for the main body" *(OED).* Truly a modest claim. His conclusion, while longer, makes no elaborate claims and is a fair summary of his work.

> In the course of this disquisition, you have often smiled at "all such reading, as was never read:" and possibly I may have indulged it too far: but it is the reading necessary for a Comment on *Shakespeare.* Those who apply solely to the Ancients for this purpose, may with equal wisdom study the TALMUD for an Exposition of TRISTRAM SHANDY. Nothing but an intimate acquaintance with the Writers of the time, who are frequently of no other value, can point out his allusions, and ascertain his Phraseology. The Reformers of his Text are for ever equally positive, and equally wrong. The Cant of the Age, a provincial Expression, an obscure Proverb, an obsolete Custom, a Hint at a Person or a Fact no longer remembered, hath continually defeated the best of the our *Guessers:* You must not suppose me to speak at random, when I assure you, that from some forgotten book or other, I can demonstrate this to you in many hundred Places; and I almost wish, that I had not been persuaded into a different Employment.

Farmer had many "forgotten" books, and he had studied them to good effect.

Although the *Essay* was devoted almost wholly to the matter of Shakespeare's learning, Farmer had on occasion questioned certain textual decisions made by previous editors. There are nine of these occasions; all of them resulted in changes in the 1765 Johnson *Shakespeare* when it was revised in 1773 by Johnson and Steevens. The changes are additions, in the form of footnotes, from the *Essay.* I give them in the order of appearance in the *Essay.* Octavius says that Antony made Cleopatra "Of lower Syria, Cyprus, Lydia, / Absolute Queen," which John Upton emended to "Lybia" from the Greek of Plutarch, but which Farmer refuted by pointing to the translation of "the French of *Amyot,* by *Thomas North,* in *Folio,* 1579" where the error, "Lydia," originated (10–11). Hence, the 1765 reading "Lybia" is revised to "Lydia" in 1773, and Farmer is quoted in a note. In IV.i of the same play Octavius says "Let the old ruffian [Antony] know, / He hath many other ways to die: mean time, / Laugh at his challenge." "He" of the second quoted line was Sir Thomas Hanmer's emendation for "I," an emendation Farmer was able to demolish (11–12). The

The Essay on the Learning of Shakespeare   115

1773 edition restores "I," quotes Upton on the emendation, repeats Johnson's note, "I think this emendation deserves to be received [despite the restoration of the received reading]. It had, before Mr. Upton's book appeared, been made by sir T. Hanmer," and adds Farmer's proof as an addition to Johnson's. In *Julius Caesar* there is a minor crux in the provisions of Caesar's will, the dead emperor willing certain lands "On this side Tyber" to the people (12). Theobald emended to "that side Tyber," and Johnson printed the emendation in his text but restored the old reading in 1773 and added Farmer's statement in proof of the validity of the old reading.

Johnson accepted Warburton's emendation of "ouphen heirs" for "orphan-heirs" toward the end of *The Merry Wives of Windsor*, but reverted to the received text in 1773, again adding Farmer's remarks (20–21). An emendation in the names of the gates of Troy in the Prologue to *Troilus and Cressida*, accepted in 1765 and revised to the original reading, resulted from another of Farmer's remarks.[23] Reference is made in *2 Henry VI* to "Bargulus the strong Illyrian Pirate," and Warburton noted that "Bargulus Illyrius latro" occurs in Cicero's *Offices*. Johnson adds Farmer's remark (52) that Shakespeare could have met with the same description of Bargulus in two translations to Warburton's note in 1773. Prince Hall exclaims "*Rivo*, says the drunkard," and in 1765 Johnson noted "*Ribi*, that is, *drink*. Hanmer. All the former editions have *rivo*, which certainly has no meaning, but yet was perhaps the cant of *English* taverns." Farmer quoted John Marston's *What You Will*, "Rivo drink deep," in defense of the old reading (80). In 1773, "Rivo" is restored, and Steevens adds to Johnson's note, "This conjecture [Johnson's] Mr. Farmer has supported by a quotation from Marston," and corroborates with two more parallels. Gremio says to Petruchio, "*Baccare*—you are marvellous forward," and Warburton, ever ready with an emendation, stated that "We must read *Baccalare;* by which the *Italians* mean, thou arrogant, presumptuous man!" Johnson accepted the emendation in the 1765 text, but restored *Baccare* in 1773, quoting Farmer (81–82), who had adduced two examples of *"Backare"* from John Heywood's *Epigrams*. Finally, Richard III, before the battle of Bosworth, calls the Earl of Richmond "a paltry fellow, / Long kept in Bretagne at our Mother's cost," which Theobald had emended to "his Mother's cost" and which Johnson had accepted. In 1773, because of Farmer's recourse to Holinshed (92), Johnson restored the old reading. While there can be no extravagant claims for these nine additions to the restoration of Shakespeare's text, they are nonetheless a valuable byproduct of the *Essay*.

Farmer contemplated a fourth edition of the *Essay* and went so far

116   The Essay on the Learning of Shakespeare

as to mark up an interleaved copy of the third edition, but, as with the history of Leicester, the fourth edition proved abortive. The third edition with Farmer's additions and corrections is now in the Folger Shakespeare Library in Washington, D.C. (S.a. 138) and is quoted with permission. The revision of the third edition follows much the lines of that of the first, although one cannot be sure of the exact extent of the added matter as one cannot know how much of the marginal additions would have been kept. There is the occasional peripheral remark, the very first of which, opposite the title-page, points to the existence of a hitherto unknown edition of the *Essay:* "D^r. *Domvile* of *Dublin* inform'd me, that this Essay (I suppose, the first Edit) was printed in *Ireland*."[24] Or this, on William Guthrie, who had adversely reviewed the *Essay*, and who had quoted from Saxo Grammaticus "with a *small* variation from the *Original*." Farmer's remark, "Criticism at *second hand* very rarely escapes Detection," is keyed to the footnote on page 57. Evidently Guthrie's criticism of the *Essay* had rankled, for Farmer had at him again. On page 48 of the *Essay* Farmer had written, "it cannot therefore be credited, that any man, when the *Original* was produced, should still choose to defend a *cant* acceptation, and inform us, perhaps, *seriously,* that in *gaming* language, from I know not what practice, to *tye* is to *equal!*" His marginal comment reads, "this however appears to have been done by Mr *Guthrie* his profession would not suffer him to be fallible." At the bottom of page 5 of the preface: "Sterne in the 9th Vol. of *Tristram Shandy,* calls *Reviewers* with good humour, 'Critics in keeping.'" It may be unnecessary to do other than state that the marginalia provide further eivdence of the ways and byways of Farmer's reading.

Two large divisions emerge from what is a considerable body of marginalia. The first, and more obvious, is the very subject of the *Essay,* i.e., the extent of Shakespeare's learning. The second is those parts of the marginalia that are of some interest to the biographer and the bibliophile. As the first division consists of additions which do not change Farmer's original contention that Shakespeare was much less learned than previous scholars had argued, I shall quote a few of these additions and rather more of those of a more personal nature. Sometimes the two divisions coincide. Thus, on a blank page, the first of seven before the preface, Farmer wrote "Sh.^e instead of forgetting his School learning as Capell supposes, really increased it by his Stage-practice. Merchant of *Venice* was certainly written before the *Merry Wives* He pronounces Stephāno in the first, & Stephăno in the last. *This* & all the Notes relative to *Sh.*^s Learning in the late Edits should be inserted." Farmer had more to say about Capell. He added this to a

The Essay on the Learning of Shakespeare 117

note on the matter of the Shakespeare apocrypha: "See Capell's Pr.[olusions] *Merry Devil*—mistaken for Birth of *Merlin*—founds his Merit on his Accuracy!" (76, note 1.). On the word "proface": "Capel (5.102) puts a note of admir^t after *proface*—certainly did not understand it" (79).

Back, however, to the matter of Shakespeare's learning. Farmer was puzzled by the fact that none of Shakespeare's books were extant: "It is remarkable that none of *Sh.*'s Books remain, that I know of—many of *Jonson*" (Preface, 2).[25] He quoted (opposite page 4) from William Duff's *Essay on Original Genius* (1767), "The Truth is a Poet of original Genius has very little occasion for the weak aid of Literature: he is self-taught. He comes into the world as it were completely accomplished," providing the page reference. And still on Shakespeare's natural genius from the prologue to Sir Robert Stapleton's "Comedy of the Sleighted Maid 1663 No Jonson's Art, no Shakespeare's Wit in Nature For men are shrunk in Brain, as well as Stature" (opposite page 10): "When *Ben Jonson* observed to Drummond of "*Hawthornden* that *Shakespeare wanted Art,* he plainly meant—knowledge of the ancient Laws of the *Drama,*" an important distinction (21). "Almost every Fable & every Fact of Antiquity can be found in Gower and Lydgate" (37), to which Shakespeare would have had access. As further proof that Shakespeare need only have gone to works written in English, Farmer gave another parallel, a passage in the play *Robert Earl of Huntington* (1601), for the word "proface" and one from Marlowe's *Jew of Malta* for "Rivo Castiliano" (opposite pages 80, 81). One more example of this line of reasoning must suffice. Charles Gildon is quoted on page 32 of the *Essay* to the effect that Shakespeare "was acquainted with the *Fables* of antiquity very well: that some of the Arrows of *Cupid* are painted with lead, and others with Gold, he found in *Ovid*." Farmer's marginal note reads, "John Lilly in his *Sapho & Phao* introduces Vulcan & the Cyclops making *golden,* silver'd and leaden ones, & Venus afterwards describes various darts."

Farmer's marginalia reinforce what is known about him, particuarly his virtually encyclopedic knowledge of the literature of many languages and many centuries. A note on page 16 of the *Essay* identifies two early translations of Anacreon, "By *Henry Stephens* and *Elias Andreas. Par.* 1554," to which information Farmer could add, "The latter is sometimes dated 1555, which caused a difference between 2 of the most intelligent Bibliophilists, that the Lord ever saw, A Fabricius & Michael Mattaire." He knew and recorded the existence of "*La Giulietta,* Novella di M. *Luigi da Porto* 'Romeo de' Montecchi ama la Giulietta de' Cappulletti, de' pietosi casa' Lately pr.^d in a Collection of old Novels, at *Venice*," his "lately" being 1754 (opposite page 83). On page 67 of the *Essay* Farmer had written that he had met with Sir John Harington's *Metamorphosis of Ajax;* in his marginal note he gave the subtitle, "A new discourse of a stale subject," adding "tho' Mrs *Cooper* & *The. Cibber* suppose it never to have been printed at all," correcting two popular biographical-bibliographical compilations.[26] Having occasion (in a footnote to pages 61 to 63 of the *Essay*) to quote some lines of a sonnet by Petrarch and to observe that Sir Thomas Wyatt had translated the sonnet without "any notice of the Original," he told where it could be found other than in the 1574 edition of "*Songes and Sonettes,* by the Earle of *Surrey* and Others," i.e., "See it pr.^d in *Harington's Nugae Antiquae,* V. 3. P. 249." As was his wont, he was ready with the exact bibliographical reference.

Farmer had come upon three errors, uncorrected in the three editions of the *Essay*. He had quoted the opening line of Prospero's address to his attendant Spirits in *The Tempest* as "Ye Elves of Hills, of standing Lakes, and Groves" (page 44), correcting the words "of standing Lakes" to "Brooks, Standing Lakes," the original misquotation unnoted by D. N. Smith. Hard upon this, in a note to page 46, Farmer observed of *"The Optick Glasse of Humors"* that he believed it was written by *T. Wombwell*. His marginal comment is, "So I imagin'd from a Note of Mr *Baker;* but I have since seen a copy in the Library of *Canterbury* Cathedral, p. 1609 and ascribed to T. Walkington of St John's Cambridge." The latter ascription is the correct one. The third error was of a trivial nature; its correction giving rise to a memorable phrase. On page 64 of the *Essay,* Farmer, writing about early performances of *The Comedy of Errors,* noted that "it was exhibited in *German* at *Nuremburgh,* by the celebrated *Hanssach* the *Shoemaker*." In the margin Farmer wrote "Hans Sachs" and at the bottom of the page, "Probably the name from this or other subsequent Exhibition—plainly auricular Orthography."

There are many more remarks that I am tempted to quote, but enough have been quoted to show what a fourth edition of the *Essay* would have contained. I may note in conclusion that Farmer's two cronies, George Steevens and Isaac Reed, knew of the projected revision of the *Essay*. On pages 56–57 of the *Essay* Farmer had discussed Saxo Grammaticus and the novel titled *"Hystorie of Hamblet."* In one margin Farmer wrote "Mr *Steevens";* in the other were the words "This appears similar" in Steevens's hand. Reed knew of Farmer's correction of the authorship of *The Optick Glasse of Humors* from Wombwell to Walkington, quoting the correcting passage from "Dr. Farmer's MSS" in a note to his 1803 *Shakespeare* (II.47) in a reprint-

The Essay on the Learning of Shakespeare 119

ing of Farmer's *Essay.* Since Steevens, who also reprinted Farmer's *Essay* in his 1793 *Shakespeare,* did not correct the originally mistaken attribution, it is more probable that Farmer undertook his revision of the *Essay* some time between 1793 and his death in 1797. I have not discovered that either Steevens or Reed made any use of Farmer's marginalia other than the information about Walkington. Perhaps, too, it should be remarked that the sale catalog of Farmer's library lists three copies of the third edition of the *Essay,* two on large paper, and "Another Copy, said to be the 4th edition, *Spurious*" (my italics).[27]

6

A Letter . . . to Mr. Steevens

Samuel Johnson, it may be recalled, enlisted Farmer's aid in the 1773 *Shakespeare,* and Farmer responded with an appended *Letter* to his friend George Steevens which must rank with the *Essay on the Learning of Shakespeare* as his greatest contributions to Shakespeare studies. It is not generally known, however, that Farmer's contribution to the 1773 edition extended to more than the appended *Letter.* He commented on six different passages, five of them coming in the actual text of the plays, the sixth appearing in Appendix II (02^r), a comment on T.T.'s (Thomas Tyrwhitt's) remark that Shakespeare, in *Richard III,* and Henry Lacey, in a Latin play on the same subject, coincided in one circumstance, arousing the supposition that "one of the poets must have profited by the others performance." Farmer wrote that "This circumstance is not an invention of either poet, but taken from *Hall's Chronicle*" and then quoted the pertinent passage. He commented in the text on Warburton's emendation of "orphan-heirs" to "ouphen heirs" in *The Merry Wives of Windsor* (I.301.4). He admitted the plausibility of Warburton's emendation, "But," he wrote,

I fancy, in acquiescence to the vulgar doctrine, the address in this line is to a part of the *troop,* as mortals by birth, but adopted by the fairies: *orphans* in respect of their real parents, and now only dependent on *destiny* herself. A few lines from Spenser will sufficiently illustrate this passage:

> The man whom *heavens* have *ordayned* to bee
> The spouse of *Britomart* is *Arthegall.*
> He wonneth in the land of *Fayeree,*
> Yet is no *Fary* borne, ne sib at all,
> To elfes, but sprong of seed terrestriall,
> And whilome by *Faries* stolen away,
> Whiles yet in infant cradle he did crall &c.
>
> Edit. 1590. B.3 St. 26.

A Letter . . . to Mr. Steevens   121

He elaborated on his remarks in the *Essay* on the Prologue to *Troilus and Cressida* (IX.[3].1). He wrote a long, almost page-length, note on Romeo's "O brawling love! O loving hate," in which he quoted Watson, Turberville, Chaucer, and Petrarch and cited Wyatt's translation of the Sonnet of Petrarch, noting that "This kind of antithesis was very much the taste of the Provencal and Italian poets; perhaps it might be hinted by the ode of Sappho preserved by Longinus," another casual display of wide reading (X.13.4). And, again on *Romeo and Juliet,* he commented on the designation "the County Paris" by a quotation from Fairfax's translation of Tasso (X.99.7).[1] The last of the notes is on Hamlet's "distraction in's aspect" (X.228.3), Steevens citing Farmer as his authority for "aspect" being accented on the second syllable in Shakespeare's time. Of greater interest is the fact that Farmer performed some editorial duties for Steevens. The Rev. Michael Tyson, writing from Cambridge to Richard Gough on 18 March 1772, said that he "saw at his [Farmer's] room, the other day, Steevens's proof-sheets of the new edition of Shakspeare. Farmer is making additions" (*Lit. Anecd.,* VIII.587). What is more, Steevens was accused of having withheld "the Notes on Shakspeare with which Mr. [Tom] Davies had furnished him, on the pretence 'that the distribution of the Notes in the Edition of 1773 was lodged with Dr. Farmer; whose answer to a letter on that subject" is quoted, many years after the fact:

> Sir   *March* 2, 1785.
> An accidental avocation has deprived me of the opportunity of giving you an answer by an earlier post. Give me leave to assure you, that though I have read your *printed* Notes on Shakspeare [he refers to Davies's *Dramatic Miscellanies,* 3 vols., 1783–84] with pleasure, if not always with conviction, and shall be glad to read more; yet I never saw, or asked to see, or was offered to be *shewn,* any manuscript Note of yours in my life. I hope this fully answers your question; and that you will believe me, Sir, your most obedient servant. (*Lit. Anecd.,* IX. 665)

It will not escape notice that Farmer did not deny that he had "the distribution ['distributing' in Davies's Appendix] of the Notes of the Edition of 1773." There is one additional bit of information about Farmer's involvement in the 1773 edition, for in his appended *Letter* to Steevens he writes of the caskets scene in *The Merchant of Venice,* "I know not whether Dr. *Johnson* communicated to you a passage in a letter, which I wrote to him above a year ago, relative to the business of the three caskets in this play. I informed him, that the story was taken from an old translation of the *Gesta Romanorum,* first printed by *Winkin de Worde*" (pp. 14–15).[2]

APPENDIX II.

A
LETTER

FROM THE REV.

Mr. FARMER of Emanuel College, Cambridge,

AUTHOR OF

AN ESSAY ON THE LEARNING OF SHAKESPEARE,

TO

MR. STEEVENS.

Dear Sir,

I HAVE long promifed you a fpecimen of fuch obferva-
tions, as I think to be ftill wanting on the works of our
favourite poet. The edition you now offer to the publick,
approaches much nearer to perfection, than any that has yet
appeared; and, I doubt not, will be the ftandard of every
future one. The track of reading, which I fometime ago
endeavoured to prove more immediately neceffary to a commentator on *Shakefpeare*, you have very fuccefsfully followed, and have confequently fuperfeded fome remarks,
which I might otherwife have troubled you with. Thofe I
now fend you, are fuch as I marked on the margin of the
copy you were fo kind to communicate to me. and bear a
very fmall proportion to the mifcellaneous collections of this
fort, which I may probably put together fome time or other:
if I do this I will take care by proper references to make them
peculiarly ufeful to the readers of your edition.

An appendix has little room for quotation—I will be therefore as concife as poffible.

VOL.

A Letter . . . to Mr. Steevens   123

Farmer's notes in the second Appendix to the 1773 *Shakespeare* were presented with no little formality. It should not go unnoted that Farmer states that the notes in this *Letter* "bear a very small proportion to the miscellaneous collections of this sort, which I may probably put together some time or other: if I do this I will take care by proper references to make them peculiarly useful to the readers of your edition." As with others of Farmer's projects, this one also came to naught.

One would expect the preoccupations and methods, and even some of the prejudices, of the *Essay on the Learning of Shakespeare* to resurface in the 1773 Appendix, and one would not be mistaken. Some reversals might also be expected. Since Capell had criticized the *Essay,* it is not surprising that Farmer should seize this public opportunity to pay him back in kind. In the very first note in the Appendix, Farmer began his attack, not naming him, true, but recognizably Capell from the quoted words: "So little did a late editor know of his author, when he idly supposed his *school literature* might perhaps have been lost by the *dissipation of youth,* or the *busy scenes* of publick life!" (2). Capell, always referring to Johnson's 1765 *Shakespeare* as "the late edition," had won himself the description as "a late editor." As one more example, the first note on *The Merry Wives of Windsor* reads, "The Adventures of *Falstaff* in this play seem to have been taken from the story of the *Lovers of Pisa,* in an old piece, called *'Tarleton's Newes out of Purgatorie.'* A late editor pretended to much knowledge of this sort; and I am sorry that it proved to be only pretention."[3] Farmer refers caustically to William Kenrick, who had adversely reviewed Johnson's edition (8), and to William Guthrie (31), whose theory about Lady Macbeth he had refuted in the *Essay.* Richard Warner, who had very politely differed with Farmer's *Essay,* is described as "A gentleman of great merit" (2) and as a "gentleman [who] has treated me with so much civility" (34), although he is treated with less than subtle irony in one other reference (33).

The notes in the 1773 appendix are, as was the *Essay,* a personal document. Just as he had referred graciously to his friend Michael Lort in the *Essay,* so did he have kind words for others of his friends. Dr. Anthony Askew is remembered as "my very learned friend" who had a "MS. of Lidgate" (15), and Mrs. Askew is described as "a very ingenious lady, with whom I have the honour to be acquainted, Mrs. *Askew* of Queen's Square, has a fine copy of the second *folio* edition of *Shakespeare,* which formerly belonged to king *Charles* I. and was a present from him to his Master of the Revels, Sir *Thomas Herbert*" (21). Thomas Warton is "my very ingenious friend" (4), as is Percy exactly (19). Johnson is gently corrected in three notes and agreed

124   A Letter . . . to Mr. Steevens

with in one.[4] Farmer, who proposed thirty-four emendations in the 247 notes of the appendix was particularly proud of one. Lord Salisbury, in *King John,* vows to forego various pleasures "Till I have set a glory to this hand / By giving it the worship of revenge" for the death of Arthur. "I should think," wrote Farmer, "it should be 'a glory to this *head'*—Pointing to the dead prince, and using the word *worship* in its common acceptation. *A glory* is a frequent term: 'Round a quaker's beaver cast a *glory*,' says Mr. *Pope:* the solemn confirmation of the other lords seems to require this sense. The late Mr. *Gray* was much pleased with this correction" (25). The lines are one of the cruces in the play, with two pages devoted to them in the New Variorum edition where Farmer's note is quoted (341–42). One other emendation must be noted. In act III, scene iii of *Romeo and Juliet,* the Nurse is given two lines, "O woeful sympathy! / Piteous predicament!" Farmer wrote, "One may wonder the editors did not see that this language must necessarily belong to the *Friar"* (37). The New Variorum editor quotes Farmer's note as it appeared in the 1803 *Shakespeare* edited by Reed, i.e., with a first sentence, "The old copies give these words to the Nurse," and in his textual notes writes "Given to 'Friar' by Steev. 1778 (Farmer and S. Walker conj.)" (182), which is surely misleading. Farmer, not Steevens, was first. Maybe one should be reminded that the notes in the *1773* Appendix are in the form of a letter to Mr. Steevens, who made extensive use of them in 1778. Steevens acknowledged the source of his emendation, writing "Dr. Farmer's emendation may justly claim that place in the text to which I have now advanced it" (1778. X.104.8).

It was inevitable that Farmer should return to the question of Shakespeare's learning in the Appendix. Twice he referred back to the *Essay,* once to establish that an earlier play on Macbeth had been given in Latin but also in English, and the second time to demonstrate that the old play on Richard II was also in English.[5] Don Armado of *Love's Labour's Lost* is given to fantastic wordplay, as witness "Doth the inconsiderate take salve for *l'envoy,* and the word *l'envoy* for a salve?" a pun that goes unremarked in the 1773 edition. But in the appendix Farmer protested, "I can scarcely think that *Shakespeare* had so far forgotten his little school learning, as to suppose that the *Latin* verb *salve,* and the *English substantive, salve,* had the same pronunciation; and yet without this, the quibble cannot be preserved" (10). Twice Farmer is almost surely attributing too much learning, albeit in English, to Shakespeare. He could not help think that Shakespeare knew and was intending "a stroke at a passage in a famous old book, call'd 'The gentleman's Academie in Hawking, Hunting, and Armorie,' written originally by *Juliana Barnes* and re-

A Letter . . . to Mr. Steevens

published by *Gervase Markham, 1595*" (29). And he thought "*Shakespeare* had probably in view a very popular book of his time, The *Beehive of the Roman Church*" (40) for Iago's "Or to be naked with her friend in bed / An hour, or more, not meaning any harm?" Lord Littleton thought Shakespeare had derived an incident from William of Malmsbury's Latin history of England. Farmer wrote, "I do not however believe that lord *Littleton* supposed *Shakespeare* to have read this old *Monk*. The story is told likewise by *Matthew Paris* and *Matthew of Westminster;* and by many of the *English* Chroniclers, *Stowe, Speed,* &c. &c." (27).

In a note on Hamlet's reference to "the satirical slave," Warburton had claimed Shakespeare was plainly alluding to Juvenal's tenth *Satire*. Farmer refuted Warburton and stated that Shakespeare "could not possibly have read any one of the *Roman* poets," and pointed out that there was a translation of the tenth *Satire* although he could not tell if it had been printed in Shakespeare's time (38). And, about a supposed parody of a passage in a *French* poem by *Garnier* in *As You Like It,* he concluded that "one may remark once for all, that *Shakespeare* wrote for the *people;* and could not have been so absurd to bring forward any allusion, which had not been familiarized by some accident or other" (38). At one juncture Farmer proclaimed flatly that Shakespeare "was little acquainted with literary history" and had thought the name Dr. Caius denoted "a *foreign quack*" (27). He recalled a passage in the old play, *The Return from Parnassus* in which Burbage and Kempe are introduced, and Kempe says "Few of the university . . . pen play well; *they* smell too much of that *writer Ovid,* and that *writer, Metamorphosis:*—why here's our *Fellow Shakespeare* put them all down" (18). In a long note on Macbeth's famous "Daggers / Unmannerly breech'd with gore" lines, Farmer suggested a French source for the passage, one which Shakespeare "had read in the English," adding "but had he been able to have read the *French* on the other page, even as a *learner,* he must have been set right at once" (23). Shakespeare, then, had little or no French.

Farmer continued to wear his erudition lightly, although he could refer facetiously at the end of his *Essay* to "all such reading as was never read," quoting Pope's *Dunciad*. One hundred and thirty-four of the works quoted or cited in the notes in the appendix were works Farmer owned. Thus, of the seven works referred to on the first page of the notes, Farmer had six. A few examples of his wide reading, beginning with the first note, shall do the duty for many others. William Collins had told Thomas Warton that the romance on which Shakespeare had founded *The Tempest* was an Italian chemical romance called *Orelia and Isabella*. Farmer knew better. "The romance

126 A Letter . . . to Mr. Steevens

alluded to is not ORELIA, but AURELIA and *Isabella*," he wrote. "I know not by what mistake the late Mr. *Collins* in his information to Mr. *Warton,* could give it the epithet of *chemical.* There is an edition of it in four languages, printed at *Antwerp, 1556*" (2). His own copy, number 2251 in the sale catalog of his library, is "Histoire d'Aurelio et Isabelle, fille du Roy d'Ecosse, Fr. &. Itasl. *Paris,* 1553." When it came to the words "flight" and "bird-bolt" in a passage in *Much Ado about Nothing,* Farmer quoted Harleian "Catalogue of MSS. vol. I. n. 69" and then remembered "the title-page of an old pamphlet" which he found "still more explicit. 'A new *post*—a marke exceeding necessary for all mens arrows: whether the great man's *flight,* the gallant's *rover,* the wiseman's *pricke-shaft,* the poor man's *but-shaft,* or the fool's *bird-bolt*" (9). The Harleian Catalogue is number twenyt-three in the sale catalog of Farmer's library; the old pamphlet is absent. Zachary Grey had quoted "Rastal in his *Chronicle*" for the line "Richard that robb'd the lion of his heart" in *King John* for the derivation of "lion-hearted," i.e., the monarch's tearing the heart out of a lion put into the cell in which he was imprisoned. Farmer was able to add, "I have an *old black lettered history of Lord Fauconbridge,* whence *Shakespeare* might pick up this circumstance" (24). It should be remembered that Steevens is addressed directly in a number of these notes. Hence, in one, having occasion to invoke "Kendall" for one parallel, Farmer thought of something else: "I forgot to observe to you that in *Kendall*'s collection there are many translations from *Claudian, Ausonius,* the *Anthologia,* &c." (28). Farmer refers to Timothy Kendall's *Flowers of Epigrammes, out of sundrie the moste singular authours selected, as well auncient as late writers,* 1577. The quotation of a few notes in order to suggest the range of Farmer's reading and the retentiveness of his memory, as well as the treasures of his private library, is a futile effort. There is virtually no note, wrong though it may be, that does not bear witness to all the above.

Farmer expressed strong views about the Shakespeare canon in the *Essay;* he had more to say on the subject in the 1773 appendix. Probably the most interesting is what amounts to a reversal of the previously held opinion that Shakespeare had no hand in *Pericles.* When he came to the famous image in *Twelfth Night* Farmer wrote,

> This celebrated image was not improbably first sketched out in the old play of *Pericles.* I think, *Shakespeare*'s hand may be sometimes seen in the latter part of it, and there only:———two or three passages, which he was unwilling to lose, he has transplanted, with some alteration, into his own plays.

A Letter . . . to Mr. Steevens 127

"She sat like patience on a monument,
Smiling at grief."———

In *Pericles,* "Thou *(Marina)* dost act like patience on king's graves, and smiling extremity out of act."
Thus, a little before, *Marina* asks the *bawd,* "are you a woman?" Bawd. "What would you have me to be if not a woman?" *Mar.* "*An honest woman or not a woman.*"———Somewhat similar to the dialogue between *Iago and Othello* relative to *Cassio.*

"I think, that he is *honest.*
Men should be what they seem.
Or those that be not would they might seem *none.*"

Again, "She starves the ears she feeds, says *Pericles,* and makes them hungry, the more she gives them speech." So in *Hamlet.*

"As if *increase of appetite* had grown
By what it *fed* on." (19–20)

The first of the parallels, that of *Twelfth Night,* has been accepted; the other two are not mentioned in the New Variorum edition, although the parallel to *Hamlet* ought surely to have been noticed, especially as there is no note on the lines.
Farmer had dismissed "this horrible Piece," *Titus Andronicus,* from the Shakespeare canon in the *Essay.* He returned to it in the appendix, declaring, "There is every reason to believe, that *Shakespeare* was not the author of this play. I have already said enough upon the subject." Whereupon he added four more paragraphs, covering half a page, on the subject, concluding with, "It has been said, that this play was first printed for *G. Elves,* 1594. I have seen in an old catalogue of *tales,* &c. the history of *Titus Andronicus*" (33). Farmer could call another play, actually the *Henry VI* plays, a "*doubtful* performance" in the *Essay)* (53), but later made the confusing statement, "I have no doubt but *Henry the sixth* had the same Author with *Edward the third,* which hath been recovered to the world in Mr. *Capell's Prolusions*" (88). Capell had said of *Edward the Sixth* that it was "thought to be writ by Shakespeare." Farmer's statement in the Appendix is unambiguous,

I have already given some reasons, why I cannot believe, that these plays were *originally* written by *Shakespeare.* The question, who did write them? is at best, but an argument *ad ignorantiam.* We must remember, that very many old plays are *anonymous;* and that *play-writing* was

128 A Letter . . . to Mr. Steevens

scarcely yet thought reputable: nay, some authors express for it great horrors of repentance.—I will attempt, however, at some future time to answer this question: the disquisition of it would be too long for this place.

One may at least argue, that the plays were not written by *Shakespeare* from *Shakespeare* himself. The *chorus* at the end of *Henry* V. addresses the audience

> —————"For *their sake,*
> "*In your fair minds let this* acceptance take."

But it could be neither agreeable to the poet's judgment or his modesty, to recommend his new play from the merit and success of *Henry* VI.!———His claim to indulgence is, that, tho' *bending* and unequal to the task, he has ventured to *pursue the story:* and this sufficiently accounts for the connection of the whole, and the allusions of particular passages.

The disquisition never materialized.

Farmer's doubts about Shakespeare's part in *The Taming of the Shrew,* voiced in the *Essay,* were reinforced in the appendix (18). New to the appendix were his reservations about *Henry VIII* and his assertion that certain lines in *Two Noble Kinsmen,* a play he had not mentioned elsewhere, were by Shakespeare. He wrote, of the first,

> I intirely agree in opinion with Dr. *Johnson,* that *Ben Jonson* wrote the *prologue and epilogue* to this play. *Shakespeare* had a little before assisted him in his *Sejanus;* and *Ben* was too proud to receive assistance without returning it. It is probable, that he drew up the directions for the parade at the *christening,* &c. which his employment at court would teach him, and *Shakespeare* must be ignorant of: I think, I now and then perceive his hand in the dialogue. (31)

The question of the extent of collaboration on this play is still unsettled, but only Farmer thought he discerned Jonson at work in the coronation scene and "now and then" in the dialogue. As for *Two Noble Kinsmen,* Farmer had "no doubt" that the "beautiful lines" spoken by Emilia of a rose, beginning "It is the very emblem of a maid" and continuing for six more lines, "were written by *Shakespeare*" (35). Modern scholarly opinion differs, assigning act II, scene ii, in which the lines appear, to John Fletcher. Farmer was not alone, however, in thinking that the play *The Puritan* was "ridiculously ascribed to *Shakespeare*" (23).

Steevens, it has been seen (p. 124 above), was given credit for an emendation in *Romeo and Juliet* suggested to him by Farmer. He is also given credit by the editor of the New Variorum *King John* (281) for suggesting a passage in Lyly's *Mydas* as a parallel for the affectation of melancholy in that play; Farmer made the suggestion in the appendix (24). The editor of the New Variorum *Love's Labour's Lost* devotes over two full pages of commentary on Boyet's question, "Who is the shooter?" (126–28), beginning with "At the suggestion of FARMER [good!], who found here a 'quibble,' STEEVENS changed this to *suitor*, and remarked that 'suitor' was anciently pronounced *shooter*." Steevens gave an example of such usage, but the textual note gives "Var.'85" as the source of the emendation, with nothing to indicate that the original suggestion was made twelve years earlier. This is also true of a parallel for "male-varlet" in *Troilus and Cressida* (34) which the New Variorum editor assigns to 1778. These are but a few instances of the rather haphazard way in which modern editors have treated Farmer's notes, that is, when they have not entirely neglected them. There is more than a fair sprinkling of notes by Farmer in the New Variorum editions, but there has also been criminal neglect. Other modern editions of Shakespeare's plays are usually very light on commentary and almost silent about parallels, and I shall give examples of only a few instances where the commentary in these editions should have included something by Farmer. Necessary to be stressed again is that Farmer's 247 notes are an appendix to the text and commentary of the ten volumes of the 1773 *Shakespeare* and that many of them owe their existence to the need to correct, add to, or corroborate the notes of the scholars whose notes are printed in that edition.

The following series of notes is those which should be in the New Variorum editions of the various plays represented. Trinculo says of Caliban, "He were a brave monster indeed, if they [his eyes] were set in his tail," and Farmer writes, "I believe this to be an allusion to a story that is met with in *Stowe*, and other writers of the time. It seems, in the year 1574, a whale was thrown ashore near *Ramsgate*. A *monstrous fish* (says the *chronicler*) but not so *monstrous* as some reported—for his *eyes* were in his *head*, and not in his *back*" (*Summary*, 1575, p. 562 [p. 3]). There is no note in the New Variorum edition on this line. A reference to a "corporal of the field" in *Love's Labour's Lost* produced three parallels.

> *Giles Clayton* in his *Martial Discipline*, 1591, has a chapter on the office and duty of a *corporal of the field*. In one of *Drake's Voyages, it appears, that the Captains Morgan* and *Sampson* by this name, "had commandement over the rest of the land captaines." *Brokesby* tells us, that "Mr. Dodwell's father was in an office then known by the name of *Corporal of the Field*, which he said was equal to that of a captain of horse." (10)

130   A Letter . . . to Mr. Steevens

The *OED,* quoted in the New Variorum edition (106) corroborates. "Brokesby" is Francis Brokesby, who wrote *The Life of Henry Dodwell* (1715); Farmer had a copy (number 4011). In the same play Boyet is told "you can carve; / Break up this capon," explained as "open this letter" by Theobald, who gave parallels from French and Italian. It remained for Farmer, however, to offer parallels in English: "Henry IV. Consulting with *Sully* about his marriage, says, 'my niece of *Guise* could please me best, notwithstanding the malicious reports, that she loves *Poulets* in paper, better than in a *fricasee.*'—A message is called *a cold pigeon,* in the letter concerning the entertainments at *Killingworth Castle*" (10). And while Theobald was scandalized that the Princess, still in *Love's Labour's Lost,* should say "Pox on that jest," thinking she meant the venereal disease, Farmer quoted the poetry of Davison and a letter of Donne's in exemplification of the reference as one to smallpox (12).

Helen of *A Midsummer Night's Dream* asks "Can you not hate me, as I know you do / But you must join in souls to mock me so?" and Hanmer, Warburton, Johnson, and Tyrwhitt tried emendation, while Steevens explicated, "i.e. join heartily, unite in the same mind." Only Farmer gave a parallel: "We meet with this phrase in an old poem by *Robert Dabourne,* '————Men shift their fashions— / They are *in souls* the same'" (13), but the New Variorum editor did not include it. Farmer was evidently the first to state that part of the story of *The Merchant of Venice* derived from "the *Gesta Romanorum,* first printed by *Winkin de Worde*" (14–15), although Tyrwhitt's priority in this matter seems implied in the New Variorum edition (305). One other note on the same play should have a place in any future edition. Gratiano says, "Now by my hood, a Gentile, and no Jew," and Johnson wrote, "A jest rising from the ambiguity of *Gentile,* which signifies both a *heathen* and *one well born.*" Johnson's note is enshrined in the New Variorum (100), but Farmer's addition, one that puts the matter beyond doubt, is not. "There is an old book by one *Ellis,*" he wrote, "entitled 'The *Gentile* Sinner, or England's brave Gentleman'" (15).

Farmer was first to state that in the Clown's song in *Twelfth Night,* the words "Lady, Lady" were the "*burthen,* and should be printed as such," i.e., in italics rather than the roman letter in which they were printed in the 1773 *Shakespeare,* and he was the first to call attention to the presence of a stanza from it in Percy's *Reliques.* At the same time he noted that Mercutio's "lady, lady, lady" in *Romeo and Juliet* was also the burthen and should be so printed (19). The New Variorum encloses the words in single marks of quotation and attributes mention of the stanza in Percy's *Reliques* to Staunton in 1857! The letter Malvolio is deceived by includes the words "Remember who commended thy yellow stockings, and wish'd to see thee ever cross-gartered." The New Variorum gives Steevens's parallel from Ford's *Lover's Melancholy* made in the 1778 edition, but neglects the earlier parallel, the first such parallel, in Farmer's note: "Sir *Thomas Overbury* in his character of a *footman* without *gards* on his coat, represents him as more upright than any *crosse-garter'd* gentleman-usher" (20).

Another first for Farmer was his note identifying "Whoop, do me no harm, good man" in *The Winter's Tale* as "the name of an old song. In the famous history of *Fryar Bacon* we have a ballad *to the tune of, 'Oh! do me no harme, good man'* " (22). And, in the same play, Camillo's reference to a "sitting" prompted Theobald to emend to "fitting," Warburton to explain "council-days being, in our author's time, called, in common speech, the 'sittings,' " and Farmer to afford the first parallel: "*Howel,* in one of his letters, says, 'My lord president hopes to be at the next *sitting* in York' " (22). Theobald and Warburton are quoted in the New Variorum edition; Farmer is not. The editor of the New Variorum *Macbeth* was particularly chary of having recourse to Farmer's notes. Macbeth's "gouts of blood" is explained as "Clarendon [Press, 1869]: Drops, from the French *goutte,* and, according to stage tradition, so pronounced" (121). Almost a century earlier Farmer had stated that "*Gouts* for *drops* is frequent in old *English*" (22). Pope and others were content to emend "maggot-pies" to "magpies," and the New Variorum editor was equally content to quote Skeat's, "also called *maggoty-pie,*" with his etymological derivation (228). Farmer pointed out that in "*Minshew's Guide to the Tongues.* 1617, we meet with a *maggatopie:* and *Middleton* in his *More Dissemblers beside Women,* says 'He calls her *magot o' Pie*' " (23). A last sin of omission on the part of the New Variorum editor is his failure to quote Farmer's note on the apparitions in the fourth act. Farmer wrote, "Lord *Howard,* in his *Defensative against the Poison of supposed Prophecies,* mentions 'a notable example of a conjuror, who represented (as it were, in dumb show) all the persons who should possess the crown of *France;* and caused the king of *Navarre,* or rather a wicked spirit in his stead, to appear in the fifth place, &c.' " (23–24). Geoffrey Bullough quotes the same passage in his *Narrative and Dramatic Sources of Shakespeare,* but there is no mention of Farmer, to whom we must credit another important first.[6]

Agamemnon tells Aeneas " 'Tis done like Hector, but securely done"; Warburton correctly glossed "securely" in the Latin sense, i.e., "A negative security arising from a contempt of the object opposed";

132   A Letter . . . to Mr. Steevens

and Farmer provided needed parallels: "Mr. *Warner* in his ingenious letter to Mr. *Garrick,* thinks this sense peculiar to *Shakespeare,* 'for, says he, I have not been able to trace it elsewhere.' This gentleman has treated me with so much civility, that I am bound in honour to remove his difficulty."

It is to be found in the last act of the *Spanish Tragedy,*

"O damned devil! how *secure* he is."

In my Lord *Bacon's Essay on Tumults,* "neither let any prince or state be *secure* concerning discontents." And besides these, in *Drayton, Fletcher,* and the vulgar translation of the bible. (34)

Warburton is quoted in the New Variorum edition; Farmer is ignored. Richard Warner, it is obvious, could not compete with Farmer in breadth of reading. In the same note Farmer helped Warner in the latter's unsuccessful "researches for the word *religion* in its *Latin* acceptation," quoting "*Hoby's* translation of *Castilio,* 1561" and citing Ben Jonson's use of "both the *substantive* and the *adjective* in this sense." And, to round matters off, Farmer noted that "the word *Cavalero,* with the *Spanish* termination, . . . is to be found in *Heywood, Withers, Davies, Taylor,* and many other writers," thus countering Warner's argument that Shakespeare knew the Spanish word else he would have written "Cavalier."

The opening sentences in the New Variorum edition's section on the "Source of the Plot" of *Romeo and Juliet* read, "MALONE. The story on which this story is formed was originally told by Luigi da Porto, of Vicenza, who died in 1529. His novel did not appear till some years after his death, being first printed at Venice in 1535" (397). Malone's note first appeared in the 1790 *Shakespeare,* edited by him. In the first volume of his Supplement to the 1778 Johnson–Steevens *Shakespeare,* Malone had printed the Italian of the conclusion of da Porto's story for comparison with Arthur Brooke's *Tragicall History of Romeo and Juliet.* In the 1773 Johnson–Steevens *Shakespeare,* Steevens had written that the "story on which this play is founded, is said to have been a true one. It was originally published by an anonymous Italian novelist in 1549 at Venice, and again in 1553 at the same place" (X.[5]). It was not, therefore, until Farmer's Letter to Steevens was printed that the anonymous Italian novelist was named. Here is Farmer's note.

This story was well known to the *English* poets before the time of *Shakespeare.* In an old collection of poems called "*A gorgeous gallery of gallant Inventions,* 1578," I find it mentioned.

A Letter . . . to Mr. Steevens   133

"Sir *Romeus* annoy but trifle seems to mine." and again, *Romeus and Juliet* are celebrated in "*A poor Knight his Palace of private Pleasures, 1579.*" I quote these passages for the sake of observing, that if *Shakespeare* had not read *Painter's* translation, it is not likely that he would have altered the name to *Romeo*. There was another novel on the subject by *L. da Porto; which has been lately printed at Venice.* (36–37)

The novel had appeared in the second volume of the four volumes of *Del Novelliero Italiano*, Venice Siena, 1754. To Farmer, and not to Malone, must go the credit of first naming Luigi da Porto.

Two more examples of neglect of Farmer's notes in the 1773 appendix follow: Hamlet's letter to Ophelia is headed "*To the celestial, and my soul's idol, the most beautified Ophelia,*" which last phrase Polonius characterizes as "vile." Theobald emended to "beatified," which Capell accepted, since both "celestial" and "idol" would seem to demand a religious term. Johnson, noting that Hanmer and Warburton had also followed Theobald, tentatively opted for the original reading, with the qualifying remark that "*Beautified* seems to be a 'vile phrase,' for the ambiguity of its meaning." There is no note by Steevens in the 1773 edition. The New Variorum editor cites Theobald and Capell, quotes Johnson, and then gives a parallel by Steevens. But Farmer had been beforehand with Steevens, "*Heyward* in his *History of Edward VI.* says, 'Katherine Parre, queen dowager to king *Henry VIII.* was a woman *beautified* with many excellent virtues'" (38). In more than one instance, it is clear Steevens has been cited or quoted although he had been anticipated by Farmer. "Put out the light, and then put out the light," a line which merits two pages of commentary in the New Variorum edition of *Othello* (194–96), is represented by a single note in the 1773 *Shakespeare* as Warburton's emendation of the punctuation. Farmer's full note reads,

> This has been considered as a very difficult line. *Fielding* makes *Betterton* and *Booth* dispute about it with the *author himself* in the other world. The punctuation recommended by Dr. *Warburton,* gives a spirit to it which, I fear, was not intended. It seems to have been only a *play upon words. To put the light out* was a phrase for *to kill.* In the Maid's tragedy, *Melantius* says,"————'Tis a justice and a noble one, / To put the light out of such base offenders." (40)

The New Variorum editor quotes Warburton and Farmer, the latter only partially, so that the reference to Fielding is omitted entirely as is the reference to and quotation from *The Maid's Tragedy.* Thus, when the editor remarks parenthetically that "Both Steevens and Malone cite many instances from Shakespeare, his predecessors, and contemporaries, to prove that 'to put out the light' means 'to kill or die,' "

134   A Letter . . . to Mr. Steevens

one might think that Farmer was at a loss for an example when, in fact, he was the first to adduce one.

When the editor of the Arden *Merry Wives of Windsor* (1971) came to Falstaff's "Send me a cool rut-time, Jove, or who can blame me to piss my tallow?" he allowed that "Shakespeare's authority may well have been Turberville, ch. 17, first cited by Farmer" (136). He did not, however, make use of Farmer's note on Nym's "I will possess him [Ford] with yellowness, for the revolt of mine is dangerous," noting that Pope had emended "the" to "this" and Theobald "mine" to "mien." His own note reads, in part, "(Presumably) this rebellion of mine against Falstaff" (27). The note on these words in the Riverside *Shakespeare* (1974) reads, equally tentatively, "casting off my allegiance (?)" (295). Steevens's note in the 1773 edition reads, "*The revolt of mine* is the old reading. Nym, who is about to quit his master, may be made to observe, with propriety, that the desertion of servants is dangerous to the interests of their masters. *Revolt of mien,* was there any authority for such a reading, would signify *change of countenance,* one of the effects he had just been ascribing to jealousy" (I.213.7). Farmer wrote that the old reading, "mine," is "authority enough for *the revolt of mien* in modern orthography. 'Know you that fellow that walketh there? says *Eliot,* 1593—'he is an alchymist by his *mine,* and hath multiplied all to moonshine' " (5–6). "Eliot" is John Eliot, *Ortho-epia Gallica, Eliots fruits to the french.* Recourse to the *OED* reveals that "mien" was spelled in various ways, "meane" in Spenser, "meen" in some writers, and "mine" in "J. Eliot, Fruits 167" with the same quotation in Farmer's note. Suckling, by the way, also wrote "mine" for "mien." This all points to the conclusion that Farmer, again neglected, almost surely had the answer to the question posed by "the revolt of mine."

Two of Farmer's notes on *2 Henry VI* should have found a place in the New Arden edition of that play, despite the economy of commentary practiced in the series. Buckingham urges Henry to "retire to Killingworth," which Steevens needlessly emended to "Kenelworth," adding that "perhaps *Killingworth* might be the old pronunciation." Farmer puts matters right: "In the letter concerning *Q. Elizabeth's* entertainment at this place, we find, 'the casttel hath name of *Kyllelingwoorth;* but of truth, grounded upon faythfull story, *Kennelwoorth*' " (30). Even more striking is the omission of the second note. Jack Cade says of the severed heads of the Duke of Suffolk and Lord Say, "Let them kiss one another; for they lov'd well, when they were alive," and Farmer quite properly remarked, "This is from the *Mirrour for Neighbours* in the legend of *Jack Cade.*

With these two heads I made a pretty play,

A Letter . . . to Mr. Steevens 135

> For sight on poales I bore them thro' the strete,
> And for my sport made *each kisse other* swete."
>
> (39)

How *"Magistrates"* became *"Neighbours"* may be put down to Farmer's execrable scrawl, for it is the *Mirrour for Magistrates* he quotes, the compositor also falling foul of "pight" (not "sight") in the second line. This is a remarkable oversight on the part of the New Arden editor, for he quotes the addition to the *Mirrour* but five lines before Cade's words (128). Geoffrey Bullough writes, of *2 Henry VI*, "There is no reason to suppose that Shakespeare was indebted to *A Mirror for Magistrates* in this play, so citation from that book is limited to an excerpt from the 'tragedy' of Suffolk."[7] One can only hope that future editors and scholars will turn to Farmer's notes.[8]

A few scattered notes, quoted in no particular order, will serve to give some further idea of the variety of subject matter and interests revealed in Farmer's Letter to Steevens. In a note on *The Tempest,* on Ferdinand's question to Miranda, "If you be maid, or not?" Farmer who had had occasion in the *Essay* on Shakespeare's learning to refute the claim that Virgil lay behind this passage, wrote, among other things, "When we meet with an harsh expression in *Shakespeare,* we are usually to look for a *play upon words,*" a statement which may prompt research.[9] In the last scene of *A Midsummer Night's Dream* Puck says, "I am sent, with broom, before, / To sweep the dust behind the door." Farmer's note, *"To sweep the dust behind the door* is a common expression, and a common practice in large, old houses; where the doors of halls and galleries are thrown backward, and seldom or never shut" (14), is quoted in the New Variorum edition (237) where Halliwell's "more cleanly interpretation," i.e., "to sweep away the dust which is behind the door" is favored. Possibly Hallilwell was right, but he wrote in 1841; Farmer, in 1773. Another of Farmer's notes on *domestica facta* is accepted by the editor of the New Variorum *King Lear* (129). The stage direction "Stocks brought out" was occasion for Farmer to point out that "formerly in great houses, as still in some colleges, there were moveable *stocks* for the correction of the servants" (36). Sometimes Farmer assumed more familiarity with earlier English literature than was true. Feste, in *Twelfth Night,* says, rather cryptically, "So that conclusions to be as kisses, if your four negatives make your two affirmatives, why then the worse for my friends, and the better for my foes," making for a minor crux. Farmer offered apposite parallels, one from *Lust's Dominion,* and one from Sir Philip Sidney, who "has enlarged upon this thought in the sixty-third stanza of his *Astrophel and Stella*" (20). The note is quoted in the New Variorum edition (279), but the editor did not

136 A Letter . . . to Mr. Steevens

think it necessary to verify the reference to Sidney's poem. The un-quoted lines in question are, "For Grammar sayes (to Grammer who sayes nay) / That in one speech two Negatives affirme."

The editor of the New Variorum *Winter's Tale* devoted one and a half pages of his Preface to the play's "sea-coast in Bohemia" (viii–ix), noting that Ben Jonson was the first to cavil at this, and that Sir Thomas Hanmer went so far as to change "Bohemia" to "Bithynia" at its every appearance. "Some time after the baronet's edition appeared [1744]," he wrote, "attention was called to the fact that the 'sea-coast of Bohemia' was mentioned in GREENE's novel of *Dorastus and Fawnia*, out of which SHAKESPEARE had moulded his 'Winter's Tale.'" The editor of the New Arden edition quotes Uncle Toby in Sterne's *Tristram Shandy* on the absence of a seacoast in Bohemia from "Bk. 8, Ch. 19" (66). Farmer's note, anticipating the Sterne reference among other matters, called attention to the fact that Shake-speare took the phrase from Greene, whose novel was anterior to Shakespeare's play:

> Sir *Thomas Hanmer* gave himself much needless concern that *Shake-speare* should consider *Bohemia* as a maritime country. He would have us read *Bithynia:* but our author implicitly copied the novel before him. Dr. *Grey*, indeed, was *apt to believe* that *Dorastus and Faunia* might rather be borrowed from the play, but I have met with a copy of it, which was printed in 1588.—*Cervantes* ridicules these geographical mistakes, when he makes the princess *Micomicona* land at *Ossuna.*—Corporal *Trim's* king of *Bohemia* "delighted in navigation, and had never a seaport in his dominions;" and my lord *Herbert* tells us, that *De Luines* the prime minister of *France,* when he was embassador there, demanded, whether *Bohemia* was an *inland Country,* or lay "upon the Sea?"—There is a similar mistake in *Two Gentlemen of Verona,* relative to that City and *Milan.* (21)

In *Two Gentlemen of Verona* Valentine goes "from Verona to Milan," both inland places, by sea.[10]

A few more notes should suffice, if only to touch on one or two areas. In the matter of parallels Farmer was the equal of his friends Steevens and Reed. As an example, Bassanio is confronted with the three caskets in *The Merchant of Venice* and apostrophizes the leaden, "Thy paleness moves me more than eloquence." Warburton emended the original "paleness" to "plainness," the emendation being elevated into the text in the 1773 edition. Warburton had explained that "Bassanio is displeased at the golden *casket* for its *gaudiness,* and the silver one for its *paleness,*" and in defense of his emendation, "plainness," added that it "characterizes the lead from the silver, which *paleness* does not, they being both *pale*. Besides, there is a beauty in the *antithesis* between *plainness* and *eloquence;* between *paleness and eloquence* none." Bassanio had described silver as "thou pale and common drudge," and it was this that commanded Farmer's attention. He wrote, "It may be that Dr. *Warburton* has altered the wrong word, if any alteration be necessary." "I would rather give the character of *silver,*"

> ———— "Thou *stale,* and common drudge
> " 'Tween man and man."————
> The *paleness* of *lead* is for ever alluded to.
> "*Diane* declining, *pale* as any *ledde.*"
> Says *Stephen Hawes.* In *Fairfax's Tasso,* we have
> "The Lord *Tancredie, pale* with rage as *lead.*"
> Again, *Sackville* in his Legend of the Duke of Buckingham,
> "Now *pale* as *lead,* now cold as any stone."
> And in the old ballad of the *King and the Beggar,*
> ———— "She blushed scarlet red,
> "Then straight again, as *pale as lead.*"

As to the *antithesis, Shakespeare* has already made it in the *Midsummer Night's Dream:*

> "When, says *Theseus,* I have seen great clerks look *pale,*
> I read as much, as from the rattling tongue
> "Of fancy and audacious *eloquence.*"
>
> (15–16)

Whatever one thinks of Farmer's emendation, it did find favor with some, but of his talent for parallels there can be no doubt.

Farmer was not always right. One of his major errors was in supposing that "many" of Shakespeare's sonnets "are addressed to his beloved nephew *William Harte,*" an opinion of which he was disabused by Malone. In this same note Farmer took issue with Steevens. Hamlet and Laertes are at Ophelia's grave, both protesting their great sorrow. Hamlet challenges Laertes, "Woo't drink up Esil? eat a crocodile," the word "Esil" causing difficulty, as it was printed in italic type in former editions, suggesting it was the name of a river. Theobald was "persuaded the poet wrote "*Wilt drink up* Eisel? *eat a* crocodile," "Eisel" being "vinegar." Steevens would have none of this, stating, among other matters, that "no authors later than Chaucer or Skelton make use of *eysel* for *vinegar:* nor has Shakespeare employed it in any other of his plays." Farmer's reminder was gentle: "You forgot our author's 111th sonnet, "I will drinke / Potions of *Eysell*"

138   A Letter . . . to Mr. Steevens

(39–40). It should not go unremarked, finally, that Farmer's explanation of Iago's description of jealousy "which doth mock / The meat it feeds on" and elsewhere in *Othello*, "to *mock* seems the same with to *mammock*," i.e., to "ruminate" or "chew," was anticipated by Zachary Grey's "Mr. Smith" (Variorum, 176).

And so, with five more notes on *Othello*, the last play in the 1773 *Shakespeare*, Farmer came to the conclusion of his *Letter* to Steevens, modestly stating, "Thus have I, dear Sir, accomplished my promise, as well as the short notice you have given me, and my many avocations would permit me. I have no value for any of the corrections that I have attempted: but I flatter myself, that I have sometimes irrefragably supported the old text against the attacks of former commentators." And as this was in the form of a letter, he signed himself, "I am, dear Sir, Your very obedient servant, RICHARD FARMER."

7

Further Notes on Shakespeare

Johnson and Steevens revised their 1773 edition of Shakespeare in 1778 and included all but two of the 247 notes of Farmer's *Letter* to Steevens. One omitted note is on the passage in *2 Henry IV* in which Poins says that an "answer is as ready as a borrow'd cap" (V.406.4 in the 1773 edition). Warburton had objected to "borrow'd" and proposed to emend to "borrower's," with Steevens defending the old reading in his comment on Warburton's note. Farmer, in the *Letter* in the 1773 Appendix, had written, "I think Dr. *Warburton's* correction is right. A cap is not a thing likely to be *borrowed,* in the common sense of the word: and in the sense of *stealing,* the sentence should be a cap *to be borrowed.* Besides, *conveying* was the cant phrase for *stealing*" (28), thus disposing of Steevens's argument that "to *borrow* was the common cant term for the act of stealing." The 1778 text reads "a borrower's cap," Warburton's note is quoted, Steevens's comment is omitted, and thus the necessity for Farmer's note disappears. Steevens later restored the note in his 1793 *Shakespeare,* but it had continued absent in 1785 and in Malone's 1790 *Shakespeare.* The other note omitted in 1778 was Farmer's mistaken comment in the Appendix on the "Count Palatine" of *The Merchant of Venice,* of whom he wrote, "You [Steevens] have confounded the *Prince Palatine* who married the daughter of *James I.* with *Albert a Lasco* (the *Prince Laskie,* as Dr. *Dee* calls him) who was in *England* in the reign of *Elizabeth*" (15). Warburton, commenting on a passage in *Coriolanus* containing the words "the virginal palms of your daughters," added a rationale for invoking a coinage from the French where the English word in the text seemingly made no sense. He adduced a line in *Tarquin and Lucrece,* "To dry the old oak's sap, and cherish springs," arguing that "cherish" should be "tarish" from the French *"tarir."* Johnson suggested "perish springs," to which Farmer added, "Whether the word *perish* be right or not in this place, Dr. Johnson truly observes, that it is sometimes used actively. In the *Maid's Tragedy:*—'Let not my sins,' says Evadne to Amintor, *'Perish* your noble youth'" (VII.476.3). With but a few exceptions, the notes in the

Letter to Steevens were reprinted in edition after edition through 1821. Edmond Malone, almost surely in the interest of saving space for his own long notes in his 1790 *Shakespeare*, shortened a number of Farmer's notes and omitted more of them than any previous editor. Steevens restored most of the omissions in 1793, both whole notes and parts of notes. In 1790 Farmer added a note on "Atalanta's better part" in *As You Like It* (III.322.3) as well as the date to the comment originally made in his *Essay* on the old play on Richard III to the effect that "A childish imitation of Dr. Legge's play was written by one Lacy, 1583; which had not been worth mentioning, were they not confounded by Mr. Capell."

Edmond Malone's *Attempt to Ascertain the Order in which the Plays of Shakespeare were Written* was first published in volume I of the 1778 Johnson–Steevens *Shakespeare*. Malone had only recently taken up permanent residence in England, having left Ireland on 1 May 1777, although he had visited London twelve years earlier. At that time he had met and become intimate with Samuel Johnson, a relationship which afforded the best of all possible entrees into literary and scholarly circles.[1] In the *Attempt* Malone had recourse to some of Farmer's opinions in the *Essay on the Learning of Shakespeare,* but there is nothing to suggest any acquaintanceship between the two men. Malone had asserted in the 1778 *Shakespeare* and repeated in the 1785 edition that a reference to "Hamlets" in an epistle of Thomas Nashe's prefixed to Robert Greene's *Arcadia* was *not* in italics and hence *not* a clue to the date of Shakespeare's tragedy. In 1785, however, a note by Farmer, keyed to the statement about no distinguishing italics, reads "It is so printed [i.e. in italics] in edition 1589" (I.309). Consequently, in 1790, Malone revised his original position, noting that "the word *Hamlets* being printed in a different character from the rest" of the passage convinced him that it *is* a reference to Shakespeare's play. At another juncture in the 1785 reprinting of the *Attempt* there is another footnote by Farmer. Malone, in discussing the date of *The Merry Wives of Windsor,* cited Farmer's concurrence with Thomas Warton that the "imperfect copy" of the play must have been "revised and considerably augmented" in 1607. Farmer's note reads "Not before 1607. Probably some years after; at least not acted, as the imperfect copy was reprinted 1619" (I.319).

Malone and Farmer knew each other as least as early as 5 July, 1780,[2] and their acquaintance ripened, as can be seen from the letter of that date and in the revised *Attempt* in Malone's *Shakespeare,* 1790. In this latter there are a number of suggestions by Farmer, two

Further Notes on Shakespeare — page 141

prefaced by "Dr. Farmer is of opinion"—neither being in the *Essay* on Shakespeare's learning nor in the 1773 Appendix, further evidence of the greater degree of intimacy that had developed between the two men.[3]

Between 1773 and the spate of notes in the *Letter* to Steevens and 1778 when the revised Johnson–Steevens *Shakespeare* was published, Farmer seems not to have concerned himself with Shakespearean scholarship. Having been elected Master of Emmanuel College in 1775, he busied himself with college affairs, and within six months, having been made Vice-Chancellor, he undertook larger responsibilities. In 1778, the very year of the revised Johnson–Steevens *Shakespeare*, he was appointed Principal Librarian of the University Library, in which post he was able further to gratify his bibliomaniacal desires, buying rare books and manuscripts for the Library.

Farmer's next contributions to Shakespearean scholarship were in Malone's *Supplement to the Edition of Shakespeare's Plays Published in 1778,* itself published in two volumes in 1780. In the Advertisement prefixed to his *Supplement* Malone expressed his "warmest acknowledgments" to Percy, Steevens, Thomas Tyrwhitt, Samuel Henley, and to "the reverend Dr. Farmer." Curiously enough, in a letter of 5 July 1780 to his friend Lord Charlemont, to whom he was sending eight sets of his *Supplement,* Malone wrote that he "was in hopes to have had very considerable contributions [to the *Supplement*] from Dr. Farmer, but he has been so ill all the winter that he was not able to revise his papers. However, he has promised to arrange them this summer, and to turn out his whole Shakespeare drawer in the form of a printed letter to me. I long much to see his dissertation on the three parts of King Henry VI, which he thinks he can prove not to have been originally written, but only revised and improved by Shakespeare."[4] The "printed" letter to Malone, like others of Farmer's projects, never saw publication, nor was the dissertation on the three parts of *Henry VI* ever completed. In 1767 Farmer had written in his *Essay* that he had "no doubt but *Henry the sixth* had the same Author with *Edward the third,* which hath been recovered to the world in Mr. *Capell's Prolusions*" (88). Earlier in the same *Essay* he had described the Henry VI plays collectively as "this *doubtful* performance" (53), while Capell had described *Edward III* as "thought to be writ by Shakespeare." Farmer returned to the subject of the authorship of the three parts of *Henry VI* in the second Appendix to the 1773 *Shakespeare,* there writing, "I have already given some reasons [in the *Essay*], why I cannot believe, that these

142   Further Notes on Shakespeare

plays were *originally* written by *Shakespeare*. . . . I will attempt, however, at some future time, to answer this question ['who did write them']: the disquisition of it would be too long for this place" (Qqʳ).

Farmer's "disquisition" continued to be promised in subsequent editions of Shakespeare, although it was obvious that Malone had taken over the project with Farmer's blessing. Malone's "Dissertation on the Three Parts of King Henry VI" was finally printed at the end of *3 Henry VI* in his edition of Shakespeare (1790), after the notes of Steevens and Tyrwhitt, both of whom argued for Shakespeare's authorship of the three plays. In the 1785 *Shakespeare,* however, in a note at the end of *3 Henry VI,* Malone had agreed with Dr. Johnson in thinking the three plays were by Shakespeare. Malone had written to Bishop Percy on 28 September 1786 about the progress on his edition of Shakespeare, remarking, among other matters,

> I am at present very busy in arranging an Essay which is to be subjoined to the 3ᵈ part of Henry VI and is to go to press in about a fortnight, the object of which is to prove that the *Henries* were not written originally by Shakespeare, but were a *rifacimento*. As this is our friend Dʳ Farmer's own ground, I shall be a little mortified if he should not give me some support, and mean to run down to Cambridge for a few days to press him into the service; but he is so lazy that I doubt whether he will do anything, though he has half promised me. (*Letters,* I.34–35)

Malone was right, Farmer was too lazy. On 9 August 1787 Farmer wrote to Malone:

Eman: Aug 9.
1787.

My Dear Sir,
I HOPED to have seen you in my way thro' town, but I spent only one day there, and that at the other end of it.
You should have heard from me a post or two sooner, but our Registrar was out of the University, and I could not earlier get into the office. I find that Henry Earl of Southampton was admitted to the degree of B.A. in 1589, and proceeded no further; and, luckily examining the Book of Matriculations, I at last fell upon "Hen. Comes Southampton, impubes, 12 anº." of St. John's Coll. Decʳ. 11, 1585. Here we have his age as well as College. Essex was of Trin. June 1, 1579.
, I know not what to say as to the picture you mention. To be sure I could not cry out with Falstaff that "I am ashamed of my Company;" but as there is a print from it already, would not the property be invaded? Indeed, neither the one nor the other is a favourite. Romney supposed, as the picture was for a College, that it would be hung in a high room; and the engraver has not allowed for this exaggeration.
[*Some casual remarks on other matters are here omitted.*]

Further Notes on Shakespeare 143

By the way, this reminds me of a letter in the hands of Mr. Boswell, which will effectually demolish Mr. Colman's idea, that in the Preface to my Pamphlet, I meant to compliment *Mr. Steevens*. It appears from the date of that letter, that I had no acquaintance with him till long after that publication, and I wish Mr. Colman was informed that I alluded to *Dr. Johnson*, whose words I am sure I took down to a syllable: "I have not read a book which better answers the purpose for which it was written, and the question is for ever decided." Mr. Reed just shewed me this squib of Colman's. He cannot himself think that any thing else deserves notice.

Whatever you may have fancy'd, I solemnly declare to you, that I always meant to send you my Notes on the *Henrys*, if I could find them, and I flattered myself they might be among some papers at Canterbury. I cannot yet find them, and you want no assistance. As I remember, you have *some* of my arguments, but not *all*. I have supposed the plays originally *Marlow's*, and altered after his death by *Shakespeare;* this I argued from *Stile and Manner,* with many quotations, from passages contradictory to others in Shakespeare's genuine Plays, and others *clashing* in the Henrys *themselves,* which shew *different hands,* &c. &c. Besides, Marlow was so much hung up as an example of divine vengeance for *Atheism,* that nothing would go down under his name. That poor wretch, Capell, besides his conundrum of Shakespeare's *underwriting himself on purpose,* quotes two lines to prove the *whole Shakespeare's* "What! will th' aspiring blood of Lancaster sink in the ground? I thought it would have mounted." It is curious that *Marlow* has the same phraseology in his Edw. II. "Scorning that the lowly earth should drink his blood, mounts up to th'air." So much for Master Capell. After all, if any thing turns up you shall have it. In the last Edition, many things taken from *conversation,* on a *pencil'd margin,* by *Reed* or *Steevens,* when they were with me, are egregiously blundered, and sometimes *sheer nonsense.*

We shall be happy to see you at the *Fair.*

Yours affectionately,
R. FARMER

Calamo rapidiss.[5]

Soon thereafter, on August 29, Farmer wrote again, presumably in answer to a letter from Malone with further questions. As will be seen from the postscript, the matter of the *Henry VI* plays was still being discussed.

My dear Sir/   Eman. Coll. Aug. 29, 1787.

I have been spending a little Time with the Bp. of *Elphin,* & if his *Lordship* has made me too late for the *Devil,* I am very sorry for it.

I find a *Henry Constable* of S^t. *John's* B.A. 1579. I suppose this to have been the *Poet*—had he been an *Oxford* graduate, *Wood* would have said so. He got his Account, not from Winstanley, but a M.S. of *Bolton's* Hypercritica, which is $pp.^d$ at the end of *Hall's* Edit. of Triveth.[6] I will

144   Further Notes on Shakespeare

transcribe lest the book should not be at hand—"Noble *Henry Constable* was a great Master in English Tongue, nor had any Gentleman of our Nation a more pure, quick, or higher Delivery of Conceit, witness among all other that Sonnet of his before his Majesty's *Lepanto*. I have not seen much of Sir *Edw. Dyer's* Poetry, &c." Constable appears in the *Helicon,* which I believe you allude to, & in *England's Parnassus* 1600—I do not find him in *Dainty Devises,* or *Phoenix Nest,* &c. We will consider—if it must be so—about the *Print*. Perhaps I had better get a *head* or Chalk-drawer for 2 or 3 Guines, when I go thro' Town, than set *Steevens* a quarrelling about *Jones—that* was all his doing.

Your's affectionately,
R. Farmer.

P.S. I have found a few pencil'd *Mem.s* about the *Henrys*—if I can make them out, I will send them. Possibly I shall lead Mr *Boswell* into a Correspondence with Miss *Lawrence.*[7]

As a result of this letter Malone visited Cambridge on September 30, the only visit recorded in Reed's *Diaries* (154–57), and he remained for two weeks. He was, however, in Cambridge in 1784 for the bicentenary celebration of the founding of Emmanuel College. In 1788, writing on January 7 to Lord Charlemont, Malone, referring to his recently printed dissertation on the Henry VI plays, said that "Dr. Farmer has pointed out to me a passage which renders it much more probable that Marlowe was the co-adjutor," i.e., that Marlowe helped Robert Greene write *The Whole Contention of the Two Famous Houses of York and Lancaster,* which was a source for Shakespeare in the second and third parts of *Henry VI* (Charlemont MSS. II. 67). Hence, in the 1790 *Shakespeare,* Malone reversed himself, writing that although he had "formerly coincided with Dr. Johnson on this subject," a more attentive examination of "the two old plays published in quarto under the title of *The Whole Contention of the two famous houses of York and Lancaster,* in two parts" had caused him to change his mind, his reasons being given "in a distinct Essay on the subject," i.e., the following Dissertation. At the end of this Dissertation Malone wrote that he produced his arguments "with the more confidence, as they have the approbation of one who has given such decisive proofs of his taste and knowledge, by ascertaining the extent of *Shakespeare's learning,* that I have no doubt his thoughts on the Present question also, will have that weight with the publick to which they are undoubtedly entitled. It is almost unnecessary to add, that I mean my friend Dr. Farmer; who many years ago delivered it as his opinion, that these plays were not written *originally* by *Shakespeare*." Malone availed himself of Farmer's *Essay* for one of his arguments, recorded his indebtedness to him for several suggestions, and so

Further Notes on Shakespeare   145

worded the last sentences of his Dissertation as to inspire the belief that he had discussed it extensively with Farmer or, indeed, that Farmer had read it before publication. It is possible Farmer was temperamentally incapable of carrying to a successful conclusion the disquisition he had promised, or possibly he was too busy with other matters. It is to his credit that he recognized Malone's abilities and that he gave freely of his advice. What is more, in 1790, in Malone's revised essay on the chronology of Shakespeare's plays, Farmer's opinions on the *Henry VI* plays are acknowledged (I.i.271–83 passim). It is also worth noting that Farmer, with characteristic laziness and generosity, "again recommended to me," wrote Reed in his diary, "the republication of Butler's Works for the executn. of which he lent me the materials he had collected" (161).

Farmer's contributions to Malone's *Supplement* are of great interest. The two men had met; we know they were in correspondence. In volume one of the *Supplement,* given over to the "supplemental observations" on the 1778 edition and to Shakespeare's poems, there are a few notes by Farmer. He cites, and quotes to the extent of some four pages, the source for the bond scene in *The Merchant of Venice* (124–28), i.e., *The Orator,* to give it its short title, *"Written in French by Alexander Silvayn, and Englished by L.P.* [i.e., Lazarus Pilot] *London, printed by Adam Islip, 1596."* Geoffrey Bullough, who reprints the pertinent part of *The Orator* in his *Narrative and Dramatic Sources of Shakespeare's Plays,* fails to mention Farmer, the first to call attention to this source. Farmer quotes an exact parallel passage to Costard's "O sweet guerdon" speech in *Love's Labour's Lost* from *A Health to the Gentlemanly Profession of Serving-Men, or The Serving-man's Comfort* (110). He tells a very amusing anecdote in a gloss on *duc ad me* in *As You Like It* (129), and he notes to Steevens that it was remarkable that Shakespeare "has written no lines on the death of any poetical friend, nor commendatory verses on any living author, which was the constant practice of Jonson, Fletcher, &c.," adding that "Perhaps the singular modesty of Shakespeare hindered him from attempting to decide on the merits of others, while his liberal turn of mind forbad him to express such gross and indiscriminate praises as too often disgrace the names of many of his contemporaries" (193). He also tells another anecdote, this one in explication of Hamlet's "There's a divinity that shapes our ends, / Rough-hew them, how we will" (362).[8] The note on *duc ad me* is worth quoting, Steevens noting that "Dr. Farmer observes to me, that, being at a house not far from Cambridge, when news was brought that the hen-roost was robbed, a facetious old 'squire who was present, immediately sung the following stanza, which has an odd coinci-

146 Further Notes on Shakespeare

dence with the ditty of Jacques: *Dame,* what makes your ducks to die? / *duck, duck,* duck.———— / *Dame,* what makes your chicks to cry? / chuck, chuck, chuck."

Farmer's share in the establishment of the text and the explication of Shakespeare's poems begins with his furnishing Malone with the 1600 edition in 12mo. of *Venus and Adonis* (I.403) and includes a few suggestions for emendations as well as one note of somewhat larger moment. Venus says,

> Were I hard-favour'd, foul, or wrinkled-old,
> Ill-natur'd, crooked, churlish, harsh in voice,
> O'er-worn, despised, rheumatick and cold,
> Thick-sighted, barren, lean, and lacking juice.

Farmer informed Malone that the word "juice" is "so pronounced [joice] in the midland counties" (I.410.9), a note given a place in the New Variorum *Poems*.[9] According to Hyder E. Rollins, "Farmer was the first scholar of note to examine the *P.P.* [*Passionate Pilgrim*] of 1612 and to understand its connection with the *Poems* of 1640," a connection he had discussed in his *Essay* in 1767 as well as having given information on the subject to Edward Capell.[10] Farmer's interest in the *Passionate Pilgrim* is evidenced by one emendation (I.716) and by one gloss. The latter is worth quoting as another slight example of Farmer's knowledge of early English literature. The word in question is "threne," and Malone's note reads "This *funeral song.* A book entitled David's *Threanes,* by J. Heywood, was published in 1620. Two years afterwards it was reprinted under the title of David's *Tears:* the former title probably was discarded as obsolete. For this information I am indebted to Dr. Farmer" (I.736).

Volume II of Malone's *Supplement* contains the apocryphal plays, *Pericles, Locrine, Sir John Oldcastle, Lord Cromwell, The London Prodigal, The Puritan,* and *A Yorkshire Tragedy.* Farmer's interest in *Pericles,* one which later prompted him to suggest that Malone include it in his 1790 *Shakespeare,* is seen in five notes, three of which suggested emendations and may be forgotten. One is the explication of a difficult passage. The First Fisherman says, "what a man cannot get, he may lawfully deal for—his wife's soul," so reads the text in the *Supplement* (48). Farmer tentatively suggested the explication: "What a man cannot get, there is no law against giving, to save his wife's soul from purgatory" (48). The Riverside *Shakespeare* (1974) dismisses the passage as "not satisfactorily explained: no doubt the text is corrupt," an understandable view since the preferred text does not set off the last three words. The last note is on the vexed matter of

Further Notes on Shakespeare

authorship, Malone stating that "Dr. Farmer, whose opinion in every thing that relates to our author has deservedly the greatest weight, thinks the hand of Shakspeare may be sometimes seen in the latter part of the play, and there only" (159). Farmer mistakenly supposed Thomas Heywood to have written both *Sir John Oldcastle* and *Lord Cromwell* (270), and he thought *The Puritan* to have been written by an Oxford man, because of a unique use of the term "battling," the equivalent of what in Cambridge was termed "sizing" (543). He detected a sneer at *Macbeth* in *The Puritan* (616), and he declared categorically of *A Yorkshire Tragedy* that "most certainly it was not written by our poet at all" (675).

Most eighteenth-century editions of Shakespeare contained one or more appendices as final gathering places for afterthoughts and notes contributed too late for inclusion, and Malone's *Supplement* was no exception, boasting of two appendices, one for each volume, although both were printed at the end of the second. Farmer's interest in *Pericles* is again attested by three notes in the second appendix (722 and 723). One is an emendation, another confirms Steevens's reading of a line, and the third sees an allusion to Cicero's *dies honestissimus* in a reference to "a day [that] fits you." His note reads, "May not here be an allusion to the *dies honestissimus* of Cicero?—'If you like the day, find it out in the almanack, and nobody will take it from you.'" Francis Douce later added, "The allusion is to the lucky and unlucky days which are put down in some of the old calendars." Both notes are ignored in the New Cambridge edition. The editor of the New Arden edition cites neither note, altogether either might be the basis for his own suggestions. The Riverside *Shakespeare* (1974) offers an interpretation based upon acceptance of an emendation by Malone. Farmer's suggestion deserves a place in the commentary on this passage. Modern editors, unable themselves to do better, have ignored the two notes.

Three years later Malone published *A Second Appendix to Mr. Malone's Supplement* . . . , in which he added his second thoughts to the extent of sixty-seven pages. With the exception of two suggestions or bits of information, one from the Rev. John Bowle (1) and one from Farmer (31), Malone was unassisted. Farmer's assistance came at that juncture in *2 Henry IV* where Henry V assures his brothers that they need have no fears, for "This is the English, not the Turkish court: / Not Amurath an Amurath succeeds, / But Harry Harry." He directed Malone to the account of Amurath the third, sixth Emperor of the Turks, whose eldest son had his brothers strangled on the death of their father. Malone's note concludes, "It is highly probable that Shakspeare here alludes to this transaction; which was pointed out to

148 Further Notes on Shakespeare

me by the Revd. Dr. Farmer." The absence of notes by anybody else may be taken as a further sign of the intimacy between Farmer and Malone, but Farmer spent most of his time in Cambridge, and Malone, in London. Occasionally they coincided in London, where at one dinner, Malone, the host, had as guests Farmer, Boswell, Lort, Reed, and Courtenay. Boswell, in his laconic journalistic fashion, noted, "supt and was jovial. Home late" (*Diaries,* 275n.).

When, either through a real need or through one conceived by the booksellers, the Johnson–Steevens *Shakespeare* was to be revised once more, the task of editing the volumes fell to Isaac Reed, described on the title-page of the first volume as "The editor of Dodsley's Collection of Old Plays," a collection published in 1780. Reed had been suggested by Steevens; Farmer also urged him to undertake the edition. Reed had contributed two notes to the 1778 edition, in one of them explaining "slip" in Mercutio's witty exchange with Romeo as "a counterfeit piece of money" and bolstering up his explanation with passages from a prose piece by Robert Greene and from Ben Jonson's *Magnetic Lady* (X.69.3). Reed's other note concerned the change of name from Oldcastle to Falstaff in the Henry IV plays (V.522.4). That Farmer took an active interest in the 1785 edition and that the annual trips to Cambridge on the part of Reed and Steevens were spent in something other than mere high living is seen in the number of new notes contributed or suggested by him. There are sixty-eight of these. Before analyzing them, it will be well to quote again the letter Farmer wrote to Malone on 9 August 1787. "In the last edition [the 1785 *Shakespeare*], he wrote, "many things taken from conversation in a pencil'd margin by Reed and Steevens when they were with me, are egregiously blundered, and sometimes sheer nonsense."[11] There is no way of knowing which of Farmer's penciled marginalia Reed or Steevens mistook, leaving some of the comments "sheer nonsense." What one *can* deduce from the notes and suggestions added to the 1785 edition by Farmer is that he was unselfish in sharing his knowledge and opinions. Fifty-two of the sixty-eight new suggestions appear in the notes of Steevens (48), Reed (3), and Malone; Farmer puts his name to sixteen only. The only references in Reed's *Diary* about work done on Shakespeare in Cambridge occur on 30 September 1792 when he writes, "This Morning I was employed chiefly in correcting the Sheets of Shakespeare," and October 2 when he writes that he "Dined in the Hall then returned to my room and read two sheets of Shakespeare" (194–95). On September 16 Reed had noted that he read "Mr. Steevens's intended preface to Shakespeare" (192), but he says nothing to indicate that he suggested any changes in it. Steevens's edition of Shakespeare, nominally Reed's,

Further Notes on Shakespeare

was published in 1793. One can be quite sure that Farmer was consulted more than once in the new edition.

Further deducible from Farmer's notes and suggestions in 1785 are his willingness to try his hand at emending Shakespeare's text, for twenty of his sixty-eight contributions are suggested emendations. Additionally, one has some further light on the kind and variety of his reading and knowledge of books. In one note he informs Steevens that Shakespeare "took the name of his Jew from an old pamphlet entitled, '*Caleb Shillocke,* his Prophesie, or the Jewes Prediction.' London, Printed for T.P. [Thomas Pavyer.) No date" (III.[140].3). Perhaps, too, one may deduce from the number of notes (ten, five of which are emendations) on *The Merry Wives of Windsor* and on the two parts of *Henry IV* (another ten) that his favorite character was Sir John Falstaff, a suspicion that would be strengthened by the evidence of the *Letter* to Steevens, for there one finds twenty-seven notes on those two plays. Farmer was the first to explain the allusion to "a pension of thousands to be paid from the Sophy" in *Twelfth Night,* writing that it was to "Sir *Robert Shirley,* who was just returned in the character of *embassador to the Sophy.* He boasted of the great rewards he had received, and lived in London with the utmost splendor" (IV.229.8). And he was right in his assertion, prompted by Hamlet's question to Polonius, "My lord, you play'd once i' the university, you say?", that "the common players were likewise occasionally admitted to perform there," quoting from a "passage in vice chancellor Hatcher's letter to Lord Burghley Ch. June 21, 1580," a work he probably had consulted because the same quoted passage contains a reference to "the Right Honourable the Lord of Leicester his servants" (X.389.8).

Angelo, in *Measure for Measure,* asks, "having waste ground enough, Shall we desire to raze the sanctuary, / And pitch our evils there?" Reed, as editor, noted "*Evils,* in the present instance, undoubtedly stands for *foricae.* Dr. Farmer assures me he has seen the word *evil* used in this sense by our ancient writers; and it appears from *Harrington's Metamorphosis of Ajax,* &c. that privies were originally so ill-contrived, even in royal palaces, as to deserve the title of *evils* or nuisances" (II.55.6). *OED* gives "Meaning uncertain" for the obsolete use of "evil," adding "(some Commentators explain it as 'a jakes, privy'; there seems to be no ground for this exc. in the two passages themselves, where 'hovel' would suit equally well. But identity with prec. seems quite possible)." The two passages are the one from *Measure for Measure* and one from *Henry VIII,* "Let 'em look thy glory not in mischief / Nor build their evils on the graves of great men." The desecration of former holy places, especially by the drop-

150 Further Notes on Shakespeare

pings of animals, is not uncommon in literature, hence Farmer, first to interpret "evils" in the sense that he did, may indeed have encountered the word in that context among "our ancient writers."[12]

Farmer had a keen eye for puns. He was the first to note the pun on the Clown's response to the thief Abhorson, who was destined to hang, "for your kindness, I owe you a good turn," explaining it as "a turn of the ladder. He quibbles on the phrase acording to its common acceptation" (II.121.1). King Claudius chides Hamlet: "How is it that the clouds still hang on you?" to which Hamlet replies, "Not so, my lord, I am too much i' the sun." Samuel Johnson had invoked the proverb "Out of heaven's blessing into the warm sun," but Farmer was the first to "question whether a quibble between *sun* and *son* be not here intended" (X.276.3).[13] He was able, incidentally, to corroborate and add parallels to Johnson's statement that to turn one's girdle was proverbial, quoting examples from "Winwood's Memorials, fol. ed. 1725. vol. 1 p. 453" and "Cowley *On the Government of Oliver Cromwell*" (II.373.4). He was first to note that Costard's reference to "a northern man" meant "*Vir Borealis,* a clown. See Glossary to Urry's Chaucer" (II.536.2). While Farmer is given credit for the last two notes in the New Variorum edition, he is also properly taken to task for attributing certain verses to John Florio that were not his (4).

Other notes on which Farmer was first, or provided an apt parallel, or explicated a difficult locus in the 1785 *Shakespeare* are not wanting. Petruchio tells Katherine that "Women are made to bear, and so are you," to which she replies "No such jade, sir, as you, if me you mean." Farmer, knowing that "jade" was usually a feminine word, tentatively proposed "jack," but added, "However, there is authority for *jade* in a male sense. So, in *Soliman and Perseda, Picton* says of *Basilico,* 'He just like a *knight?* He'll *just* like a *jade*'" (III.470.7). OED quotes another passage in *The Taming of the Shrew* in exemplification of "jade" as "Rarely applied to a man," usually in the sense of a "contemptuous name for a horse." Farmer saw, what others had not seen, that "captious" in "this captious and intenible sieve" in Helen's speech in *All's Well that Ends Well,* was "a contraction of "capacious" (IV.38.8), an observation that has also found favor with modern editors. The first Witch says, "But in a sieve I'll thither sail," and the editor of the New Variorum *Macbeth* gives Steevens credit for an incident told in *News from Scotland,* evidently ignoring the fact that Steevens gives Farmer as the discoverer of the scarce pamphlet *News from Scotland* (IV.468.4). Farmer is again robbed of his due, for the New Variorum editor gives Halliwell (1865) credit for a note on Macbeth's "Tomorrow, and to morrow, and to morrow" (333) that was originally made by Farmer. "This repetition," writes Steevens, "as

Further Notes on Shakespeare

Dr. Farmer observed to me, occurs in *Barclay's Ship of Fooles,* 1570: '*Cras, cras, cras,* to-morrow we shall amende' " (IV.633.3).

Farmer observed to Steevens that Falstaff's reference to his "vocation" was "undoubtedly a sneer on Aegremont Ratcliffe's *Politique Discourses,* 1578. From the beginning to the end of this work, the word *vocation* occurs in almost every paragraph" (V.287.7). The Emmanuel College library has Gabriel Harvey's copy of this work, with Farmer's marginal note to that effect. Thomas Nashe's *Christ's Tears over Jerusalem* (1593) is usually quoted as a source for Falstaff's "vocation," and while it is closer in phrasing to the entire line, there appears to be but the one use of the word. Shakespeare would, however, probably know Nashe's work rather than Ratcliffe's. Samuel Johnson correctly noted that "*Shot* is used for *Shooter,* one who is to fight by shooting" in *2 Henry IV* (V.564.7), and Farmer was ready with the apposite quotation from "the *Exercise of Armes for Calivres, Muskettes, and Pykes,* 1619," with which "instance" he "furnished" Steevens. It was Farmer who first called attention to Richard Knolles's *General History of the Turks* in explanation of the newly crowned Henry the Fifth's assurances to his brothers, "This is the English, not the Turkish court; / Not Amarath an Amurath succeeds, / But Harry, Harry," (V.621.3), having first pointed it out in Malone's *Second Supplement* (1782).[14] Finally, when Richard, Duke of Gloucester, decrees the death of Hastings, Farmer notes, "For this circumstance see *Holinshed, Hall,* and *The Mirror of [sic] Magistrates*" (VII.90.8), a remark that is ignored in the *Richard III* New Variorum, but one that underlines the popularity of the circumstance.

One attempt at emendation must not go unremarked. Corporal Nym, in *Henry V,* is asked if he and Pistol were still friends. He replies, in part, "when time shall serve, there shall be smiles" which last word caused Warburton to suspect a marginal stage direction. Steevens had his own explanation of "smiles" as part of the text, but added "Dr. Farmer, however, with great probability would read—*smites,* i.e. *blows,* a word used in the midland counties" (VI.37.2). In 1803 Reed, commenting on Cleopatra's impassioned response to Antony's "Cold-hearted toward me," which reads in part, "The next Caesarian smite!" wrote "The folio has *smile.* This literal error will serve to corroborate Dr. Farmer's conjecture in *King Henry V*" (XVII.196.2). OED gives "Smite. A stroke or heavy blow with a weapon, the hand, etc., or the sound made by this. Now chiefly *rhet.*" with examples into the nineteenth century. While Farmer's emendation has not been accepted by modern editors, the note in which it occurs deserves to be remembered.

By 1790, the year of publication of Malone's *Shakespeare,* Farmer

152 Further Notes on Shakespeare

and Malone were on intimate terms, if the record of the number of times they entertained one another at dinner or were both guests at the home of mutual friends and acquaintances can be so construed. Reed notes in his diary the times at which he dined with one or both men, so that one has only a fragmentary record of their association. The meetings occur in the years 1782–90, thereafter Reed's entries become less full, especially after 1792. In 1791 and 1792 Farmer and Malone were in London; each met with Reed, but they did not coincide in his company. In 1787, and in the only such visit mentioned in Reed's diary, Malone was in Cambridge from September 30 to at least October 13, during which period he and Reed and Steevens spent much of their time with Farmer. Malone arrived before dinner on Saturday, the 29th of September, accompanied by the portrait painter Ozias Humphry. They were shown about the College and the University on Sunday and breakfasted with Steevens, Reed, and Farmer on Monday, after which they walked to Jesus College, the Castle, and St. John's College, at which last place they saw "the Pictures in the Lodge." Tuesday night they dined at "Mr. Dawses's, Peterhouse"; Humphry left on Wednesday, and what Malone did that day is unrecorded. He breakfasted with Reed and Farmer on Thursday and went with them to "the Publick Library"; on Friday he spent some time in Trinity College Library. He was on his own on Saturday, but on Sunday, after dining in Hall, he and Reed and several others went to King's College Chapel, he and Reed then going to the Drum for tea. On Monday they visited the Public Library; Tuesday: on his own; Wednesday: to Landbeach with Reed and Farmer and dined with Mr. Masters; Thursday: to the Printing Office with Reed and Farmer after breakfast; Friday: the Anatomy Schools; and Saturday departed for London with Reed. It was thus that one entertained one's friends in Cambridge in 1787. One result of Malone's Cambridge visit is revealed by part of Reed's entry in his *Diary* for 2 October 1788, for there he wrote that after breakfast he "went and sat with the Master [Farmer], who was sitting for his picture for Mr. Malone" (162). The picture was reproduced in 1790 in Malone's *Shakespeare*.

Evidently there could not have been a great exchange of ideas in Cambridge about Malone's forthcoming edition, for there are only four additions by Farmer. The Clown's use of the noun "tod" in the fourth act of *The Winter's Tale* prompted Malone to a long note, during which he wrote, "Dr. Farmer however observes to me, that to *tod,* is used as a verb by dealers in wool: Thus they say 'Twenty sheep ought to *tod*' etc." (IV.194.5). In 1785 Steevens wrote, of the Host's use of "mock-water" in *The Merry Wives of Windsor,* that "Dr. Farmer proposes to read *muck-water,* i.e. the drain of a dunghill." In

Further Notes on Shakespeare 153

1790 Malone writes, "Dr. Farmer, however, observes to me, that *Muck*-water may be the true reading, that term being used in some counties; signifying the oozing of a muck or dung-hill" (I.ii.244.5). Malone chose to print his note with Farmer's slightly expanded observation rather than Steevens's. When Pistol, in *Henry V*, misunderstands the French soldier he has captured and cries out indignantly, "Brass, cur!," Farmer, who had written a note on this in his *Essay* in 1767, offered an additional bit of information to Malone, for the latter writes that Farmer had observed to him a similar pronunciation of French in a play by Davenant (V.564.6). Farmer's fourth addition appears in the appendix in volume ten. Richard II calls John of Gaunt, among other things, a "lean-witted fool," and Farmer invoked Psalm 106 in parallel, "and sent *leanness* withal into their *soul*" (620). These additions are considerably outweighed by the omission of twenty notes first printed in the 1785 edition. Of these twenty, however, twelve were emendations which Malone evidently could not accept; one was a resurrection of a Quarto reading.

Fifteen months after the publication of Malone's *Shakespeare*, Joseph Ritson's vitriolic *Cursory Criticisms on the Edition of Shakespeare Published by Edmond Malone* (1792) appeared. Malone immediately replied with *A Letter to the Rev. Richard Farmer, D.D. Relative to the Edition of Shakespeare, published in 1790, And Some Late Criticisms on that Work*. Malone's *Letter* begins "Though you have long left the *primrose path* of poetry and criticism, for more grave and important studies, you will, I am confident, very cheerfully spend an hour with me in traversing the old Shakspearian field, where we have so often expatiated on the ever-fruitful subject of our great dramatick poet and his Commentators." On the second page Malone writes that he was "highly gratified by your warm, and I fear too partial, approbation of my labours," and farther on he manages to insert a highly laudatory reference to Farmer's *Essay* (7). Malone's reasons for addressing his *Letter* to Farmer were at least two. He wanted, as did Pope when he addressed his *Epistle* to Dr. Arbuthnot, to have a man of recognized impartiality as recipient of his answer to Ritson's attack. He also wanted the recipient of his answer to be a man of acknowledged standing in the field of Shakespearian scholarship. In the Rev. Dr. Richard Farmer he found both.

In 1793, only three years after Malone's *Shakespeare*, Steevens had his day, for in that year he published his own edition of Shakespeare. One aspect of Farmer's participation in the edition is immediately noted, for in the Advertisement one learns that "the play of *Pericles* has been added to this collection, by the advice of Dr. Farmer" (vii). It will be recalled that Farmer contributed a number of notes on *Pericles*

154   Further Notes on Shakespeare

to Malone's *Supplement* in 1780. Another way in which Farmer helped Steevens is suggested by a letter of Joseph Ritson to Steevens of 2 August 1792, the year date being conjectural but having to be before 1793. Ritson, whose part in the edition is extensive, wrote, "J. Ritson presents his compliments to mr. Steevens & sends him the two university books which he will have the goodness to deliver to dr. Farmer," evidence that Farmer was helping with the loan of books from Cambridge, where Steevens visited him in 1790 and 1792.[15] Steevens, who himself wrote the Advertisement for his edition, paid Farmer the highest possible compliment when, writing of the enormous difficulties of a definitive edition of Shakespeare, he stated that "Could a perfect and decisive edition of the following scenes [i.e., the plays] be produced, it were to be expected only (though we fear in vain) from the hand of Dr. Farmer, whose more serious avocations forbid him to undertake what every reader would delight to possess" (xi). He further wrote, in a discussion of possible omissions in Shakespeare's text, "So far from understanding the power of an ellipsis, we may venture to affirm that the very name of this figure in rhetorick never reached the ears of our ancient editors. Having on this subject the support of Dr. Farmer's acknowledged judgment and experience, we shall not shrink from controversy with those who maintain a different opinion" (xvi). Steevens, like Malone before him, knew that invoking Farmer's name lent greater weight to his own views, and he returned again in some of his notes to the authority lent by Farmer's agreement with him.

That Farmer was concerned with more than just the commentary on Shakespeare's plays is evident from a footnote on the date of Shakespeare's death as recorded in the reprinted Stratford Register that makes up part of the prolegomena in the first volume of the 1793 edition. Farmer remarks, wryly, "No one hath protracted the life of *Shakespeare* beyond 1616, except Mr. Hume; who is pleased to add a year to it, contrary to all manner of evidence" (79). In 1754, in his *History of Great Britain,* Hume had given 1617 as the year of Shakespeare's death; he later corrected the error. In the early essay, "Directions for the Study of English History," eventually printed in the *European Magazine* for June 1791, Farmer wrote, "Hume is certainly an admirable writer; his style bold, and his reflections shrewd and uncommon; but his religious and political notions have too often warped his judgment" (416). Proof that Farmer and Steevens had had a number of conversations or exchanged letters about the 1793 edition exists in thirty-one notes, only two of which are signed by Farmer (III.26.9 and 306.8). The rest are signed by Steevens, who relays Farmer's opinions. In one note Steevens quotes a manuscript "Penes Dr. Farmer" (XIV.347.3); in another, on *Hamlet,* the penulti-

Further Notes on Shakespeare

mate play in the edition, further suggesting the closeness of the association, he writes that "Dr. Farmer, however, has just favoured me with a quotation from Nicholas Breton's *Toyes of an idle Head*, 1577, which at once explains the word *wheel* in the sense for which I have contended" (XV.273.3). This last note is particularly interesting in that Steevens had glossed the word and had quoted a parallel from memory from a book the title or date of which he could not recollect. Unfortunately, the word "wele" in the quotation from Breton, cannot be construed to mean the refrain or burthen of a song, a suggestion made by Benjamin Heath in his *Revisal of Shakespeare's Text* (1765).

Farmer's most valuable contributions to the commentary reside in his notes on *Romeo and Juliet*. Steevens had had access to one of Farmer's manuscripts for a note on the play; Farmer provided him with information for three more notes, all of which are included in the New Variorum edition. Lady Capulet is praising the County Paris to Juliet and uses an extended book image "This precious book of love, this unbound lover, / To beautify him, only lacks a cover: / The fish lives in the sea," and Steevens wrote, of the last half-line quoted, "i.e. is not yet caught. Fish-skin covers to books anciently were not uncommon. Such is Dr. Farmer's explanation of this passage; and it may receive some support from what AEnobarbus says in *Antony and Cleopatra*: 'The tears *live in an onion*, that should water this sorrow" (XIV.360.6). This is the only note on the line in the New Variorum (51). On Friar Lawrence's first appearance he says he "must up-fill this osier cage of ours / With baleful weeds and precious-juiced flowers," and Farmer emerges as a critic of literature, not simply as a scholar. Steevens writes, "Shakespeare, on his introduction of Friar Lawrence, has very artificially [i.e., artfully] prepared us for the part he is afterwards to sustain. Having thus early discovered him to be a chemist, we are not surprised when we find him furnishing the draught which produces the catastrophe of the piece. I owe this remark to Dr. Farmer" (XIV. 413.8). The New Variorum editor (110) omits the last sentence, and Farmer is again robbed of his due. In a verbal passage at arms with Romeo the Nurse says "Ah, mocker! that's the dog's name. R is for the dog. No; I know it begins with some other letter," with "dog" as Tyrwhitt's emendation for a blank in the text, an emendation that Steevens adopted, but then added "though Dr. Farmer has since recommended another which would seem equally to deserve attention. He would either omit *name* or insert *letter*. The dog's letter, as the same gentleman observes, is pleasantly exemplified in *Barclay's Ship of Fools*, 1578:

> This man malicious which troubled is with wrath,
> Not els soundeth but the hoorse letter R.

156 Further Notes on Shakespeare

> Though all be well, yet he none aunswere hath
> Save the *dogges letter* glowming with nar, nar"
>
> (XIV.435.5).

The New Variorum editor shortens Steevens's note but quotes the four lines with credit to Farmer (140).

One speech of Ariel's in *The Tempest* ends "Yea, his dread trident shake," and Prospero's answer completes the line, "My brave spirit." The new Variorum editor notes that "To read this line metrically FARMER would make a dyssyllable of 'shake' " (53), which does less than justice to Farmer's explanation: "Lest the metre should appear defective, it is necessary to apprize the reader, that in Warwickshire and other midland counties, *shake* is still pronounced by the common people as if it were written—*shaake,* a dyssyllable" (III.26.9). Another note demonstrates Farmer's knowledge of country matters. Mrs. Page asks, "Do not these fair yokes [horns] / Become the forest better than the town?" and the editor of the New Arden *Merry Wives of Windsor* remarks that Falstaff's horns were so called "because they resemble the oxen's yoke in shape" (143). Farmer observed to Steevens that "the extremities of *yokes* for cattle, as still used in several counties of England, bend upwards, and rising very high, in shape resemble *horns*" (III.493.3). Farmer's note has pride of place in explication of Jacques's "What, for a counter, would I do, but good?" Farmer observed to Steevens "that about the time this play was written, the French *counters* (i.e. pieces of false money used as a means of reckoning) were brought into use in England. They are again mentioned in *Troilus and Cressida:* '——will you with *counters* sum / The past proportion of his infinite?' " (VI.61.3).

Antonio, in *The Winter's Tale,* says he would "land-damn" the villain who spread the false rumors. Commentary on this line occupies two full pages in the New Variorum edition (84–86), the editor concluding, "we can all grasp the meaning of the last half of 'Land-dam,' and I would add, that to understand half of Shakespeare's meaning in a difficult passage is something to be not a little proud of." Farmer's proposal is conveyed, as usual, in a note by Steevens: "After all these aukward struggles to obtain a meaning, we might, I think, not unsafely, read—'I'd *laudanum* him,'—i.e. poison him with *laudanum*. The word is much more ancient than the time of Shakespeare. I owe this remark to Dr. Farmer" (VII.56.4). This is Farmer at his worst, and the New Variorum editor makes the most of it: "It is hard to believe that the 'Puck of Commentators' [Steevens] did not take a malicious pleasure in thus recording the solemn nonsense of his learned friend. Although he adopted the emendation, he knew

well enough that it would not be associated with his name" (85).
OED gives 1602–3 as the earliest use of the word. Did Farmer know
whereof he spoke?

Not everybody thought highly of Farmer's endeavors, as witness
Thomas James Mathias in *Pursuits of Literature: A Satirical Poem in
Four Dialogues.*[16] Farmer, usually linked with Steevens, is satirized
for his notes to Shakespeare in the 1793 edition. One example will
suffice. Dr. Samuel Parr, himself an Emmanuel man, had written that
"*Malone, Reed, Farmer,* and *Tyrwhitt,* have come forward as the
GUIDES OF THE PUBLIC TASTE." Mathias seized on this and
wrote that "when the title of *Guides of the Public Taste* is given to
Malone, Reed, Farmer, and *Tyrwhitt,* who are note-makers alone by
profession, I find myself constrained to look into my English Dictionary for the meaning of the words *guide* and *taste.*"[17] But Mathias,
satirizing Farmer as a note-taker, had good words for him in a
footnote to still another swipe at him: "I lament that Dr. Farmer never
published his intended HISTORY OF LEICESTER. I lament it, but
do not reprobate the Doctor, as he behaved in a gentlemanly manner
when he declined prosecuting that work, which is a real loss to the
antiquary and lover of topography" (47n.). Mathias, at one time a
Fellow of Trinity College, Cambridge, would, of course, have known
Farmer. His *Pursuits of Literature* was almost universally criticized,
De Quincy noting that it was "marred by much license of tongue,
much mean and impotent spite, and a systematic pedantry without
parallel in literature."[18]

Farmer's involvement in the edition is further attested by Steevens's
acknowledgment of some areas of fundamental agreement that Steevens felt lent considerable authority to certain of his editorial principles. Thus, of a proposed omission in a line in *Macbeth,* Steevens
wrote,

> I am aware, that for this, and similar rejections, I shall be censured by
> those who are disinclined to venture out of the track of the old stage-
> waggon, though it may occasionally conduct them into a slough. . . . For
> my own sake, however, let me add, that throughout the present tragedy no
> such liberties have been exercised, without the previous approbation of
> Dr. Farmer, who fully concurs with me in supposing the irregularities of
> Shakespeare's text to be oftener occasioned by interpolations, than by
> omissions. (VII.496.7)

He returned to this consideration in a note on *Richard II,* taking
exception to Malone's statement that "it is always safer to add [to
Shakespeare's text] than to omit" by remarking that "in Dr. Farmer's

judgement as well as my own, the irregularities of our author's measure are too frequently occasioned by gross and manifest interpolations" (VIII.298.3). The whole vexed matter of the comparative authority of the first and second Folios was one upon which Steevens and Malone wasted much ink. At one juncture, in a note on *Measure for Measure,* Malone had noted that "The alterations made in that copy do not deserve the smallest credit. There are undoubted proofs that they were merely arbitrary; and in general they are also extremely injudicious," to which Steevens added, "I am of a different opinion, in which I am joined by Dr. Farmer, and consequently prefer the reading of the second folio to my own attempt at emendation" (IV.278.6). Steevens, to go on to another matter, felt that "*The Tempest* was evidently one of the last works of Shakspeare; and it is therefore natural to suppose the metre of it must have been exact and regular. Dr. Farmer concurs with me in this supposition" (III.113.7). Steevens justifies one of his emendations by writing that it "has met with the approbation of Dr. Farmer, or it would not have appeared in the text" (VII.501.6) and another by stating that "Dr. Farmer joins with me in suspecting this passage to be corrupt, and is satisfied with the emendation I have proposed" (XI.588.3). He had thrown the gauntlet down when, retorting to John Monck Mason's objection to one of his emendations, he wrote,

> Being nevertheless aware that Mr. M. Mason's gallant effort to produce an easy sense, will provoke the slight objections and petty cavils of such as restrain themselves within the bounds of timid conjecture, it is necessary I should subjoin, that this present emendation was not inserted in our text on merely my own judgement, but with the deliberate approbation of Dr. Farmer.—Having now prepared for controversy—*signa canant!* (VIII. 357.3)

From the first to last, from the seven suggestions on *The Tempest* to the one on *Othello,* from the advice to include *Pericles* to the footnote on the reprinted Stratford Register, and from the approabation of and the concurrence in Steevens's emendations and editorial principles, Farmer's presence in the 1793 *Shakespeare* made itself strongly felt.

Farmer died on 8 September 1797; Steevens survived him for less than three years, dying on 22 January 1800.[19] They had evidently continued to discuss Shakespeare and to look forward to a revision of the 1793 edition until Farmer died. When Steevens died, he left his own copy of the 1793 edition, with his revisions, to Reed, whose advertisement to the revised 1793 edition, published in 1803, explains that the 1803 edition "contains the last improvements and corrections of Mr. Steevens, by whom it was prepared for the press"

Further Notes on Shakespeare

and that it is "faithfully printed from the copy given by Mr. Steevens to the proprietors of the preceding edition, in his life-time; with such additions as, it is presumed, he would have received [i.e., accepted], had he lived to determine on them himself." Reed apologizes for not accepting the assistance of various gentlemen, as he was "fearful of loading the page." There are, however, a number of new notes, other than those by Steevens himself and by Malone. Among these are twenty-four suggested to Steevens by Farmer or taken from Farmer's papers. Only five are signed Farmer. Evidently Steevens was given or had access to Farmer's "Shakespeare memoranda," for he so refers to them in the prolegomenous matter and in two notes on *Hamlet* (XVIII.200.3 and 372.4) and two on *All's Well that Ends Well* (VIII.86.5 and 293.3). In a footnote to Malone's "Historical Account of the English Stage," Steevens wrote,

> Among the *memoranda* of my lamented friend, Dr. Farmer, was found what he styles "Index to the Registry of the University of *Cambridge* [loose papers]." From this I have made the following extract of theatrical occurrences in our University:
> 6.104. Complaint of a riot at the plays at Trinity, 1610.
> 9.78. Dominus *Pepper* at certain interludes, with his habit, &c. 1600.
> 11.110. Decree against Plays and Games upon Gogmagog Hills, 1574.
> 13.12 Windows broke during the comedy at *Kings,* 1595.
> 13.51. Letter recommending the Queen of *Bohemia's* players, 1629.
> 13.117. Players at Chesterton, 1590. (III.39.7)

This is another indication of Farmer's close interest in the history of the acted drama. In a preliminary note on *Titus Andronicus,* Steevens quotes some rough notes on the authorship of that play "from a loose scrap of paper, in the handwriting of Dr. Farmer":

> *Kyd*—probably original author of *Andronicus, Locrine,* and play in *Hamlet.*—Marloe, of H. 6.
> Ben Jonson, *Barthol. Fair*—ranks together *Hieronymo* and *Andronicus,* [time and stile]—first exposed him to the criticks—shelter'd afterwards under another's name.
> *Sporting* Kyd [perhaps wrote comedy] and Marloe's mighty line—*Jonson.* [might assist Lily,] Perhaps Shakespeare's additions *outshone.*
> Tamburlaine mention'd with praise by *Heywood,* as Marloe's might be different from the bombast one—and that written by Kyd. (XXI.[6])

The remaining notes are on seventeen plays, with the largest number (four) devoted to *1 Henry IV,* possible further evidence of Farmer's preference for that play and its fat knight. Perhaps the most delightful

160   Further Notes on Shakespeare

note is that in which Farmer has his say on Edward Capell who "thought that *Edward III* was Shakespeare's because *nobody* could write so, and *Titus Andronicus* because *every body* could! Well fare his heart, for he is a jewel of a reasoner!" (XXI.139*.). There is one more glancing swipe at Capell, who had noted of Hamlet's "Marry, this is miching mallecho; it means mischief," that the Poisoner in the dumb show was compared "to the character called Iniquity, in the ancient moralities." Farmer, whose own conjecture on this passage I reserve for later discussion, remarked "If, as Capell declares (I know not on what authority) *Malicho* to be the *Vice* of the Spanish Moralities, he should at least be distinguished by a capital" (XVIII.200.3).

Farmer's twenty-four notes in the 1803 *Shakespeare* may be considered a minor blaze of glory, as virtually all of these are of some value. They are, of course, evidence of his continuing interest in the annotation of Shakespeare's plays and of his diffidence about claiming credit for his observations. He, with others but to a much lesser extreme, was given to the sin of emendation; eight of the new notes in 1803 are such conjectures.[20] He invoked a Quarto reading, "sieve" for "fame" in Troilus's "nor the remainder viands / We do not throw in unrespective fame/Because we now are full." He noted that "in several counties of England, the baskets used for carrying out dirt, &c. are called *sieves*" (XV.304.1.). There is no such definition in the *OED*, the nearest being "a kind of basket used chiefly for market use," with one example being Steevens's note to that effect to which Farmer had added his comment. One of Farmer's notes has been egregiously ignored by one editor of the New Variorum editions. Falstaff says "Now shall we know if Gadshill have set a watch," but Malone and Steevens and Farmer all preferred the Quarto's "match" for "watch." Malone quoted *Bartholomew Fair,* and Steevens wrote, "As no *watch* is afterwards set, I suppose *match* to be the true reading. So, as Dr. Farmer observed, in *Ratsey's* (Gamaliel) *Ghost,* b.1. 4to (no date) about 1605: 'I have, says he, been many times beholding to Tapsters and Chamberlaines for directions and *setting of matches*' " (XI.204.1). The editor of the New Variorum *1 Henry IV* lists the same quotation from *Ratsey's Ghost* from "Collier (ed. 1842)"! Farmer's note was half a century earlier.

One of Farmer's memoranda has been quoted (p. 159); I give the others in order of appearance. Touchstone says to Corin in *As You Like It,* "God made incision in thee! thou art raw," and the New Variorum offers no parallels, although one early critic calls it ("to make incision") a "common proverbial saying" and a nineteenth-century editor says it "evidently had a well-known colloquial significance" (141).[21] Steevens learned from Farmer's memorandum that in

Further Notes on Shakespeare
161

"*The Times Whistle, or a new Daunce of Seven Satires:* MS. about the end of Queen Eliz. by R. E. Gent. now at Canterbury: The Prologue ends—

> Be stout my heart, my hand be firm and steady;
> Strike, and strike home,—the vain worldes vaine is ready:
> Let ulcer'd & goutie humors quake,
> Whilst with my pen I doe *incision make.*"
>
> (VIII.86.5).

This is precisely the kind of note that should be in a variorum edition, particularly since no other parallel has been adduced. And Steevens learned that "*The Life and Death of St. George,* a ballad, begins as follows:

> Of Hector's deeds did Homer sing,
> And of the sack of stately Troy:
> What grief fair Helen did them bring
> Which was Sir Paris' only joy"
>
> (VIII.239.3),

in parallel to the Clown's song in *All's Well That Ends Well,*

> Was this fair face the cause, quoth she,
> Why the Grecians sacked Troy?
> Fond done, done fond,
> Was this king Priam's joy.

Again, this should have a place in a variorum edition.

The next one of Farmer's memoranda invoked by Steevens does neither much credit, that is, Farmer for noting it and Steevens for resurrecting it. Hamlet's "miching mallecho" elicited this from Farmer: "At the beginning of *Grim the Collier of Croydon,* the ghost of *Malbecco* is introduced as a prolocutor." Steevens added, "Query, therefore, if the obscure words already quoted, were not originally:—— 'This is *mimicking Malbecco';* a private gloss by some friend on the margin of the MS. Hamlet, and thence ignorantly received into the text of Shakspeare" (XVIII.200.3). Here Steevens has done his friend a disservice. In the last of the memoranda (XVIII.372.4) Farmer quotes *Ratsey's Ghost* again in exemplification of the qualifications of the player who, in the dueling scene in *Hamlet,* is described as "fat and scant of breath." Farmer's quotation from this work underlines the importance of the role.

Ratsey's Ghost served Farmer well, for two more of his notes were

162 Further Notes on Shakespeare

from that work, one already quoted above (p. 160). The third comes at the juncture in *1 Henry IV* where Falstaff lists various circumlocutions for "thieves," one of them being "minions of the moon." Steevens's note reads, almost formulaically, "Thus, as Dr. Farmer observes, Gamaliel Ratsey and his company 'became servants to the *moone,* for the sunne was too hot for them' " (XI.192.8). The note is quoted in the New Variorum edition (29). *Ratsey's Ghost, Time's Whistle,* the ballad *Life and Death of St. George*—all obscure corners of Farmer's reading. And there were others. Ariel sings, and his song ends, "Hark! now I hear them—ding-dong, bell.

[Burden, ding-dong."

Farmer's brief, signed note, reads "It should be—Ding-dong, *ding-dong, ding-dong* bell" (IV.46.4), albeit based on the transposition of lines which put the Burden below the quoted line rather than above, where it should be. The point, however, is that Farmer knew but did not name the source for his suggestion. The editor of the New Variorum *Tempest* notes, however, that in a collection of songs and ballads of 1660 the Burden line was omitted and Farmer's suggestion was there exemplified (82). In a note on the crux "cry hem" in *Much Ado About Nothing,* Farmer suggested an emendation that should be forgotten, but which is quoted from George Withers's *Philarete* (VI.143.1).

   Other notes must be considered. A rather startling omission in the New Variorum *Macbeth* is Farmer's note on Macbeth's "The very stones prate of my whereabout," which Malone had paralleled with a very apposite passage from "*A Warning for faire Women,* 1599" and to which Farmer added a line from "Churchyard's *Choise:* 'The stepps I tread, *shall tell me my offence*' " (X.105.3). Both notes should have found a place in the New Variorum edition and so, too, with the notes of both men on the description of the ghost of Hamlet's father with "his beaver up." Malone explained that though "beaver" was the part of the helmet which was let down to allow the wearer to drink, Shakespeare always used it as the part that raised up exposing the face. "In Bullokar's *English Expositor,* 8vo. 1616, *beaver* is defined thus:—'In Armour it signifies that part of the helmet which may be *lifted up,* to take breath more freely.' " Farmer added, "So, in Laud's *Diary:* 'The Lord Broke shot in the left eye, and killed in the place at Lichfield—his *bever up,* and armed to the knee, so that a musket at that distance could have done him little harm'" (XVIII.49.8). The editor of the New Variorum *Hamlet* quotes Bullokar exactly as did Malone, without giving him credit, and ignores Farmer.

Further Notes on Shakespeare

This "pitch, as ancient writers do report, doth defile," pontificates Falstaff. Steevens quoted an ancient ballad; Thomas Holt White added a quotation from Lyly's *Euphues;* and Steevens, in another note, wrote that "Dr. Farmer has pointed out another passage exhibiting the same observation, but omitted to specify the work to which it belongs: 'It is harde for a man to *touch pitch,* and not to be *defiled* with it.'" It remained for William Harris, co-editor of the 1803 *Shakespeare,* to identify the source in "the apocryphal Book of *Ecclesiasticus,* xiii. 1: 'He that toucheth *pitch* shall be *defiled* therewith'" (XI.305.4). Farmer had a source, albeit he had forgotten it.

Three notes remain to be considered. Johnson explained the "garters of an indifferent knit" in *The Taming of the Shrew* as "*indifferent, or not different,* one from the other," and Steevens gave two examples of the same usage in Shakespeare's plays. And, he added, "In Donne's *Parodoxes,* p. 56, Dr. Farmer observes, that we find 'one *indifferent* shoe;' meaning, I suppose, a shoe that would fit either the right or left foot" (IX.127.9). Farmer was able to corroborate another of Johnson's glosses. Othello apostrophizes Desdemona as "Excellent wretch!" and Johnson explained that it was "now, in some parts of England, a term of the softest and fondest tenderness," to which Steevens, after adding a parallel, wrote, "I am assured by Dr. Farmer, that *wretch* is provincial in Staffordshire for *a young woman*" (XIX.366.1). Pistol asks King Henry V, "Trailest thou the puissant pike?" and Farmer's is the only note on this in the 1803 *Shakespeare:* "So, at the beginning of Chapman's *Revenge for Honour:*——a wife / Fit for *the traylor of the puissant pike,*" as apt a parallel as one could wish for and precisely the sort of note Farmer was able to provide time after time (XII.425.7).

Farmer had concluded his 1773 *Letter* to Steevens in characteristically modest fashion. "I have no value for any of the corrections that I have attempted," he wrote, "but I flatter myself, that I have sometimes irrefragably supported the old text against the attacks of former commentators." Adopting the stance of most eighteenth-century editors of Shakespeare, he deprecated his attempts at emendation and was orthodoxically in line with others in their statements of belief in the sanctity of "the old text." Despite his and similar statements by others, the temptation to emend was great, and he, like others, often succumbed. His contribution to the study of Shakespeare's text consists primarily of the wealth of parallel passages from works of all description, from the earliest printed books to last month's periodical—as witness his use of the report of a murder trial in the 1770 *London Magazine* in illustration of the word "lethal." It is not surprising that Farmer, an enthusiastic playgoer, both in London and at

164 Further Notes on Shakespeare

Stourbidge Fair in Cambridge, should so very often quote or cite plays of the sixteenth, seventeenth, and eighteenth centuries. He knew and quoted plays by Ben Jonson, Lyly, Beaumont and Fletcher, Davenant, John Heywood, Massinger, Middleton, Marston, Dekker, Webster, Kyd, Dryden, Shirley, Brome, Machin, Rowley, Colman, Field, and various anonymous dramatists. He even remembered a line by the walk-on second watchman in Lyly's *Endymion*.[22] Further, he agreed with and strengthened Steevens's belief in the chief cause for corruption of Shakespeare's text, i.e., interpolations. With Steevens, whose editorial consultant he was, he did not undervalue the readings of the second Folio. And he, like many eighteenth-century editors and commentators, and unlike their modern counterparts, was not averse to calling upon personal observation in the elucidation of this word or that allusion in Shakespeare's plays—as witness various remarks on rural dialects and practices. Perhaps Farmer's greatest contribution to eighteenth-century Shakespearan scholarship is impossible to assess, for it lay in the stimulus he afforded to the great editors of the period, to Steevens and Reed especially, and to Malone to a lesser degree. They visited him in Cambridge and they dined with him in London, and whatever else they discussed, one can be certain that the problems of editing Shakespeare's plays were never distant for long from their minds. Farmer was highly regarded by the great eighteenth-century editors of Shakespeare: Johnson, Steevens, Malone, Reed. Most of those who attacked him—George Colman, Richard Warner, Joseph Ritson—did so rather gently. Indeed, Ritson, on the occasion of a visit to Cambridge, wrote to a friend on 6 August 1781, "I have been lately at Cambridge, where I saw a great many curious books, made a great many important discoveries: and, what is better than all, became intimately acquainted with Dr. Farmer, whom I found a most sensible, benevolent and worthy man" (see p. 39). And when, in May 1783, less than two years after this letter, Ritson published his notorious *Remarks* on the 1778 *Shakespeare* and Malone's *Supplement,* he said that he hoped he would not be thought to speak disrespectfully of Farmer, Steevens, and Tyrwhitt, a hope that was realized only for Farmer and Tyrwhitt. George Tollet disagreed with an emendation Farmer had proposed in *Henry VIII;* he wrote "Dr. Farmer has displayed such eminent knowledge of Shakespeare, that it is with the utmost diffidence I dissent from the alteration which he would establish here" (1793, XI.148.7). Similar expressions of esteem and deference appear in the notes of other commentators.

The story of the Shakespeare forgeries, the work of William Henry Ireland, is a well-known one.[23] One reader of the prospectus for publishing a folio volume of what he termed "Shakespearian novel-

Further Notes on Shakespeare

ties" was induced to write to the March 1795 *GM* protesting some of the terms of the prospectus. K.S., not otherwise identified, wanted especially to know where these treasures had lain concealed for two hundred years. He suggested that the "publick would certainly have been gratified to know, that these extraordinary MSS. had been deemed genuine by Dr. Farmer, Messrs. Steevens and Malone; whose literary characters might have served as letters of credence" (209–10). An anonymous reply to K.S. appeared in the April *GM*, the writer taking exception to K.S.'s question whether the MSS. had been deemed genuine by "Dr. F——, Messrs S. and M." and asking "And are none others to be believed? Is all knowledge of S—— and of old papers stored in the breast of this triumvirate?" (285). K.S.'s rebuttal came in June. He stated, among other things,

> It is asked whether Dr. F. Messrs. S. and M. have *applied* for admission to see the Shakspeare papers? I ask in return, is it be expected any of these gentlemen would risk such an application, after having been given to understand (as I am credibly informed they were) that the company of Shakespeare's editors was not wished.
>
> It is farther asked, "Are none others to be *believed*," beside Dr. F. Messrs. S. and M.? or, as I take the question to imply, are no other persons competent to become umpires on the present occasion. I beg leave to answer, many others may be competent; but I know of none whose opinions, individually taken, would have equal influence with the publick.

He went on to suggest that a committee be formed of "Bishop Percy, Messrs. Porson, Pinkerton, Astle, Ayscough, Gough, Reed, Ritson, Chalmers, and Douce" to decide on the authenticity of the papers (457). Possibly K.S. was deferring to Farmer's ecclesiastical position in naming him before the well-known editors Steevens and Malone; whatever his reason, Farmer, in 1795, almost thirty years after the first edition of his *Essay*, but with a third edition in 1787, was still highly regarded as a Shakespeare scholar.[24] James Boaden linked Farmer's name with those of Dr. Johnson, Tyrwhitt, Malone, and Steevens as leading Shakespeareans in his *Letter to George Steevens, Esq.*, his critical examination of the Shakespeare papers, published in 1796 (10). And it was Malone, in his *Inquiry* (1796) into the authenticity of the papers, who stated that he, and Farmer and Steevens, did not visit Norfolk House lest their visit be construed as acceptance of the genuineness of the papers (22).

When the *GM* printed "the names of those who are said to have expressed their opinions FOR and AGAINST the authenticity of the late Shakespearean discoveries" in April 1796, none of the proposed committee was listed as FOR. Indeed, those against were many more

166 Further Notes on Shakespeare

than those FOR. One division of those AGAINST read Lord Orford, Bishop of Dromore, Rev. Mr. Henley, Rev. Dr. Farmer, Geo Steevens, esq. Edmond Malone, esq. Isaac Reed, esq. Joseph Ritson, esq. Holt White, esq. commentators on Shakspeare" (p. 267). Whatever modern Shakespeareans may think of Farmer's *Essay* and his subsequent notes on various editions, his contemporaries held him in high esteem.

8

Summing Up

Other Writings

Farmer's sole separately printed work is his *Essay* on Shakespeare's learning, although his appendix to the 1773 Johnson–Steevens *Shakespeare* equals it in length and scope. The only other of his fairly extended efforts that saw print is his "Directions for the study of English History" which, while written much earlier, appeared in the *European Magazine* for 1791. There Reed, writing as "C.D." stated that the Directions were "written many years ago to a Friend by a Gentleman of great eminence, yet living, whose name at present cannot be disclosed" (415). Soon after Farmer's death Reed wrote an account of him for William Seward's *Biographiana* (1799) and named him as "the Gentleman of great emminence," explaining that "Dr. Farmer, when a young man, at the request of a friend, wrote the following Directions for studying the English history, which, with his permission, were printed in his lifetime in the European Magazine for June 1791" (583–84). What Reed did not know, and what Nichols did know, was that the "Letter on English History," so titled by the latter in the *GM* in 1818 (ii.291–93), was "From a Distinguished Scholar at Cambridge, *to a Young Nobleman, Written about the Years 1764, 1765*" (my emphasis). The Directions are reprinted in *Biographiana,* pages 584 91, from which I quote some extracts, not to demonstrate young Farmer's extensive knowledge of English historiography, but to isolate some of his opinions. He seems not to have had any great fondness for David Hume as a historian. Writing of the "Monkish" historians, Farmer noted that "Hume often puts their names in his margin; but I fear all he knew of them was through the *media* of other writers. He has some mistakes, which could not have happened had he really consulted the originals" (584). Further on he could admit that "Hume is certainly an admirable writer; his stile bold, and his reflections shrewd and uncommon; but his religious and political notions have too often warped his judgments" (590). As a scholar and critic, Farmer could applaud Hume as a man of letters

168   Summing Up

(bar some errors), but as a churchman and staunch Tory, Farmer could only conclude that Hume's judgment was warped.

When he came to the matter of the original inhabitants of "our island," Farmer remembered a curious corner of his reading, occasioning him to remark, "I may just mention, that some writers would cavil at the word *island* just above, and insist that we were formerly joined to the French continent" (585). "The best authors" for the period before the Conquest, "are Milton and Sir William Temple; the latter more pleasing, but the former more accurate. Milton's prose works are exceedingly stiff and pedantic, and Sir William's as remarkably easy and genteel; but he should have attended more to the *minutiae* of names and dates" (586). At the juncture where he mentioned "Hollinshead or Stowe," he added another personal note, admitting his "love of black letter" (587), and hard upon that admission he professed his admiration for Samuel Daniel: "The most elegant old history we have is that by Samuel Daniel, a poet of no mean rank. Though he wrote more than a half century before Milton, his stile appears much more modern" (58). And, finally,

> The last observation I shall trouble you with is, that sometimes a single pamphlet will give us the better clue of a transaction than a volume in folio. Thus we learn from the Duchess of Marlborough's "Apology," that the peace of Utrecht was made by a quarrel among the women of the bedchamber! Hence Memoirs, Secret Histories, Political Papers, &c. are not to be despised; always allowing sufficiently for the prejudice of the party, and believing them no farther than they are supported by collateral evidence.

S. C. Roberts summarized the pioneering importance of Farmer's little essay in these words: "When it is remembered that, in the eighteenth century, Cambridge scholarship was largely concerned with mathematics, theology and the literature and history of ancient Greece and Rome and that the first professorship of modern history was not founded until 1724, it will be recognized that Farmer's interest in English history and literature was that of a man in advance of his time."[1]

In the text of the "Directions" in the *European Magazine,* the second of Farmer's remarks on David Hume is followed by "[Mrs. Macaulay has just now published against his account of the Stuarts, but I have not yet had an opportunity of reading her book]." The first volume of Catherine Macaulay's *History of England from the Accession of James I to that of the Brunswick Line* was published in 1763, when Farmer was twenty-eight years old, and still a "young man."

Summing Up — 169

That the reference in the "Directions" is to the first volume is borne out by David Hume's letter to Catherine Macaulay, dated 29 March 1764, reprinted in the *European Magazine* in November 1783, with her reply to him (331–32). Hume politely and briefly restates the fundamental differences in their interpretations of events; she, as politely and briefly, agrees upon the fundamental differences that exist between them. Since the second volume of her *History* was not published until 1766, the date of the "Directions" must be 1763.

Reed noted that the "Directions" were printed with Farmer's permission. No permission was needed for Farmer's letter to Reed, 28 January 1794, printed in June of that year in the *European Magazine* (412–13). The letter is about John Dennis, more precisely about the account of him in the revised *Biographia Britannica,* edited by Dr. Andrew Kippis. Kippis, the presumed writer of the account of Dennis, refused to believe the story of Dennis's expulsion from Caius College for attempting to stab a person in the dark. Kippis knew the story from Reed's *Biographia Dramatica,* but Reed had had it from Farmer's *Essay* on Shakespeare's learning. Farmer's letter rehearses a bit of Cambridge University history, for he notes that "it was formerly by no means uncommon for a man, after the severest censures of his own college (were he not actually expelled the *University*), to gain admission into another, from interest or from party, or perhaps sometimes from the little emoluments he brought to his new society. This at length produced a grace in the Senate in 1732, which put an end to this infamous traffick." He quotes the grace, *De migrantibus ab uno collegio in aliud,* and then turns to and quotes the Caius College "Gesta Book": 4 March 1680. "At a meeting of the Master and Fellows, Sir *Dennis* mulcted £3. his scholarship taken away, and he *sent out of College,* for assaulting and wounding Sir *Glenham* with a sword." The moralist condemned "this infamous traffick"; the scholar went to the primary source.

Farmer played a very minor role in the Chatterton affair, brought into it through his friendship with Steevens and his acquaintance with Walpole. Walpole insisted that he had never received the two letters from Chatterton, which it was alleged he had in a history of Bristol where they had been printed. In the April 1792 *GM* a correspondent from Cambridge who signed himself Christ. Seltzer asserted that Walpole never wrote any letter to Chatterton, although "about six weeks ago a letter appeared in the *World* said there to be written by the Hon. Henry [*sic*] Walpole (now Earl of Orford) about the year 1768, to Thomas Chatterton," adding, "Indeed, when such a report was rife a year or two ago in the University of Cambridge, many of the noble Earl's friends, and particularly Dr. Farmer, the present worthy

170   Summing Up

and learned Master of Emanuel College in that University, declared
that they were especially authorized and enjoined by him to contra-
dict the report of his ever having any such correspondence whatever"
(p. 296). Farmer replied in the next month's *GM* and clarified a matter
that should never have been muddied by the pseudonymous Christ.
Seltzer.

> Mr. URBAN, *Emman. Coll. May 25.*
> I SEE in your Magazine of the last month, p. 296, a letter with the
> signature of *Christ. Seltzer;* a gentleman of whose existence I am as
> doubtful, as of that of old *Rowley* himself.
> The subject is, whether Mr. *Walpole,* the present Earl of *Orford,* had
> any correspondence with the unfortunate *Chatterton;* and it is there
> asserted, that Mr. *Walpole* never wrote to him *any Letter whatever:* and
> that I, amongst others, was *authorized and enjoined* by him to contradict
> the report of such correspondence.
> Now is it possible, that Lord *Orford* should deny, or enjoin others to do
> so, what he himself has *publickly* declared to be *true,* and suffered you to
> tell all the world in your Magazine for *May,* 1782?
> The fact is, and all that I know about it—more than two years ago, my
> friend Mr. *Steevens* gave me the following information, which at that time
> I occasionally mentioned in the University:
> "Mr. *Walpole* has authorized his friends to declare, that he never saw
> those Letters from *Chatterton,* which Mr. *Barrett* has printed, till they
> appeared in the new History of *Bristol.* Mr. W. also expresses his ap-
> prehensions, that, after his death, some pretended answers to them will be
> produced."
> Yours, &c. RICHARD FARMER. (398)

Farmer, who knew everybody in Cambridge that might conceivably
write such a letter, inaccurate as it was, was correct in doubting the
existence of a real Christ. Seltzer. In the 1788 edition of Walpole's
Works, Walpole referred to Farmer's letter, writing that "Dr. Farmer
has shown the absurdity of supposing Mr. W should for no possible
reason deny a letter, of which he himself had given the first account by
memory, and is one of the many proofs of his veracity in his relation of
his correspondence with Chatterton" (IV.242).

One of the more memorable visits to Cambridge during Farmer's
years there was that of the celebrated Samuel Johnson. In a letter to
Percy, dated 25 February 1765, six days after Johnson's departure,
Farmer gave his impression of the great man.

> Since I last heard from you, I have had the unexpected pleasure of M[r]
> JOHNSON'S Company at *Cambridge*—a Character the most extraordi-
> nary, that it has ever been my fortune to meet with.—I admire him, and I

Summing Up   171

pity him: You will not ask me a reason for the former—his Compass of [k]nowledge, and his manner of expressing that knowledge are really admirable. but he has *pitiable* infirmities both in body and mind. I can excuse his *Dogmatisms* and *Prejudices;* but he throws about rather too much of what some *Frenchman* calls the *Essence of* BUT: in plain *English,* he seems to have something to *except* in every man's Character. *Hurd* for instance comes off badly, and *Shenstone* still worse: he pitys *You* for your opinion of the latter. indeed what he takes from *you,* he gives to your better half—Mrs Percy's judgment is, he assures me (where there has been an equall opportunity of information) much to be prefer'd to her husband's! He was in good spirits, and seem'd pleased with us: the latter he confirm'd, by promising another visit towards summer. I wish, you may contrive to meet him; but it must be in No term, for his hours are not very Acade[mic] and I have been obliged to work double tides ever since. I had little opportunity to speak to him about *Shakespeare:* he ask'd my assistance, and refused my Subscription. I told him, that my time just now is too much employ'd—but I suspect I shall have enough before his Publication.—I am to thank you for the favourable Opinion, he seems to entertain of me. (*Letters,* II.84–85)

A month later, on March 26, Percy wrote to Farmer and mentioned, "I see Johnson often, who speaks of you respectfully and without a *But*" (*Letters,* II.87). In later letters Percy informed Farmer of Johnson's interest in and attempt to help with the history of Leicester, his great admiration for the *Essay* on Shakespeare's learning, and of his remark that he wished Farmer "would throw together all [his] Knowledge about Shakespeare and old English Writers in general and give us a large Volume."[2]

At least two other accounts of Dr. Johnson's visit exist, other than Boswell's brief mention (*Life,* I.487). Dr. John Sharp, later to be Archdeacon of Northumberland, described the visit twenty years later in the *GM* (1785.i.173); the only reference germane to present purposes is to Johnson's telling Sharp that he would return quickly and that he was promised "an habitation in Emanuel College." He never returned, but on 22 July 1777, twelve years later, he wrote to Farmer asking him if there was anything in Thomas Baker's manuscripts or materials elsewhere in Cambridge of possible use for his projected *Lives* of the poets. Johnson would employ a transcriber, but if "you think my inspection necessary, I will come down, for who that has once experienced the civilities of Cambridge would not snatch the opportunity of another visit?" Three years later he asked Farmer for information about "Ambrose Philips, Broome, and Gray who were all at Cambridge," and two years later, writing to Malone on 27 February 1782, he pleaded illness as the reason he could not meet with him and Dr. Farmer.[3] Boswell reports only the one meeting, that at Cam-

172 Summing Up

bridge, between Johnson and Farmer. In 1818 The Reverend Baptist Noel Turner of Emmanuel wrote an account of the visit that is inaccurate in some details. I quote the pertinent parts from volume six of Nichol's *Illustrations* where Turner's account is reprinted from the *New Monthly Magazine*. Turner had written to the *New Monthly Magazine* (II.525), under the pseudonym of Humfree Tellfair, about "Johnson-Farmer," stating that "Early in 1765 he had the singular happiness of introducing these two literary luminaries to their first personal interview, at Emanuel-college, Cambridge, and of enjoying the intellectual banquets that ensued" (147). He now was ready to give a full narrative of Johnson's visit. He claimed that he was several times the bearer of messages "between Johnson and Farmer" and that it was at his suggestion that Johnson made the visit to Cambridge (149). Turner's account of the visit is long and rambling, and I quote only what is relevant to Farmer and Johnson together. Turner eventually got to his *pièce de résistance:*

> The long-wished-for interview of these unknown friends was uncommonly joyous on both sides. After the salutations, said Johnson, "Mr. Farmer, I understand you have a large collection of very rare and curious books." Farmer. "Why yes, Sir, to be sure I have plenty of all such reading as was never read." Johnson. "Will you favour me with a specimen, Sir?" Farmer, considering for a moment, reached down "Markham's Booke of Armorie," and turning to a particular page, presented it to the Doctor, who, with rolling head, attentively perused it . . . he exclaims, "Now I am shocked, Sir—now I am shocked!" which was only answered by Farmer with his usual ha! ha! ha! for even blasphemy, where it is unintentional, may be so thoroughly ridiculous as merely to excite the laugh of pity! (154)

On a later occasion, where Farmer was present with Johnson, Lort, Turner, and Turner's friend Mr. Leycester, the host of the evening in "Neville's-court, Trinity College," Turner reported,

> In the height of our convivial hilarity, our great man exclaimed: "Come, now, I'll give you a test; now I'll try who is a true antiquary amongst you. Has any one of this company every met with the History of Glorianus and Gloriana?" Farmer, drawing the pipe out of his mouth, followed by a cloud of smoke, instantly said, "I've got the book." "Gi' me your hand, gi'me your hand," said Johnson, "you are the man after my own heart." And the shaking of two such hands, with two such happy faces attached to them, could hardly, I think, be matched in the whole annals of literature! (157)

Dr. Frank H. Stubbings, former librarian of Emmanuel College Li-

Summing Up 173

brary, provides a correction to Turner, pointing out that one of the books in the sale catalog of Farmer's library was "Dedekindi Grobianus et Grobiana *Lug. Bat.* 1642" (Lot 1960).[4]

In Isaac Reed's manuscript "Memoranda taken at Cambridge During my stay in Emanuel College Septr 1782," one memorandum reads, "Dr Johnson was Usher at the School at Market Bosworth. During his residence at Birmingham he wrote Essays in a Newspaper published by Warren." The next memorandum is of greater significance, as it almost surely adds to the accounts of Johnson's visit: "3 Sept. 1782 Dr Farmer told me that Dr Johnson actually was the Translator of Lobo's Voyages. It was printed at Birmingh.^{m} by one *Warren* (I think) a Printer there in whose house Johnson then lived. The inform.^{n} came from a person then a Journeyman who afterwards set up at Leicester. He said also that Dr Johnson wrote the Dedication to Percy's Ballads."[5] The information about the Birmingham stay is corroborated by Boswell, who names Warren's printer as "one Osborn," about whom nothing else is known, but who may be the "Journeyman" in Reed's note. What is of importance is that Johnson probably told Farmer this during his visit, as the two may never have met again. And while it is possible that the "Journeyman" who migrated to Leicester, Farmer's native city, may have told him of the Lobo translation, he could not have known about the Dedication to Percy's *Reliques of Ancient English Poetry*. It was not until 1800 that Percy, in a letter to Robert Anderson, wrote that "the former Dedication [omitted in the fourth edition of the *Reliques*], though not wholly written by him, owed its finest strokes to the superior pen of Dr. Johnson, and I could not any longer allow myself to strut in borrowed feathers." Percy added that he believed that Johnson "never mentioned" this "himself to any one."[6] Boswell knew of Johnson's connection with the Dedication, but cancelled the pertinent page in the *Life,* and so Percy, in 1800, still thought Johnson had not mentioned his part to any one. But Farmer knew it in 1782 and could only have had the information from Johnson himself.[7] The "He" of Reed's memorandum could not have been the journeyman printer, who would have had nothing to do with Percy's *Reliques,* published thirty years after the Lobo translation. Reed's memorandum makes the case for his authorship of a lengthy account of Johnson in the *European Magazine* (December 1784 through April 1785), of which he was editor in all but name, much stronger. There Reed, if it was he, wrote that the Dedication "it has been surmised was wholly or in part the production of his pen."[8]

There is the possibility that Farmer and Johnson met more than once. Dyer relates two anecdotes which would lead one to believe that

174 Summing Up

they may have met in London. "Farmer," he writes, "at the mutual desire of Dr. Johnson, and an eminent scholar of Cambridge, had engaged to bring about an interview between them in London. Previously to the introduction, he had, however, informed Johnson, that his friend about to be introduced, was a warm Whig." In a second anecdote Farmer interrogates Johnson on the omission in Johnson's life of Isaac Watts the fact that Watts was both "a dissenter and a Whig," whereupon Johnson replies, "Sir, you did not know the man; he was a religious, not a political Dissenter" (404–5). The first anecdote certainly would seem to indicate an actual meeting, with Farmer introducing the "eminent scholar of Cambridge"; the second might conceivably have been effected by correspondence.

All this is prelude to a discussion of a piece of prose, a letter, albeit not intended for public consumption, which has recently been attributed to Farmer. As the letter is an important document in the matter of Samuel Johnson's royal pension, it merits close consideration. On 21 February 1793 John Stuart, Earl of Bute, wrote to James Boswell, "Mr. Boswell's attention to collect every thing, which in any shape concerns the late Doctor Johnson, induces Lord Bute to send him, with his compliments, copies of two letters addressed to his late Father." Lord Bute's late father, the third Earl of Bute, was Secretary of State in 1761 and became Prime Minister in 1762. One of the enclosed letters was from Cambridge, dated 15 November 1761 and was a plea that Johnson be granted a royal pension. The second letter, printed in the *Life* by Boswell, who elected not to print the other, was Johnson's acknowledgment of the intended pension. The first, and anonymous, letter is printed in full by Marshall Waingrow, who makes no attempt to discover the identity of the anonymous writer."[9] The writer stated that he had never seen Johnson, but had "made many enquiries into his character, who tho' tarnished with some human failings is on the whole extremely aim[i]able and benevolent." He added that he "purposely" wrote the letter "in a handwriting quite different from what I commonly use." Bertram H. Davis has studied the matter and has concluded that Farmer wrote the letter, using Edward Blakeway, his and Percy's friend, and a Fellow of Magdalene College, as his amanuensis.[10]

Davis believes that Thomas Percy, "a frequent Johnson companion since 1756," proposed the letter, and that Blakeway was chosen to act as scribe because Farmer's almost illegible scrawl would have been a giveaway. The theory is perhaps based upon certain unsupported assumptions. For example, "Farmer was thoroughly familiar with Johnson's works, and he was a close friend of Thomas Percy" (37). There is no proof for the first part of that statement, and the *closeness* of the friendship in 1761 is debatable. Nor is it known or established

Summing Up 175

that Blakeway was "an intimate Cambridge friend" of Farmer's (37). The two men were nearly contemporary; Blakeway was admitted to Magdalene as a sizar on 10 March 1752, aged fifteen. It may or may not be significant that when, on August 18 and September 2, 3, and 4, Percy dined at Emmanuel, Blakeway was not one of the guests on any of these occasions, and when Percy was with Blakeway on August 18 and 19 and September 3, Farmer was not present. At least their names were not included as being guests on these occasions. However, on at least two occasions, 19 May 1761 and 11 November 1761, Blakeway's name appears as witnessing Farmer's withdrawal of books from the Emmanuel College Library.[11] Whatever the degree of intimacy that may have existed between the two, the case for Farmer's authorship comes down to this. He was at Cambridge; he was unacquainted with Johnson; he could readily get together with Blakeway, and his knowledge of Johnson from Percy and from Johnson's works was all that an astute person like Farmer would have needed to write such a letter. Hence, any one of Blakeway's Cambridge acquaintances with a recognizable handwriting, personally unacquainted with Johnson, and astute enough to make the very general remarks about Johnson that the letter contains—there is no mention of any work by Johnson, except possibly the *Dictionary* in the words "who has . . . immortalized as it were our language"—could have written the letter.

Some objections to the theory occur. On or about 9 October 1762 Percy wrote to Farmer, informing him, "I have lately heard an account how Johnson came by his Pension. It seems my Lord Bute had procured a pension of the same value for Hume: and some of his friends (my Lord Melcome, say some) remonstrating, that to prevent an odium he ought [e]qually to distinguish English Literati: he tho[ught] it necessary to do this for one of the most Eminent, and at the same time, most necessitous of them" (*Letters*, II.12–13). There is no mention of or allusion to the letter that Farmer allegedly wrote at his, Percy's, suggestion. The correspondence was private, and the pension had been granted, but there was no congratulatory note, no matter whose efforts got Johnson his pension. And from the anonymous letter itself: "I have long meditated such a design, but the oddness and unusualness of the attempt for a long time discouraged me." How long a time? Years? In 1761 Farmer was twenty-six years old, eight years from the date of his admission to Emmanuel, eight *full* years. Would he have been considering such a letter for a long time? Finally, there is the tone of the letter itself. There is the seemingly unnecessary tentativeness and repetitive awkwardness of "I never, that I know of, ever saw Mr. Johnson." Surely one knows if he has seen or been in the company of greatness. There is a mealy-mouthedness about the description of Johnson's character, "which tho' tarnished

176   Summing Up

with some human failings is on the whole extremely aim[i]able and benevolent," which runs contrary to all we know about Farmer. Nor does the apologetic suggestion that Lord might look upon the letter "as the production of one whose intellects have been, by some accident overturned" sound like Farmer. The writer admits that he did not aim "at elegance in the composition," but wrote it "immediately from the feelings of the heart." Perhaps he could not do better, but that he was Farmer remains to be demonstrated.[12]

Percy, in a letter to Farmer almost surely misdated "[June 16, 1763]" in the edition of Percy's *Letters,* asked his friend, "Have you yet resolved to give us at some future period the *Athenae Cantabrigienses*? I wish you would seriously undertake it. I would come over and make interest to be admitted *ad eundem* in your celebrated and ancient University, if it were only to gain admittance into your work" (II.44). On 28 February 1799 Rev. Mr. Samuel Denne wrote to Richard Gough, telling him, among other matters, "my late valued friend Dr. Farmer talked to me of an account that he had kept of his contemporaries at Emanuel. I shall, when I have the opportunity, inquire if this manuscript be existent, and into the accuracy of its information. He professed to me, that he had noticed the situation of the members of our college, pointing out any changes in it, and an account of their literary productions" (*Lit. Illustr.,* VI.762). If Farmer actually got down to the task of compiling an *Athenae Cantabrigienses,* he would have had the assistance of these manuscripts, listed in the sale catalog of his library: 8020 Charles Mason, sen. Fellow of Trinity, his Collections relative to the University and Town of Cambridge; 8021 Miscellaneous Collections relating to the County and University of Cambridge, by William Ingram, An. 1600, containing many curious particulars;[13] 8022 List of Graduates in the University of Cambridge, by Dr. Richardson, late Master of Emanuel College; 8025 Alphabetic List of the Members of Emanuel College; and 8030 Miscellanies relative to the University of Cambridge. Charles Mason was Professor of Geology from 1734–62; he died in 1771. It is curious that his collections should have strayed out of Trinity College and into Farmer's hands. Rev. Mr. Samuel Denne could not have had too much time to search out Farmer's manuscript, as he died on August 3, five months after his letter to Gough.

Help to Others

While it has been seen that Farmer's published scholarship was more extensive than has been previously acknowledged, the fullest

Summing Up

177

estimate of his accomplishments must take into account the help he afforded other scholars. Nichols, it will be recalled, acknowledged Farmer's help in his history of Hinckley and more extensively in his history of Leicestershire. Nichols also thanked Farmer, with Steevens and Reed, among others, for help in his *Progresses . . . of Queen Elizabeth.*[14] Farmer's assistance to Johnson and Steevens in their editions of Shakespeare has been fully analyzed, but one should also add Farmer's help to Johnson in the latter's *Lives* of the English poets. Farmer gave Johnson the unpublished letter, dated 29 April 1730, from Pope to William Broome, his collaborator in the translation of the *Odyssey*. The letter gives a full account of Elijah Fenton, the other collaborator in the translation.[15] Indeed, Farmer helped both Johnson and Nichols in this instance, for Cole, who was allowed to transcribe the letter, had told Nichols about it. Nichols asked for a copy to use in his *Select Collection of Poems* (8 vols., 1781), but Cole, writing to him on 6 May 1781, said that Farmer had gone to London "a fortnight ago" and had given it to Johnson who would "probably print it in Mr. Fenton's Life: if he does not, the Master says, you shall have it" (*Lit. Anecd.*, I.662–63). Nichols had the use of the information and mentioned the letter in Johnson's possession in his "Additional Remarks on the Fourth Volume" of his *Select Collection of Poems* (VIII.296). The aid Farmer gave Edmond Malone on the matter of the *Henry VI* trilogy has also been set forth. That there were others who also benefited from Farmer's help will hardly come as a surprise.

It was, of course, inevitable that Farmer and James Boswell should meet, having so many friends and acquaintances in common. Reed records being in the company of both men in 1785, 1788, 1789, and 1790, while Boswell records being in Farmer's company in 1786, 1788, 1791, and 1794.[16] Farmer was on the committee for Johnson's monument and would thus have had further occasion to meet with Boswell (*Life,* IV.468). In any event, under date 8 June 1762, Boswell records,

> A lady having at this time solicited him [Johnson] to obtain the Archbishop of Canterbury's patronage to have her son sent to the University, one of those solicitations which are too frequent, where people, anxious for a particular object, do not consider propriety, or the opportunity which the persons whom they solicit have to assist them, he wrote to her the following answer; with a copy of which I am favoured by the Reverend Dr. Farmer, Master of Emanuel College, Cambridge. (*Life,* I.368)

The letter is masterly, Johnson at his best, and should be read in its entirety. I quote but one sentence: "You ask me to solicit a great man,

178   Summing Up

to whom I never spoke, for a young person whom I had never seen, upon a supposition which I had no means of knowing to be true." R. W. Chapman notes, "JB's copy . . . is not in Farmer's hand. Was the copy made surreptitiously? If not, she was a brave woman who showed it."[17] Whoever copied the letter, the original of which has disappeared, it is still thanks to Farmer that Johnson's letter is known. The temptation to quote the last sentence must not be resisted. Johnson wrote, "I have seen your son this morning; he seems a pretty youth, and will, perhaps, find some better friend than I can procure him; but, though he should at last miss the University, he may still be wise, useful, and happy." Johnson did not have a full career at University, but he was wise and useful, if seldom happy.

One of Farmer's earliest offers to help in the work of another was made through the medium of Percy. Percy was in correspondence with Dr. Thomas Birch, historian and antiquary. In a letter dated 2 July 1763 Percy wrote,

> I ought not to conclude without discharging a small commission I am entrusted with, from a very ingenious and learned friend, the Rev. Mr. Farmer, Fellow of Emmanuel College, Cambridge. He has lately been admitted Fellow of your Antiquarian Society, and is given to understand that you were pleased to interest yourself in his favour; for which he desires me to convey his acknowledgments, and to assure Dr. Birch how happy he would be in return, to discharge any business he would be pleased to entrust him with, either to explore the Cambridge libraries for him, procure him transcripts of any of their curiosities, or by any other means testify that great respect which he has for his character. (*Lit. Illustr.*, VII.569–70)

Birch died on 9 January 1766, having had two works published after the date of Percy's letter. Farmer could not have rendered Birch many services, or, if any, they were not acknowledged.

Acknowledgment was, however, forthcoming in a published work. James Granger (1723–76) is described as a print collector and biographer in the *DNB*. His *Biographical History of England, from Egbert the Great to the Revolution,* to give it an abbreviated title, was published in two quarto volumes in 1769, with a second edition in four octavo volumes in 1775. Its point of departure was the engraved portraits that accompanied the anecdotes and memoirs. Briefly, Tom Davies wrote to Granger on 6 March 1770 to tell him that "Mr. Farmer, of Emanuel College, Cambridge, has offered his assistance to your next edition," and then wrote again on May 7 of the same year to say that he "wrote last post to Mr. Farmer, at Emanuel College, Cambridge, and begged him to give all the assistance in his power to

Summing Up   179

enlarge and correct your next edition. I dare not give you hopes that it will be wanted speedily."[18] This, with the offer to help Thomas Birch, is another example of Farmer's early involvement in the works of others. How Tom Davies knew Farmer well enough to enlist his aid and to anticpate a delay in that aid remains a question. Possibly Johnson had suggested Farmer to Davies, for Johnson wrote to Granger on 12 December 1772, saying Farmer was mistaken in supposing he had given him, Johnson, "any such pamphlet or cut" (114). In any event, Farmer's help is acknowledged in the Advertisement to the second edition.

Nichols wrote of Richard Gough that he "counted some of the first Antiquaries of the Three Kingdoms among his Correspondents, but having once incorporated their observations in his various publications, he guarded their correspondence from the impertinence of modern Editors." An alphabetical list of these antiquaries, all of whose specific observations were unacknowledged, contains Farmer's name as well as Cole's, Michael Lort's, and William Bennet's—the Cambridge contingent (*Lit. Anecd.*, VI.303–4). Gough was almost exactly contemporary with Farmer, entering Bene't College in July 1752. Cole sometimes acted as middle man between Gough and Farmer, on one occasion writing to Gough on 24 July 1780, in response to questions for Farmer that he had relayed from Gough, to the effect that "you have all he says here," i.e., accompanying the letter, but unfortunately the "all" is not reprinted in the *Literary Anecdotes* (VIII.391). In this same year Cole, writing to Walpole on November 13, told him that "about six weeks ago" Farmer visited him and said that Gough had accused Robert Masters, the historian of Corpus Christi College, Cambridge, of plagiarism. He further related that Masters "was determined to write a pamphlet and expose the many gross mistakes in his book [Gough's *British Topography*]." Cole wrote, "Dr Farmer, who is much with Mr. Masters, and his friend, said at the same time that Mr Gough's book was fuller of mistakes than he had ever met [with in] one of the size" (Walpole, II.242). Some seven years earlier, 3 May 1773, Cole wrote to Walpole with Gough as the subject of discussion: "Mr Farmer of Emmanuel, a most sensible, reasonable man, told me three or four months ago that he thought the worse of the Society [of Antiquaries] for making him the Director, who, he said, was noways equal to such a task. I thought as he did, and assure you I never met with a poorer creature or duller mortal" (Walpole, I.311). Yet Michael Tyson wrote to Gough on 28 June 1777, inviting him to Cambridge, and assuring him that he would "find Farmer, Masters, and Cole with all his volumes ready to receive you," the three having been recipients of Gough's *Catalogue of*

180   Summing Up

the Coins of Canute (Lit. Anecd., VIII.626). Tyson also served as liaison between Gough and Farmer, on one occasion in 1778 noting that "Dr. Farmer will, or perhaps has already wrote to you."[19] Despite Farmer's poor opinion of Gough, he could still be of assistance to him.

John Sidney Hawkins, elder son of the unclubbable Sir John Hawkins, labored ten years on an edition of George Ruggles' satiric Latin play *Ignoramus.* When it was published in 1787, it bore an Advertisement, the last paragraph of which contained his acknowledgments of help. After a general admission of help from "many gentlemen," unidentified because they had given no permission to have their names disclosed, Hawkins wrote, "But it would be an injury to the present publication to conceal, that the Editor is indebted to the Reverend Dr. Farmer, Master of Emanuel College, Cambridge, for the knowledge of many facts which no one but himself could have furnished." Also named were Thomas Ruggles, "the now representative of the family" and Francis Douce (viii). In one note in the long introductory "Life of the Author," Hawkins gave as his source for the date of Ruggles's admission to a scholarship in Trinity College, Cambridge, "Dr. *Richarson*'s papers, penes the Rev. Dr. *Farmer*" (vii. note c). Item 8022 in the sale catalog of Farmer's library is a manuscript "List of Graduates in the University of Cambridge, by Dr. Richardson, late Master of Emanuel College." The edition, under the sponsorship of Samuel Johnson, proved very successful, and there is the possibility that it was through Johnson's good offices that Farmer provided Hawkins such "facts which no one but himself could have furnished."

On 4 October 1786 Reed, at Emmanuel, "made an Index to Mr. Herbert's *Typographcl. Ants.* to refer to," i.e., William Herbert's edition of Joseph Ames's *Typographical Antiquities,* to give it a short title. The first two volumes of Herbert's edition were published in 1785 and 1786; the third was to appear in 1790. Four days later Reed "dined at Mr. Steevens's with Mr. Seale, Mr. Herbert" and two others. And some four months later Reed "went with Dr. Farmer to Cheshunt. Dined with Mr. Herbert" (*Diaries,* 149, 150, 152). The visit to Herbert's home in Cheshunt, ten miles north of London, was in response to Herbert's letter of February 9. He wrote,

> I thank you very much for your kind notice of Dr. Farmer's intention of favouring me with his company, tho' for only an hour or two, but hope he will not confine himself to so short a period. We dine about 2 o'clock, and hope ye will make that part of the time ye can conveniently stay with me. If I knew any hour more agreeable to the Doctor, dinner shou'd be ready at that time. I am also greatly obliged to you for accompanying the Doctor;

Summing Up
181

and as we have a spare bed hope you will not think of returning to Town before the next day.[20]

Farmer had helped Herbert with titles and information from his private library. James Essex, architect and F.S.A., wrote to Richard Gough from Cambridge on 31 October 1782 and told him,

> When you see Mr. Herbert, pray present my compliments to him, and tell him his papers are still in Dr. Farmer's hands, who has had Mr. Steevens with him several weeks, and I have not been able to speak with him about them; but I hope while they are together Mr. Steevens will take note of all the black letter, or other books, in Dr. Farmer's collection, that will be useful to him. (*Lit. Illustr.*, VI. 295–96)

A year later, 8 November 1783, Essex wrote to Gough: "I received last night, by Mr. Wimbolt, three sheets of Mr. Herbert's book. Mr. Steevens being still at Emanuel, I have not found Dr. Farmer enough disengaged to put them into his hands" (*Lit. Illustr.*, VI.305–6). Farmer, it seems clear, was reading proof for Herbert well before the publication of the first of the three volumes of his work. Herbert acknowledged Farmer's help in the preliminary matter of the third volume (III.viii).

On Thursday, 25 September 1788, Reed had breakfast, went to Sturbridge Fair, and returned to Emmanuel College "and found the Master, who again recommended to me the republication of [Samuel] Butler's Works for the executn. of which he lent me the materials he had collected." Three years later, in October 1790, Reed on another annual visit to Emmanuel, "sat down to Butler's Manuscript." And another three years later, Treadway Nash's edition of *Hudibras* was published, "for which Reed had supplied Gray's [*sic*] ms. notes" (*Diaries*, 161, 185, 286). "Gray" is, of course, Zachary Grey, earliest editor of *Hudibras*. John Nichols bought a number of Grey's manuscripts in 1788, among them was "Some original Notes on Hudibras." Nichols described them in a footnote: "These were principally by Mr. Montague Bacon; and were given by me to Mr. Isaac Reed; who presented them, I believe, to Dr. Nash, previous to his publishing his very splendid edition of Hudibras in three quarto volumes, 1793" (*Lit. Anecd.*, II.547). Reed provided Nash with more than just those notes given him by Nichols, that is, the so-called "Gray's ms. notes" must have come from Farmer's colllection, for item 8100 in the sale catalog of his library, under Manuscripts, is "A large Collection of Materials, by Mr. Samuel Butler, for Hudibras, with many other Poetical Pieces, Original Letters, to and from him, &c." Items 6052–6061 are all Butler titles, 6056 being *Hudibras* "with

182   Summing Up

Hogarth's plates, and many MSS. Notes, by Dr. Farmer." Reed's help was acknowledged by Nash.[21] Farmer, through whose agency Reed got Grey's notes, is also named: "As to the MSS which after Mrs. Butler's death came into the hands of Mr. Longueville, and from whence Mr. Thyer published his genuine Remains in the year 1759; what remains of them, still unpublished, are either in the hands of the ingenious Dr. Farmer, of Cambridge, or myself" (I.xvi).

From the evidence of the Percy–Farmer correspondence, it is possible to add to the list of those who benefited from Farmer's generous help. On 2 July 1765 Percy wrote to Farmer to solicit his aid for Sir David Dalrymple, who needed copies of manuscripts in Gonville and Caius College. In addition, Percy wrote, "Sir David also would be glad to be informed of any pieces not yet published, of the unfortunate Earl of Essex: As also of Archbp. Williams, or Archbp. Harsnet. *What*, and *where* they are.—I know Your humanity and affection to the cause of Literature so well, that I need not make any apology for troubling you with these particulars: tho' I am sensible at this time you must be very busy" (II.91–92). On 8 September 1765 Percy wrote, "I will communicate the contents of your Letter to Sir David Dalrymple and will tell him to whom he is obliged" (II.93). Farmer, busy with College affairs and working on his *Essay* on Shakespeare's learning, could still take time to answer queries and perform scholarly services for somebody unknown to him. On 13 December 1766 Percy told Farmer that Percy's old friend, Edward Lye was "going on with the Impression of his Saxon Lexicon. . . . He presents his Compliments to You and desires to know if (by your mediation) he could not get a copy of *Hymni Aliquot de S. Guthlacan* (Preserved in Corpus Xti library among Abp. Parker's MSS.)—Vide Wanleij Catal. p. 128 (fol. 377. b) or at least the beginning and end of them. . . . You see, my friend, how you are applied to, in every literary Undertaking" (II.118–19). Farmer, at thirty-one years of age, with the *Essay* on Shakepeare's learning on the very eve of publication but still not in the public domain, was being "applied to, in every literary Undertaking." Incidentally, Farmer did not subscribe to Lye's *Dictionarium Saxonico et Gothico Latinum*, published six years later in 1772, although Percy, of course, did, as did George Steevens.

On 15 December 1762 Thomas Warton wrote to Percy and thanked him for "the BlLetter Bundle which will be of Use." There is a footnote keyed to the "BlLetter Bundle" added by Percy in red ink "at a considerably later date." The footnote reads, "The Black-Letter bundle here mentioned consisted of three or four small things stitched together (the property of Mr Farmer of Eman. Coll. Camb.) viz. (1) A poem by Churchyard on Archery wherein mention is made of *Prince Arthur* a popular Pageant. (2) Poem by G.D. &c. (3) Small Hist. of the 7 Champions. 4to" (*Letters*, III.74–75). Warton made use of at least one of these offerings in his *History of English Poetry*, mentioning Churchyard's poetry therein (III.381, note g.). Farmer's bundle was his response to Percy's letter to him of 9 September 1762, in which Percy, referring to Warton's *Observations* on Spenser's *Fairie Queene*, wrote, "Give his book a careful perusal and communicate to me any Remarks, that may be of use in a future Edition: I will convey them to the Author" (*Letters*, II.9).

On 3 April 1764 Warton wrote to Richard Hurd, announcing, among other matters, that he had "commenced a Correspondence with a Mr Farmer of your College; who, though an Antiquarian, seems a very sensible and ingenious Man" and asking if Hurd had ever met with "the *Teseide* of Boccace, from whence Chaucer had the *Knight's* Tale." On 19 June 1766 Warton still had not met Farmer when he wrote to him about the projected history of Leicester, offering materials that might "perhaps be of some little service." Some four months later, on 17 October 1766, Warton told Hurd, "I have been lately at Cambridge, where I gott acquainted with Mr Farmer of your College, who is a great literary Antiquarian. He is publishing a short Essay on the Learning of Shakespeare. He showed Me several curious books, which he had collected, relating to Researches of that sort. I am at present deeply engaged in finishing Theocritus; and afterwards shall execute my scheme of the History of English Poetry."[22] Warton evidently discussed the edition of Theocritus with Farmer, whether in the Cambridge visit or soon thereafter in a letter, for Farmer wrote to him on 19 November 1766. Nichols prints the letter, minus twelve lines, and gives the mistaken date December 29. The entire letter is printed in John Wooll's *Biographical Memoirs of the Rev. Joseph Warton*, 1806, 313–15, from which I quote:

> I am very glad that Joshua [Barnes] is safe arrived at Oxford. His notes, I suspect, will not figure greatly; but you will smile at his identification of *Homer* and *Solomon*. Pope (if I remember right) has a hint at his curious performance, though others have doubted its existence. I forgot to note in it that the usually accurate *Fabricius* led me into a mistake about it, except I have misquoted him. There was an edition at Rome, 1516. We have in the public library a most beautiful copy of the 1st edition, Ald. 1495; and among the archives Harry Steven's Poetae Gr. Principes, with many MS. notes (on *Theocritus* among the rest) by *Isaac Casaubon;* whether they are exhausted in his *Lectiones Theocriticae,* I could not make out upon a slight examination—so cursedly are they written; if however you have

184 Summing Up

time, I think I can get a particular friend of mine (our Greek Professor) to examine into this matter. Isaac's name is a tower of strength, whatever becomes of *Joshua's*.

Professor Taylor's Lectures on Theocritus are in the hands of a Rev. Mr. Driffield, of Chelsworth, near Hadleigh, Suffolk. Some years ago he talked of printing them—but that seems to be blown over. I cannot find any body at present that has any acquaintance with him.—Suppose you throw away a letter at him yourself.

Don't imagine that I shall be impertinent enough to say any thing more about Editors and Commentators, which you are certainly sufficiently acquainted with. Pray remember to translate Ελιξ, in the 1st Idyllium, by a less ambiguous word than Capreolus, by which unfortunate one Master *Creech* is detected of translation from the Latin.

With respect to the History of English Poetry, I flatter myself I can be of much more service: let me know your plan, &c. and command me as you please. When I have a little more time to spare, I will make you out a pretty large Spenserian packet. You talk of being idle in the summer—I wish I had been so too—my business has been solely *swearing at Engravers*. Poor *Shakespear* lies upon the table.

(*Raptim*)   Yours most affectionately,   R FARMER.

P.S. This scrawl has lain by these two days, to wait for a note to Mr. Huddesford; but I am now determined, with Master Dogberry, "If I was as tedious as a King, to bestow it all on your Worship." You may remember that we talked of a transcript of names from the Latin of Leicester MSS.; but I think we may be contented with the Preamble about the *Classes,* or somewhat to that purpose; for these sort of things have grown upon me *marvellously*. But I must trouble one of you to look at Dugdale in the Ashmolean, 6502. 12 F 2. p. 327. When I looked at his account of our Abbey, I thought it proved in the Monasticon; but, if my memoranda be right, it is not. This therefore (or what part of it *you* or *either* of you think proper) I could wish to have copied by my former amanuensis. I remember it is very legible. Can I ask likewise, at somebody's leisure, for a peep at the said Dugdale MSS. Angl. 292. No. 6491?

Warton acknowledged Farmer's offered help to the *Theocritus,* writing that he was indebted to "Dr. Farmer, then Fellow, and afterwards Master, of Emmanuel College, Cambridge, for some unedited remarks of [Joshua] Barnes, which proved of no service."[23]

Farmer was also able to help in the matter of the *Teseide* of Boccacio which Warton had brought up in the first of the two quoted letters to Hurd. In the second edition of his *Essay* on Shakespeare's learning, Farmer added a footnote about Boccacio's version of the Palamon and Arcite story, Chaucer's Knight's Tale, pointing out that it was "printed at *Ferrara* in Folio, *con il commento di Andrea Bassi,* 1475. I have seen a copy of it, and a Translation into modern *Greek,*

Summing Up 185

in the noble Library of the very learned and communicative Dr. *Askew*." Not content with this, he added "It is likewise to be met with in old *French*, under the Title of *La Theseide* de *Jean Boccace*, contenant les belles & chastes amours de deux jeunes Chevaliers Thebains *Arcite & Palemon*" (24, note y). Compare Warton in the *History of English Poetry*, "The first edition of the Italian book . . . is in the excellent library of the very learned and communicative Dr. Askew" (I.352, note t). And, in another footnote, there is reference to "La THESEIDE de Jean Boccace, contenant les chastes amours de deux chevaliers Thebans, Arcite et Palemon" (I.346, note y).[24]

On 13 February 1770 Farmer wrote to Warton, who had asked for information about the antiquarian John Leland. Nichols printed the letter.

> Dear Sir, I should have been particularly happy to have seen you at Askew's, as perhaps he has more matters worth your notice, than he himself in the multitude of his business might have time to exhibit; but I am sure he would at least be willing, for I know not a more communicative man in the world. I wish I could give you a satisfactory account of Leland. They have no registers of admissions or degrees at Christ's before the last century; nor are there any matriculations remaining of Leland's time. All I find is, from an old Proctor's book, that D^s. Leland paid for the degree of B.A. in 1522. So far I could have written some time ago; but I waited from day to day for the Antiquary of the College (one Mr. Wall), who is just now arrived at Cambridge. I hoped he might have informed me somewhat about the fellowship. Fuller, I think, is the first who calls him *fellow;* but here again I was disappointed; his list of fellows begins only in the 22d of Henry VIII. In truth, I find no reason to believe he was so. When he speaks of himself and the College, he would scarcely have omitted it: however, if any thing worth notice should occur, you shall certainly have it. You cannot oblige me more than by giving me an opportunity of hoping at least to answer your questions. Have you no job in the *History of Poetry* for your very obliged and affectionate servant, R. FARMER?
>
> P.S. Fuller calls Leland fellow of Christ's (as he pretends) on his own authority (Hist. of Camb. p. 91), and quotes his *Vita Seberti* (Sigeberti); but, if you turn to it in "Leland de Scriptoribus," or in Tanner, you will see he only says he had been a *member* of the college. Bale makes a distinct life of Sigebert; but Wall is certainly right, where he tells us there is no other than this. *(Calamo rapidiss) (Lit. Anecd., II.626–27)*

This is particularly interesting in that Warton, at Oxford, sought information from Farmer, at the same time that William Huddesford, Fellow of Trinity College and keeper of the Ashmolean Museum, was working on a life of Leland. Huddesford's *Lives of . . . John Leland,*

186   Summing Up

Thomas Hearne, and Anthony a Wood . . . was published in two
volumes in 1772, not long after Farmer's letter to Warton. Compare
part of a footnote on Leland with Farmer's letter:

> Fuller gives the preceding note, for saying LELAND was Fellow of
> Christ's College. That he studied in this College, as also at All-Souls
> College, Oxford, is not doubted; but rather as an independant Member, as
> was then customary, of both Societies; but it no where appears he was, at
> any time, Fellow of Christ's or any College, in either University. In an old
> Proctor's Book in the University of Cambridge, Dˢ. LELOND occurs,
> paying his fees for the Degree of A.B. AN. D. 1522. This probably was our
> Author, as this first Degree was frequently then granted in the early part of
> life: on this, and the above quotation, Fuller might ground his opinion that
> he was Fellow of Christ's College.

There can be no doubt that Huddesford, already a correspondent of
Farmer's, got the information for his note either directly from Farmer
or through Warton. It should not go unremarked that Huddesford
also invokes "*Leland ipse* in Scriptor. Britann, cap.lvii. De Sigeberto
rege" in the preceding footnote.[25] Huddesford acknowledged that he
had "received singular benefit from the indulgent and kind communication from Gentlemen, whose names the Editor is not at liberty to
mention" (I.vii). Farmer was one of those gentlemen.

Farmer had been of some slight assistance to Warton in another
matter. Warton had contributed some notes to the appendix of
Johnson's 1765 *Shakespeare,* one of them on the source of *The
Tempest* that Warton thought he had discovered in "an *Italian* chemical Romance called ORELIA and ISABELLA," which was called to
his attention by William Collins. Farmer wrote to Percy around the
middle of March 1768, telling him, among other matters, "*Warton*
sends me word, that he has found the Novel of the *Tempest.*" Percy,
spurred on by Farmer's letter, took occasion, when in Oxford soon
thereafter, to ask Warton to show him the book. Percy's conclusion: "I
have not had time to examine it, but from peeping into it, suspected
he is misinformed" (*Letters,* II.141, 146). As a result of the combined
efforts of Farmer and Percy, Warton retracted the note in the 1773
Johnson–Steevens *Shakespeare* and explained the whole matter fully
in his *History of English Poetry* (III.477).

Warton edited Milton's minor poems in 1785 under the title of
Poems on Several Occasions, and needing information on John Goslyn, "Master of Caius College, and king's professor of medicine at
Cambridge; who died while a second time Vice-chancellor of that
university," the subject of Milton's Latin poem, *In obitum Procancellarii, medici,* he naturally turned to his Cambridge friend. In the

Summing Up   187

footnote in which the above identification of the subject of the ode is quoted, Warton acknowledged Farmer's aid.

> I am favoured in a letter from doctor Farmer with these informations. "I find in Baker's MSS. vol. xxviii. *Chargis of buryall and funeral of my brother doctor Gostlin who departed this life the* 21 *of Oct.* 1626, *and his funerall solemnized the* 16th *of Nov. following.* And so it stands in the College GESTA-BOOK. He was a Norwich-man, and matriculated Dec. 3, 1582. A benefactor of Caius and Catharine-Hall; at which last you once dined at his expense, and saw his old wooden picture in the combination room." (503)

It is possible that the following letter from Steevens to Warton, dated 29 October 1782, three years before the publication of Warton's edition of Milton's poems, has to do with that work. Steevens wrote, "Dr Farmer desires me to apologize for his not having answered a Letter of yours. The truth is that he could neither find his memoran-dums, nor time to tell you he had lost them."[26] In any event, one not only gets another instance of Farmer's assistance to Warton but also the information that Warton, and almost surely Farmer with him on that occasion, enjoyed the hospitality of St. Catharine's College.

On 9 April 1786 the Rev. John Price, librarian of the Bodleian, wrote to William Herbert to thank him for part of Herbert's edition of Joseph Ames's *Typographical Antiquities.* Herbert had asked if Price could find "the Life of Alexander" for him, and Price was reporting failure. He did, however, write that "Mr. Warton tells me (exclusive of what he took from Hearne's note to Caii Vindiciae) that what he has advanced (in vol. II p. 8 of his History of English Poetry) relative to it, was suggested to him by Dr. Farmer, Master of Emanuel College, Cambridge, who he believes has the book itself" (*Lit. Illustr.,* V.538). The work referred to is the pseudo-Callisthenes Life of Alexander of Macedon. It is possible that Farmer helped Warton on other occa-sions; he would seem to have been sufficiently helpful in any event.

If one excepts the contributions Farmer made to the various edi-tions of Shakespeare, the greatest extent of his assistance to another scholar was that which he afforded Thomas Percy, principally in the latter's *Reliques of Ancient English Poetry,* but also in other works. The two men became acquainted, so far as can be ascertained, in August 1761 when Percy went to Cambridge to copy ballads in the Pepysian Library of Magdalene College.[27] Edward Capell had intro-duced Farmer to Percy, either directly or by letter of introduction (106–7). By late 1761 Farmer must have already been well known in Cambridge, both as a collector of and expert in black-letter books. And although Percy knew Edward Blakeway of Magdalene College,

Summing Up

he probably sought out Farmer because of his reputation. In any event, the first extant letter between the two was from Percy, dated around 10 May 1762, and clearly indicated that there had been some earlier letters. Percy wrote, "I would send you some new sheets of Old Ballads from the press: but I have not one by me" (1–2), giving rise to the suspicion, later confirmed, that Farmer read proof of the whole, or a very large part, of the *Reliques*. Percy acknowledged Farmer's help in the preface to the *Reliques,* even unto the third edition, writing that "Two ingenious and learned friends at Cambridge deserve the Editor's warmest acknowledgments: to Mr. Blakeway, late fellow of Magdalene College, he owes all the assistance received from the Pepysian Library: and Mr. Farmer, fellow of Emanuel often exerted in favour of this little work, that extensive knowledge of ancient English literature for which he is so distinguished." In a footnote he added, "To the same learned and ingenious friend, now Master of Emanuel College, the Editor is indebted for many corrections and improvements in his SECOND and THIRD Edition" (1775, I.xv.).

There are three unpublished letters from Farmer to Percy in the Northamptonshire Record Office, part of the Sotheby Ecton Collection. The first is dated simply May 1762. I quote the whole.

Dear Percy

> I that was once as great as *Caesar,*
> Am now reduced to Nebuchadnezzar!

—absoluted under the *Influenza!*—are you alive in your part of the World? Faith, the *Thaxted* Gang might plunder all the Colleges in *Cambridge*—we have not above 14 effective men left—seriously, almost every body has a share of a Fever, & I as bad as any, except poor *Yeatman,*[28] who is yet dangerously ill—I think, I have more Spirits than Body, but he, God help him, has neither.—I *heaved* up a Pen yesterday, but found I could not write—"no more can you now" quoth you—come, don't be impertinent.—*Blakeway* by way of charity, call'd upon me on Sunday night—I gave him the Kennilworth Ballad, to collate with *Gascoigne's* Pleasures, as I supposed a Copy of it to be found there: he told me had got Carte in his room, & I desired him to look for *Alfred* & *Guy*—he thought he recollected something in *Hume.* you rec.'d, I hope, the Garland of Withered Roses I borrow'd for you at *Leicester*—you see I did not forget you.—*In D.ʳ Rawlinson's Catalogue appears an Edit. of Surrey in 1557*–qu? Whether the same with yours? D.ʳ Brown in his celebrated Poem, call'd *Honour* speaks of
> —"Villiers witty [Bacon wise] in vain"
You may suggest some how or other, you hope, he will not be so, when he

Summing Up 189

is read with your *Key.*—Here are the true *Aegri somnia*—nec pes, nec caput uni[29] &c. farewell—I'm tired.

R. Farmer (Ms. E (S). 1206, #4, item 34)

It is evident Percy's requests for Farmer's help came early in their friendship. The letter shows that Farmer was helping, not only with the *Reliques,* but with the contemplated edition of Surrey's poems, as well as with the *Key* to the Duke of Buckingham's *Rehearsal. The Garland of Withered Roses* eventually made its appearance in a list of works whose titles began with *Garland[s]* that made up note Ff appended to Percy's "Essay on the Ancient Minstrels." There is no "Kennilworth ballad" in the Pepys collection.

On 28 August 1762 Farmer wrote again, some of the remarks in his letter making it clear that Percy had overstepped bounds, but the tone is still cordial.

Dear Percy

I am not a little pleased, when you set me about any business, which it is in my power to perform; & equally sorry when I am disappointed, but how the Duce came you to imagine y^t such *valuable* M.S.S. as you speak of, could be got out of an University Library? I dare not own y^t I send any of the *printed* Books out of town which now & then brings me into ridiculous circumstances. (By the way, I beg you wou'd particularly send home the *Lincoln*-book—I had an angry Letter about it from Thence 2 or 3 days ago.) Kennicott indeed back'd by great Interest, the Importance of his Subject, & a Bond of £500, got from us a little while since an Hebrew M.S. or 2; but what are they to *Guy of Warwick?* after a pretty long search, I found 2 y^t you mention; but there was no occasion for the Librarian's informing me, y^t I must not transcribe any thing without the Vicechancellor's leave, for I could not read a single line, tho' they certainly may be legible to those who are conversant with old Hands. I could see however there was nothing for you in the ballad way; for the least piece took up several leaves in Folio. The printed Book you mention, I remember to have shewn you: it is in the Archives & under the same restrictions with the M.S.S. but if you will send any thing to be collated with it I will endeavor to do it. The M.S.S. at Caius I have also seen by the favour of the Master: they are tied to the Library, like the others; but the Master does not object to any Transcriptions. & Guy of Warwick seems a perfect copy, except some lines obliterated in the first page. The other is very old and rotten however, before you make up your *Corpus* of Romances, you must come over & try to decypher them. The Mem. de l'Acad. I can probably get for you in the winter, when our people have done with light reading. Pellontier is, I suppose, a modern Book, for it does not appear in our Catalogues. in Upton's Obs. upon *Shakespeare*, is a passage, which perh. you have seen. *"All the writers of the middle*

190   Summing Up

Comedy are lost. We have among the Comedies of our own Country, the Rehearsal written after this Model: for here Bays stands for Dryden; the two kings, for Charles & his brother James; & the parodies have all the cast of this ancient humour." I suppose you do not want your proof-ballads. My Compst to Mrs *Percy*, & the young ones. Yours affectionately

R. *Farmer* (item 31)

Benjamin Kennicott, a biblical scholar, mentioned as borrower of MSS. from the University Library, was active in obtaining Hebrew manuscripts. This particular transaction has gone unremarked. Percy replied on September 9: "I kiss the rod of your reproof: I am very sensible my request was unreasonable and extravagant; and thank you for your great lenity in not being before offended at it." He rather promptly asked if Farmer could procure for him "the old printed book out of the Archives," following this request with a spate of others (10–11).

From the very first, then, Percy and Farmer got on remarkably well, Percy's salutation being either "My dear Farmer" or "My dear friend," in contrast, say, to that to Thomas Warton whom he addressed as "Sir" or "Dear Sir." The editors of volume three of Percy's letters, those to Warton, remark upon this, noting that "Percy in writing to Warton, does not unbend as he does to Farmer" (1951, xxii). The close of Percy's letters to Warton are in one or more variations of the "humble, obedient servant" formula; Percy often closes with "Dear Farmer Ever yours." Percy extended many invitations to Farmer to visit him at Easton Mauduit, and while there is no direct evidence that Farmer accepted any one of the several very cordial invitations (24, 30, 44, 54, 77), Percy's letters generally close with an expression of his wife's "compliments" to or "respect" for Farmer, possible evidence that he had met her prior to Percy's taking his degree at Emmanuel. William Cole wrote to Walpole on 18 December 1769 telling him that he had dined the previous day at Emmanuel on that occasion and that Percy's wife, "who is a very handsome and agreeable woman" was also present (Walpole, I.193.n.2). Most of the letters between Percy and Farmer antedate December 1769, however.

Farmer's help took many forms: loan of books from his library and that of the University, collation of texts, acting as intermediary between Percy and other Cambridge scholars and antiquaries, and, of course, answering query after query from his profound knowledge of ancient English literature. Of a nonscholarly nature were requests for the loan of an academic gown (155), for showing guests about Cambridge (137), and for admitting a student to Emmanuel (157–58). Many of Percy's requests, sometimes couched in terms of friendly

Summing Up 191

demands, were of such sweeping character as to be deemed extraordinary. More than once he asked that University Library books sent to him be kept beyond their due date, and more than once he asked Farmer to "be so kind as collate" or, equally politely, to "examine" a work or works. On one occasion at least he asked Farmer to look over certain specified books offered in the catalogue of a firm of Cambridge booksellers and to buy them for him if they fit certain conditions (25–26). On 31 December 1763 he informed Farmer that the "whole 2^d book" of the *Reliques* "is to relate to Shakespear's ballads, your own subject" and asked him as a "great favour" to lend all the volumes of "Warburton's Shakespear. Theobald's Ditto Meres' Wits Treasury and Wit's Commonwealth[.] All your old quarto copies of Shakespear," a truly all-embracing request, as Farmer did indeed possess a number of the old quartos (57–58). Percy, at Easton Maudit, was "near twenty Miles . . . to Kettering," and it was there that parcels of books from Cambridge were sent, Percy making the trip himself or sending his servant (23). Since the books had to be returned, the chances of some loss or damage was doubled, although Farmer seems not to have concerned himself overmuch with that consideration.

Percy sought other favors from Farmer as their friendship grew. He not only sought assistance for himself, but also for those of his acquaintance. One such was John Pinkerton, Scottish antiquary and historian, with whom he carried on a correspondence of some length. On 24 July 1784 Percy wrote to Farmer to tell him that Pinkerton wished to see the so-called Maitland MS. in the Pepys Library. "Pinkerton's desires," Percy wrote,

> have not been attended with success & he thinks if I can get him an introduction from you he'll be allowed to see it. Pinkerton is probably the only person in Britain who can read the MS. or understand its contents, & the MS. is of "no use whatsoever, it is unless consulted." The MS. is in poor state & will probably become illegible before long. I would be sorry to see our archives suffer by comparison in generosity of Scotland's, Pinkerton's own country. The Advocates Library actually sent me Barrington's MS. in London, unique like this of Maitland & allowed me to keep it there two years or more on my leaving a small deposit or my note for a small sum, "I forget which."[30]

Accordingly, two days later, Percy was able to write to Pinkerton assuring him that "Dr Farmer's Letter will be the most efficacious Introduction to the [Pepys] Library."[31] Percy had himself "transcribed a great Part of the Contents" of the Maitland manuscript (*Letters*, VI.158). Pinkerton, armed with Farmer's introduction and carrying

192 Summing Up

Percy's blessing on his endeavors, accordingly visited the Pepys Library. There he inspected the folio manuscript, arranged its contents, and noted that "With these very few Alterations the Folio MS. would be rendered as perfect as possible," signing himself "J.P." and dating his reordering of the MS "Cambridge 1 Dec. 1784." In 1786 Pinkerton published a two-volume edition titled *Ancient Scotish Poems;* in his acknowledgments in the preface to that works he noted that "Dr BEATTIE, Dr FARMER, and Mr WARTON, are also entitled to thanks."[32]

I quote below more of Percy's letter of 9 September 1762 as a further example of the tone of the correspondence as well as of the variety of his requests.

> And now according to my usual custom, I must beg leave to fly to you for information on one or two subjects, which I can receive from no one else. Can you from Leland, Bale, Pitsius, or Tanner (none of which I have, tho' you have all of them in your Libraries) inform me when lived *Gilbertus Pylkyngton,* Author of the Turnament of Totterham? (See the Epistle to that Poem bound at the end of the Lincoln Book) I intend to prefix that Poem to my second Volume of Ancient Ballads, and would fain accompany it with some account of the author, at least ascertain the time he lived.
>
> Be pleased also to inform me, (as I said above) whether M. de la Curne de Ste Palaye his memoirs of ancient Chivalry (see Warton Vol. I. pag. 55.) are the same that are referred to by Mr Hurd, amongst the *Memoirs* de l'Academie des Inscriptions—because I intend [to] make Dodsley procure me Palaye's book.
>
> Lastly be so kind as to collate the inclosed song with the original in the Pepys Library, and send me all the References &c that are in Pepys's Copy: as also a Correct Copy of the Musick, which Mr Dodsley shall get engraved to accompany it.—If I mistake not in Pepys's I^{st} Volume of Old Ballads Folio, it is said that a more ancient Copy of this song is preserved in the Bodleyan Library. Please to transcribe the account.
>
> On Monday next my wife and I set out for Mr Shenstone's to spend a fortnight: at the end of that time I shall be glad of one of your very valuable and friendly Letters. We are all, thank God, well: My wife joins in best respects, with
>
>
>
> Dear Farmer
> Ever Yours
> T. Percy (10–11)
>
>

Only four of Farmer's letters to Percy are printed in volume II of the Percy *Letters.* I have quoted part of Farmer's letter in which he describes Dr. Johnson's visit to Cambridge (above, p. 170). I quote

Summing Up 193

part of another letter as a further example of the informality of Farmer's epistolary style and the range of his interests:

—When We saw Dr *Ducarrel,* he asked me for the 2^d Edition of the Essay, and promised me in return a Transcript of a small paper about *Leicester.*—I had not time to go to him, and wish you would give it him, when you see him—I cannot recollect, whether one was sent To Mr *Astle*—if not be so kind [as] to give him one and a *Pavement,* begging him to exhibit it to the Bp. of *Carlisle,* who inquired after it—I have sent you a Copy or 2 of *Jane Shore,* done by a Friend of mine with the utmost accuracy—not made fine, as a common Engraver would do it. Perhaps Mr *Walpole* would like one. (*Entre nous,* that Gentleman has made sad Mistakes about Richard 3. in *names, dates,* &c. The Parliament roll is printed in *Speed.*) The Plate of *Wyatt,* by the same hand, you may have for your *Surrey,* if you think proper. Mr *Mason* says there are some curious observations on the English language by *him* in the *Museum,* and a Translation (I think) of *Ecclesiastes.* Qu? I do not see them in the Index.

God bless You—I hope Mrs Percy is very well. N B. I wrote all this scrawl in less than 7 Minutes with a *Scout,* as You call them, standing by me.

R.F. (142–43)

In his letter of 29 December 1766 to Thomas Warton, Farmer closed with "*(Raptim)* Yours most affectionately," once more writing hurriedly. Nor should it go unnoted that while Percy was rather formal in his correspondence with Warton, as I remarked above, Farmer's warmth extended to his letters to Warton.

Sir Samuel Egerton Brydges records some of Cole's remarks on various persons. Among Cole's notes on Percy is the following as further evidence of Farmer's friendship with Percy:

In Oct. 1778, he was made Dean of Carlisle, in the room of Dr. Wilson, deceased.

Dr. Farmer told me, that on his kissing hands (yet before the change of the Ministry in March, 1782) for his Prebend of Canterbury, the people at Court were busily inquiring after a person to give the new vacant Bishopric in Ireland to, by Bishop Garnet's death, that had any royal preferment: that he immediately wrote to Dr. Percy, who had but two small livings; and the Deanery of Carlisle; and a family to provide for; and no great prospect of succeeding in England; to exchange his Deanery, and take the Irish Bishopric: which advice he followed; and Dr. Elkins accepted the exchange. April 20, 1782, he was announced in the Gazette, as Bishop of Dromore.[33]

A few years later Farmer was again of considerable service to Percy,

194   Summing Up

this time in a family matter of some delicacy. John Nichols, the
recipient of two letters from Farmer explaining the matter, later
turned the letters over to Joseph Cradock, from whose *Memoirs* I
quote them.

> Sir,   *Emanuel College, Nov. 8th*, 1781.
> I trouble you on a subject which itself must be my excuse. I know your
> friendship for Dean Percy and his family; and am sorry to inform you that
> his son, instead of proceeding to college according to his father's expecta-
> tions, has suddenly (as I am informed) left the Cambridge road for a
> scheme to London. Now, Sir, if we cannot get him hither on Monday next,
> at furthest, he will lose his Term, and probably every expectation in his
> present line of life.
> I know he has formerly been found at one of the hotels in the Adelphi,
> and it may not be amiss to enquire at Northumberland House. I hope he
> has not much money with him. You know the town better than I do, and I
> doubt not will make every proper enquiry. I will leave it to his father to
> express his gratitude.
> In great haste, yours, &c.   R FARMER.
> *To Mr. Nichols.*

> Sir,   *Emanuel College, Nov. 14*, 1781.
> I am happy to inform you. that your young man came to us time enough
> to save his Term. His excuse is, that he went to town to consult Dr. Elliot,
> his Father's physician; but as the Dean knows nothing of the case or the
> scheme, I believe (if he behaves properly in future) we had better say no
> more about it. He, however, acknowledges himself under great obligations
> for your kind attention to him, and I thank you very sincerely.
> I hope for future correspondence of a more agreeable nature; and am,
> Sir, yours, &c.   RICHARD FARMER.
> *To Mr. Nichols* (IV.96–97)

Elsewhere in his *Memoirs* Cradock adds further information about
Percy's son.

> As to the cause of the quarrel of Percy with my Emanuel friends, I can
> only speak as follows: Dr. Percy was so bright himself, that he was never
> satisfied with the progress of his son at Westminster; Mrs. Percy frequently
> lamented, and acted in this as I believe in every occurrence in life. When in
> town I would have done any things to have kept peace between the father
> and son. The latter was lost in London; Oldershaw and others at last
> found him; but the young man soon died. Percy blamed Farmer and all at
> Emanuel for placing his son in a damp apartment, and would attribute his
> death to that. I was chiefly resident in Leicestershire, and miserable to find
> such a schism amongst my best friends. Johnson questioned me about it,

Summing Up   195

and I found he strongly leaned to the Emanuel party: nothing was ever wrong in his eyes, I believe, with either Bennet, Oldershaw, or Farmer. (IV.292–93)

Young Percy died of consumption at Marseilles on 2 April 1783.

The matter of the later relationship of Percy and Farmer, a relationship that includes the alleged quarrel about young Henry Percy, has been thoroughly gone into by Cleanth Brooks, editor of the Percy–Farmer letters (II.xiv–xvii). He concludes that the two remained friends right to Farmer's death. Curiously enough, Brooks's edition of the letters was published in 1946, the same year that Reed's *Diaries* were published. In this latter, there is further evidence of the continuing friendship, for on 1 June 1792 Reed recorded, "Dined at Dr. Farmer's with Bishop Percy" (191), presumably the last time the two men met—at least in Reed's company. When Percy was told of Farmer's death in 1797, he described him to Steevens as "a friend so beloved" and to Henry Meen as "Our dear Friend Farmer."[34]

Brooks states quite unequivocally that "of all his scholarly friends, Percy seems to have depended most upon Farmer for help with the *Reliques* and with the *Surrey*" (II.ix). The extent of Farmer's help has never been analyzed, although it is possible, from the published correspondence between the two men, to determine with some exactness specific examples of that help. The order of what follows is chronological, the dates being of the letters from Percy to Farmer, unless otherwise stated. I might add initially that Percy ascribed "much of the materials used in the 'Additions and Corrections' " to Farmer and Sir David Dalrymple in an addition, in his own hand, in his copy of the *Reliques,* but he did not print that ascription.[35]

9 September 1762: "be so kind as to collate the inclosed song with the original in the Pepys Library, and send me all the References &c. that are in Pepys's Copy: as also a Correct Copy of the Musick, which Mr Dodsley shall get engraved to accompany it" (11). The song is "For the Victory at Agincourt," the music for which, supplied by Farmer, is engraved at the end of volume II. The presumption, here and elsewhere, is that when Percy asked Farmer to collate something, Farmer did so.

c. 9 October 1762: "do me the favour to collate the inclosed ballad St George and the dragon with the copy preserved in the Pepys Collection" (12).

30 January 1763: "I long impatiently to see *Thomas a beck* [*et* colla]ted" (32). Although Percy did not print the poem, "A transcript of five stanzas of this poem in Farmer's hand is preserved in Add, MS.

2822, f. 112^r" (32, n.10). "I thank you for Chaucer's *Rondeau,* which is curious; I shall soon return your Copy" (33). The poem is printed in volume II (11–12).

A digression is necessary here which will make the next quotation from Percy's letters more understandable. The third of the letters from Farmer to Percy preserved in the Northamptonshire Record Office broaches the matter of the ballad of *John Nobody.*

> Checking him said, Thou fellow dost thou see the bread born before thy face, & wilt not turn it and yet art thou glad to eat it before it be half baked." Page 21.
> "Mr *Clifford: late Master of Charter house buried in the Chancell, Dec. 13, 1677. the Duke of Bucks designed him a Monument, but dying it was turned upon the Carver's hands.*" M.S. hist. of St *Margaret's West.*^{r} trans. by *Baker.* In Strype's Annals, V. 2. P. 89. is Qu. Eliz. Sonnet "The Doubt of future Woes &c pr.^{d} in *Puttenham.* in his Memorials of *Cranmer,* P. 138 is an old satyrical song on the religious Disputes of his times, call'd *John Nobody*————I have a notion, I have seen this in *Pepys* but if you have not it, I will transcribe it for you.
> *Pepys Vol. 1, pag. 19
> In the M.S.S. at the *Museum.* N. 1174. 180. "Descent & Arms of *Farmer* of *Radcliffe* in Com. *Leicester.* Dat. AN. D . . . 1640. fol. 99. b." These were Relations of our's————& as the Matter must be very short, I should be glad, if you can procure a Transcript for me; & the Arms blazon'd (in Colours, if so on the M.S.) this I ask on supposition y^t your Friend Astle is there—who will be pleased to pay any one for ~~their~~ his trouble.
> Comp.st to Mrs Percy & Love to the Children
> from yours affectionately,
> R. *Farmer* (item 33)

On 16 June 1763, a conjectural date, Percy wrote to say that he "writ to Astle about your genealogical Business at the Museum." A footnote at this juncture (43) gives the date of Percy's letter to Astle as "14 July," but since Percy wrote to Farmer on "June 16," having already "writ" to Astle, the June 16 date must be wrong. Farmer's letter was obviously written between May 14 and some time before July 14 as there are no other letters in the correspondence between those dates.

16 June 1763: "I thank you for your offer of the Song of *Little John Nobody:* I already have got it from a Copy in the Pepys' Collection.— If you have opportunity you may see whether that Copy differs from Strype, and note the variations" (42). There are three textual variants noted, the poem appearing in volume II, pages 124–26.

9 October 1763: The engraver has finished seven plates, for the two first volumes. Your edition of Gascoigne has furnished us with one excellent design, viz. Time dragging Truth out of her well with this

Summing Up   197

Legend, *Occulta veritas tempore patet* (49). The plate is at page 209 of the second volume. Further in the same letter:

I must now beg your assistance in one of two petty researches, which my distance from competent Libraries renders me unable to prosecute sufficiently myself.

1. When did the House of commons issue out their order for taking down Charing-Cross? I know it was sometime after July 1643. I fancy Rushworth will inform you, or Whitelocke.

2do In Bp. Corbet's Song: "The mad Puritan" says of himself,
I have been in despair
Five times in a year
And been cured by reading *Greenham*.

3^{d} Item he says
I've seen in *Perkins table*
The black line of Damnation
Those crooked veins
So run in my brains
That I fear'd my reprobation.

4to I saw two in a Vision
With a flying-book between'em.

5. In another old Cavalier Song intitled "Rebellion hath broken up House," The poet sneers at

"The old wives, who on their good troth,
Lent thimbles to ruin the nation."

What particular incident in the course of the civil wars does this refer to?

Will you, my dear friend, as soon as is convenient favour me with answers to these queries particularly the four first of these numbered, (which the press waits for) and the rest at your leisure. (52–54)

Farmer found the answer to the first question in Sir Bulstrode Whitelock's *Memorials of the English Affairs,* 1682, one of the books in his library, but it came too late for insertion at its proper place and was relegated to the Additions and Corrections at the end of Volume III of the first edition. Percy's note is almost verbatim from Farmer's marginal comment, i.e., "Whitelock says 'May 4. 1643 Cheapside cross and other crosses were voted down.'" Farmer's marginal comment on Greenham reads, "One of his Treatises, a sweet Comfort for an afflicted Conscience." Percy's note reads, "See Greenham's Works, fol. 1605. particularly the tract intitled, 'A sweet comfort for an afflicted conscience.'" The reference to the "works" and the date also came from Farmer's additional comment, "Works in 2 vol. 1605." Percy's note on *Perkins table* must also have been answered by Farmer, although not in a marginal comment. It reads "See Perkins's works, fol. 1616, vol. I p. 11; where is a large half-sheet folded, containing, 'A survey, or table declaring the order of the cases of salvation, and damnation, etc.' The pedigree of damnation being distinguished by a broad black zig-zag line." So, too, with Percy's note on "flying-book": "Alluding to some visionary exposition of Zech. ch. V. ver. 1," to which he added rather considerably in the second edition (II.354). Finally, so with the fifth query, is Percy's note reading "See Grey's Hudibras, Pt. I. Cant. 2. ver. 570 &c." Farmer had accumulated much material on Butler and hence had little difficulty with this last question.[36]

Percy also asked a number of questions about *"Songs and Ballads quoted by Shakespear"* (54), among them one on "the ballad of K. Lear. (This I suppose is posterior to Shakespear. Who was the author of the old play of Lear, written before Shakespear's?)" (56). In a note on the song in the first edition, Percy remarked that both play and ballad might "be indebted to a more ancient dramatic Writer. For that an older play of KING LEIR had been exhibited before Shakespeare wrote, and is still even extant in print, I am assured upon undoubted authority, tho' I have not been so lucky as to obtain a sight of it" (I.211). In the second edition of the *Reliques* Percy was able to name and date the previous play on King Lear, i.e., *"The true Chronicle History of Leir and his three daughters . . . 1605,"* which could be found *"printed at the end of* the TWENTY PLAYS *of Shakespeare, republished from the quarto impressions by* GEORGE STEEVENS, ESQ." in 1766 (I.229) As Steevens's help is not acknowledged in the preface to any edition of the *Reliques,* and as Percy's request to Farmer antedated Steevens's *Twenty Plays* by about three years, I conclude that Farmer was the "undoubted authority" who told Percy about the older play on King Lear. That Steevens did make a suggestion for the second edition of the *Reliques,* one that Percy acted on, is known.[37] In his preface Percy had made a very generous blanket acknowledgment of Farmer's help and did not thereafter mention him by name. George Steevens is, however, named for his suggestion in the second edition of the *Reliques* ("I am indebted . . . to the friendship of Mr. Steevens," II.178), and one would think that if it was he who alerted Percy to the existence of the earlier play on King Lear, he would have been named.

28 February 1764: "I wish you would ascertain the year, when the first edition of Walton's book of fishing was published" (67). Percy's footnote, at the appropriate place, reads, "First printed in the year 1653, but probably written some time before" (I.219)

15 April 1764: "I . . . have sent the Copy of the musical Notes [to the song on the battle of Agincourt], as you have corrected them, to

Summing Up 199

the Engraver" (70). The engraving is at the end of the volume II. See the letter of 9 September 1762, quoted above, page 195.

1 February 1766: "I am much obliged to you . . . for the Original Copy in Hentzner of Q. Elizabeth's Verses" (100). The verses are at II.127.

22 October 1766: Percy asked Farmer "to look into the Preface to *Torfaei Orcades, folio* (which you once procured me out of your Libraries)" for various information about the "Icelandic *Scalds*." He wrote that "This Passage [Icelandic as a *'Court Language'*] it is of great consequence to me to quote at large; will you therefore be so kind as procure me an Extract of it" (113–14). In note O of the expanded "Essay on the Ancient English Minstrels" Percy quotes a passage from Torfaeus, noting "Vid. plura apud Torfaeii Praefat. ad Orcad. Hist. fol." (I. lxiii).

In the same letter Percy asked Farmer to "consult all the old Historians" on the story of Baldolph, who, in the reign of King Arthur, disguised himself as a minstrel in order to reach his besieged brother. Among the historians he asked Farmer to check was "G. Monmouth" (116). Farmer wrote on the margin of the letter "G. Mon. L. 9. C.1." Percy retold the story in his Essay, stating that "the above fact comes only from the suspicious pen of Geoffrey of Monmouth," mistakingly citing "Lib. 7. c.1" (I.lvii).

13 December 1766: "You have sent me a curious Extract from Queen *Elizabeth's Progress at Elvetham.* . . . Pray can you lend me the above tract" (117–18). In the Additional Notes to volume III of the second edition (1767), Percy wrote, "The Splendour and Magnificence of Elizabeth's reign is no where more strongly painted than in the little Diaries of some of her summer excursions to the houses of her nobility; nor could a more acceptable present be given to the world, than a republication of a select number of such details as the entertainment at ELVETHAM, that at KILLINGWORTH, &c. &c." (357). This is shifted to a note on "Phillida and Corydon," to which it had been added at the end of volume III of the 1767 edition, in the third edition (III.644) preceded by a note to the effect that the song was in " 'The Honourable Entertainment given to the Queenes Majestie in Progresse at Elvetham in Hampshire, by R.M. the Earle of Hertford, 1591.' 4to [Printed by Wolfe. No name of author]" (III.63).

The 22 October 1766 letter was one of the longest from Percy to Farmer, that is, eleven pages in Percy's hand, full of questions of all kinds. On 13 December 1766, in the letter already quoted, he wrote to thank Farmer: "I received your kind Favour duly and thankfully: it is replete with erudition and contains many curious articles that will appear to great advantage in my new Edition of the *Reliques:* I am

200 Summing Up

new writing the Disertation on the Ancient Ministrels, in which I shall make great enlargements and improvements" (117). At least two of these enlargements and improvements were the result of Farmer's cooperation. How many others there were must remain in the realm of conjecture unless new evidence turns up.

While it is obvious that the extant correspondence between Percy and Farmer can only scratch the surface of the total help Farmer afforded Percy in the *Reliques*, it is revelatory of the exact nature of that help. One sees from the letters that Farmer collated four texts and provided the correct musical notes for the song "For the Victory at Agincourt." The musical notes were the subject of one engraving; Farmer provided for another from his copy of Gascoigne. Chaucer's "Rondeau," titled "An Original Ballad by Chaucer" in the *Reliques*, was unknown to Percy, although it was in manuscript in the Pepysian Library. Its presence in the work is, then, another example of Farmer's help. So, too, except that the poem was known to Percy, with the verses by Queen Elizabeth. Of the many questions Percy asked Farmer, there are exact answers to five. Finally there are the extracts from Torfaei and from Queen Elizabeth's *"Progress at Elvetham."* Where exactitude is possible, it should be sought.

Percy made specific acknowledgment of Farmer's help twice in the different editions of the *Reliques*. In the first and second editions, in the head-note to "The Nut-Browne Mayd," Percy referred to "Arnolde's Chronicle, a book supposed to be first printed about 1521," adding that there was an edition of that work "preserved at the public Library at Cambridge." In a footnote keyed to the reference to Cambridge, Percy stated, "This (which a learned friend supposes to be the first Edition) is in folio: the folios are numbered at the bottom of the leaf: the Song begins at folio 75" (1767, II.26). In the third edition, "a learned friend" is revised to "my friend Mr. Farmer" (II.27n.) And in the first edition, in the essay "On the Origin of the English Stage," in a note on the abuses of tobacco smokers, even possibly in churches, Percy was able to clinch the matter by the statement that "this was really the case at Cambridge: James I. sent a letter in 1607, against 'taking Tabacco' in St. Mary's. So I learn from my friend Mr. FARMER" (I.137n.)

Some eight months before his death Farmer wrote to Malone, on 31 January 1797, answering or trying to answer questions put to him by Malone for his next edition of Shakespeare, an edition he did not live to finish, the so-called Boswell–Malone edition of 1821. After a gloomy first sentence about his health, Farmer proceded,

Notwithstanding this *Invalid* state, I should have written to you sooner, had I not waited for somewhat to say about the *Picture*. The Society of

Pembroke waited the return of their Master from *Norwich*—he is just now come, & he tells me, that if they can make it fit their Chapel, they shall be glad of the Purchase, & will order a measurement immediately: they wish however to see the *Print* that you speak of. I have many of Braithwaite's pieces, but I do not remember to have seen his *Britaines-Bath:* there is little probability of finding it in our Libraries—however I am not able to *search* at present.———I employ'd a carefull Friend at S.ᵗ *John's* (Prof.ʳ *Fawcett*) to [ex]amine their Books for some years *before* [and] *after* 1600, & he informs Me "The following Article is the only one I find on your Subject & is dated 1585—for overplus of charges att the playes for inviting the Doctoures XLVI.ˢ" I suppose the Expense was borne by Individuals, in the *Inns of Court,* & therefore never came into the College-Books. I have just dipped here & there in Mʳ *Chalmers,* & can scarcely grasp what he would be at—or whether he be in *Jest* or *Ernest.* Surely he took up the question of the *Sonnets,* without reading them—the 20ᵗʰ for instance. I wonder he did not prove the Virility of *Eliza*—from her Title of Defend*er* of the Faith. I see he gives Emanuel the honour of *John Florio's* residence 3 years before its Foundation.

I am my Dear sir, your's affectionately
R. Farmer. (Ms. Montague, d. 13)

Joseph Turner was Master of Pembroke College from 1784 to 1822 and was Dean of Norwich; I find no reference to the print in question in Aubrey Attwater's history of Pembroke College, and I have not identified [Daniel?] Braithwaite's "Britaine-Bath." The reference to Chalmers is to George Chalmer's *An Apology for the Believers in the Shakspeare-Papers which were Exhibited in Norfolk Street,* with a publication date of 1797 but evidently available by the time Farmer wrote to Malone. On page 66 Chalmers writes, "I have now closed the proofs, which have convinced me, that the sonnets of Shakspeare were addressed by him to [Queen] Elizabeth," which prompted Farmer to invoke the twentieth sonnet. The sonnet begins, "A woman's face with Nature's own hand painted / Hast thou, the master mistress of my passion" and ends, with an obvious double meaning, "But since she prick'd thee out for woman's pleasure, / Mine be thy love, and thy love's use their treasure." Despite Famer's pessimistic prediction that he would not see London again and despite his confessed inability to search the Cambridge libraries, his mind was as agile, his knowledge as wide-ranging, and his memory as fresh as when he was a younger, healthier man. He was as willing as ever to assist in the endeavors of other scholars.

Notes

Where place of publication is Cambridge (England) or Oxford, the publisher is the respective university press, unless otherwise indicated.

Chapter 1. Early Years

1. Respectively, the Wager Books for 1791–96 and 1797–99, pp. 125, 217, and p. 45.

2. Wager Book, 1791–96, p. 2 and Wager Book, 1797–99, p. 2.

3. In vol. 8 of his *Bibliotheca Topographica Britannica*, 1790, p. 740n.

4. *Leicestershire,* IV.ii.939–40.

5. *Laurence Chaderton . . . Richard Farmer* (Cambridge, 1904), 47.

6. *Literary and Miscellaneous Memoirs,* 2 vols., 1826 (J. Nichols and Sons), I.29–30.

7. Emmanuel College, MS 321, fol. 16. Farmer also noted "Tanner's Notitia [Monastica]," pp. 346 and 382 on Sir William Fermer and Richard Fermer, the former of Norfolk, the latter of Northamptonshire, fol. 1.

8. *Memoirs,* IV.90.

9. III.i.(1800), 456.

10. *Leicestershire,* I.ii.314 and 314–15.

11. A. N. L. Munby and Lenore Coral, *British Book Sale Catalogues 1676–1800* (London, 1977), 77.

12. See *The Old Town Hall Library of Leicester,* by Cecil Deedes, *et al.* (Oxford, 1919), passim.

13. *Memoirs,* IV.94.

14. D. A. Winstanley, *Unreformed Cambridge. A Study of Certain Aspects of the University in the Eighteenth Century* (Cambridge, 1935), 186. Winstanley takes his figures from E. S. Shuckburgh, *Emmanuel College* (Cambridge, 1904), 140–141, which derive from Henry Hubbard's "Book of Accounts," Emmanuel College Archives (hereafter ECA) COL. 3.2.

15. *Lit. Anecd.,* II.619 and VIII.400, respectively,

16. ECA TUT. 63. fol. 3^r, fol. 4^r and Shuckburgh, *Emmanuel College,* p. 147 where the Easter audit of 1734 to 1735 gives the dividend of "Whichcot & Sudbury to Michs. last" as 17s.11d.

17. Shuckburgh, *Emmanuel College,* p. 132.

18. Information from Emmanuel College Order Book, 1738–1839 and Parlour Book, 1769–85, passim.

19. Henry Gunning, *Ceremonies observed in the Senate House of the University of Cambridge* (Cambridge, 1838), 3 and 10.

20. Winstanley, *Unreformed Cambridge,* 73.

21. Farmer's career as librarian is described in detail by David McKitterick in

Notes   203

Cambridge University Library, the Eighteenth and Nineteenth Centuries (Cambridge, 1986), 293–351. See pp. 326–36 for the Askew sale.

22. In Emmanuel MS. 280.

23. *Diaries*, pp. 134, 135, 140, 144.

24. *European Magazine*, 37 (1800), 116.

25. The Michigan State University copy of the *Literary Anecdotes* has a manuscript note at the bottom of II.637: "She [Miss Hatton] afterwards married Hale Wortham, Esq. of Royston." The *GM* records the death of Hale Wortham, attorney of Royston, on 18 August 1793.

26. *Diaries*, pp. 119, 150, 155, respectively.

27. ECA FEL. 9.1 p. 268.

28. See p. 53, for more on Tweddell.

29. *Lit. Anecd.*, II.643–45; for Dyer, pp. 403–4.

30. Worth noting in the sale catalog is item 8171, "twenty-two Views of St. Paul's and other Cathedrals."

31. *Carmina ad Nobilissimum Thomam Holles Duces de Newcastle inscripta, cum Academiam Cantabrigiensem Bibliothecae restituendae Causa inviseret prid. kalend. Maias*, MDCCLV.

32. *History of the University and Colleges of Cambridge* (Cambridge, 1814), II.390 and *Privileges of the University of Cambridge* (Cambridge, 1824), II. 101. Dyer had the poem reprinted in the *Monthly Magazine and British Register*, vol. 17 (1804, p. 38), but the text is inaccurate in a few places.

33. Lines 15–22 in S.C. Roberts, *Richard Farmer* (Cambridge University Library) p. 261. See McKitterick, pp. 255–62 for a detailed account of the whole affair.

34. Cradock, *Memoirs*, IV.90.

35. As a young man, Farmer's toast was to a Miss Benskin. See p. 19.

36. The others were R. Richardson, B.A.; Thomas Hesilrige; Thomas Troughton Lydiatt, Alumnus; John Law, B.A.; and B. N. Turner, Scholar.

Chapter 2. Master of Emmanuel College

1. Paget Toynbee and Leonard Whibley, eds. *Correspondence of Thomas Gray*, 3 vols., continuously paged (Oxford, 1935), 1119–20, n.1.

2. In William Seward, *Biographiana*, 2 vols., continuously paged (1799) (J. Johnson), 580.

3. *Bodleian Quarterly Record*, VI., no. 72 (1931), 304, 306.

4. Bertrand Bronson, *Joseph Ritson: Scholar at Arms*, 2 vols., continuously paged (Berkeley, 1938), 393.

5. Two vols., 1834, I. 64.

6. Emmanuel MS. FEL. 9.1 and 2.

7. Pp. 13, 36. it was not until 9 October 1784 that the wagers were given dates; references are to page numbers.

8. Respectively, pp. 42, 46, 82, 136, 148, 236, and 264.

9. Letters 51 and 53 of Folger C.b.10 refer to this "annual convivial dinner."

10. P. 304; vol. 2, pp. 55, 247.

11. *Diaries*, pp. 121, 135 and 137, 155 and 169, and 163, respectively.

12. Pp. 209–10. For Coleridge's poem, see E. H. Coleridge, ed. *Complete Poetical Works*, (Oxford, 1912), I.69.

13. For Sharpe, see p. 29.

14. See S. C. Roberts, *The Family: The History of a dining club* (Cambridge,

Notes

1963), printed for the Club, for further on these Friday meetings. See also Henry Maas, ed., *The Letters of A. E. Housman,* (Cambridge, Mass., 1971), 391 and the facsimile of a letter from Housman to Roberts between pp. 202 and 203—both to do with The Family.

15. Folger MS. S.a.138; the rest is cropped.

16. Emmanuel MSS. 280A.

17. ECA COL. 14.2 See also E.G.S., "A Vicar of Stanground, *Emmanuel College Magazine,* XVIII (1907–8), 120–132.

18. Charles Henry Cooper, *Annals of Cambridge,* 5 vols. (Cambridge, 1848–1902), IV.444–45.

19. *Reminiscences of the University, Town, and County of Cambridge,* 2 vols. (Cambridge, 1855), I.232–34.

20. Gunning, *Reminiscences,* I.163 gives "Taffy" as the name of Farmer's horse.

21. Folger MS M.a.138 fol. 11.^{v}

22. The epitaph, a long and curious one, can be read in Cooper's *Annals,* IV.336–39.

23. Unfortunately the parish registers stop at 1729 and then skip to the nineteenth century.

24. John Willis Clark, *Endowments of the University of Cambridge* (Cambrige, 1904), 46.

25. University Archives, Ely Diocesan Register, H3, Swavesy, pre–1812, fol. 120–123.

26. "Affability" mistakenly becomes "assiduity" in Nichols's *Leicestershire,* IV.943.

27. COL. 19.4, unpaged.

28. Gunning, *Reminiscences,* II.5–6.

29. *Unreformed Cambridge,* pp. 24–25.

30. See Emmanuel Wager Book, 1769–85, p. 49 for Farmer as Conservator of the Cam, and Cambridge University Archives, Grace Book, 1772–1809, p. 236 for the Navigation Bill.

Chapter 3. Later Academic Career

1. University Archives, V.C.V. 23 (3), passim.

2. V.C. Ct. I.108 (1-39).

3. V.C. Ct. I.107 (1–60).

4. V.C. Ct. I.108 (16–17).

5. See V.C. Ct. I. 110 (18) under 21 October 1778 for the sentencing; also *DNB, Sub* Ewin, and Winstanley, *Unreformed Cambridge,* pp. 343–47 for a full discussion of the Vice-Chancellor's Court.

6. Gunning, *Ceremonies,* pp. 118 and 129–30, respectively.

7. *Reminiscences,* I.151.

8. *Reminiscences,* I.158. For a colorful account of the Fair in late sixteenth century, see Cooper, *Annals,* IV.318–22.

9. See Cooper, *Annals,* IV.425 for the occasion upon which the Duke of Gloucester and his son dined at Emmanuel with Farmer.

10. The address is reprinted in Cooper, *Annals,* IV.380–81.

11. *Restituta; or Titles, Extracts, and Characters of Old Books in English Literature Revived,* 4 vols. (London: Longman, Hurst, Ress, Orme and Brown, 1811–16), IV.233.

12. *Restituta,* IV.233 and Cooper, *Annals,* V.510–11.

Notes 205

13. Cleanth Brooks, ed., *The Percy Letters,* vol. 2 (1946) (Lousiana State University Press), vi, perpetuates the sledgehammer: "Farmer was capable of breaking down a door [*sic*] with a sledge hammer."

14. *Laurence Chaderton,* p. 160. He repeated this verbatim in his history of Emmanuel College, 1904, p. 160.

15. *Richard Farmer,* 1961, p. 10.

16. There is no voucher for repairs to the common chest in the University archives.

17. John Disney, ed., *The Works . . . of John Jebb,* 3 vols. (London: T. Cadell 1787), I.62 and 63–64.

18. Grace Book, Δ, 207; the wording in Cooper, *Annals,* IV.426 is somewhat different.

19. Grace Book, Δ, 208.

20. Cooper, *Annals,* IV.429 and n.6.

21. Quoted in *Lit. Anecd.,* II.643.

22. Grace Book, Δ, 207.

23. See Christopher Wordsworth, *Scholae Academicae: or University Studies in the Eighteenth Century* (Cambridge, 1877), 390.

24. See chap. I, n. 21.

25. Wordsworth, *Scholae Academicae,* pp. 57, 58.

26. *Memoirs of the Life and Writings of Robert Robinson* (London: G. G. and J. Robinson, 1796), p. 317.

27. Gunning, *Reminiscences,* I.271.

28. McKitterick, *Cambridge University Library,* p. 290.

29. Charles Sayle, *Annals of the Cambridge University Library* (Cambridge, 1916), 104.

30. McKitterick, *Cambridge University Library,* pp. 297–301.

31. Emmanuel College Order Book, 1769–85, pp. 236, 264.

32. Christopher Wordsworth, *Social Life at the English Universities in the Eighteenth Century* (Cambridge, 1874) states that "Dr Farmer's silver *tobacco pipe* is still preserved in Emmanuel College" (p. 662).

33. John Arbuthnot, *An Essay Concerning the Nature of Aliments . . . The Third Edition to which are added, Practical Rules of Diet. . .* (1735) (J. Tonson), pp. 402–3.

34. Cambridge University Library MS. 7113, no. 52.

35. See p. 188.

36. *Lit. Illustr.,* VII.14, 17, 19, 21, 45, respectively.

37. *Lit. Illust.,* VII.23, 45, 46, 25, respectively. Arbuthnot (see note 33), recommended a milk diet for sufferers from gout.

Chapter 4. The Abortive History of Leicester

1. II.621; the conditions of the Proposals are in a footnote, pp. 621–22.

2. John Nichols, *The History and Antiquities of the County of Leicestershire,* 4 vols. in 8 parts (1798–1815) (Nichols, Son, and Bentley), III.i.vi. Thomas Staveley was the author of *The Romish Horseleech . . .* and for a time Justice of the Peace for Leicester.

3. Cradock, *Memoirs,* IV.95–96.

4. Emmanuel College MS. 321.

5. Reprinted in *Notes and Queries,* 4th Series (16 January 1869), 53.

6. *Leicestershire* I.i.5.* n.7.

7. Quoted in *Lit. Illustr.,* IV.738.

Notes

8. *Leicestershire,* I.i.6.

9. F. G. Stokes, ed., *The Bletchley Diary of the Rev. William Cole, M.A. F.S.A. 1765–67,* 1931 (Constable and Co.), pp. 203–4.

10. *Annual Necrology,* 1797/98, p. 396.

11. Quoted by Nichols in *Lit. Anecd.,* II.641, hence tacitly approved.

12. Respectively, *Lit. Anecd.,* VIII.570, 575, 579.

13. See p. 120.

14. *Lit. Anecd.,* I.668n.; see also I.665 for other help Farmer rendered Nichols.

15. Pp. cxlvii–cxlix, not p. clxvii as in *Lit. Illustr.,* VI.437.

16. Nichols, *Bibliotheca Topographica Britannica,* VII.513*–514*. For Farmer's attendance, see Cole's letter to Gough, "St. Michael's, 1774" in J. P. Malcolm ed., *Letters Between the Rev. James Granger . . . and Many of the Most Eminent Literary Men of his Time,* (London: Longman, Hurst, Rees, Orme, and Brown, 1805), p. 366.

17. *Lit. Anecd.,* II. 631; the sermon, if written, is no longer extant.

Chapter 5. The Essay on the Learning of Shakespeare

1. R. W. Chapman, ed., *The Letters of Samuel Johnson,* 3 vols. (Oxford, 1952) I.233–34.

2. Chapman, *Letters,* I.249.

3. William Shakespere's *"Small Latine and Lesse Greek,"* 2 vols. (Urbana: University of Illinois Press, 1944); hereafter Baldwin. See also D. N. Smith, ed., *Eighteenth Century Essays on Shakespeare,* 2d ed. (Oxford, 1963), xxii–xxvii; hereafter Smith.

4. *Memoirs,* IV.95.

5. Bodleian Library Malone 143 [7].

6. Bodleian MS. Ashmole 1822, ff. 189–90.

7. David M. Little and George M. Kahrl, eds., *The Letters of David Garrick,* 3 vols. continuously paged (Cambridge, Mass.: Harvard University Press, 1963), 553, 633, 666, and 1063.

8. Bodleian Ashmole MS. 1822, ff. 198–99.

9. *Diaries,* p. 96; two other references to Colman in the index to the *Diaries* are actually to Dr. Colman, Master of Corpus Christi College, Cambridge.

10. An edition of the *Essay* was "Printed and sold by J. J. Tourneisen" in Basel in 1800. Colman's Appendix to his translation of Terence follows the *Essay,* and the reader is directed to Farmer's reply to Colman's suggestion about "thrasonical."

11. P. 2 on Ben Jonson; p. 24, on Boccaccio; p. 34, on Sir. C.H.W.; pp. 71–72, on Spenser; pp. 84–86, on Shakespeare editions; p. 38, on Francis Meres; and pp. 91–92, on Richard Burbage. These references are to the page numbers of the second edition and are the same in the third edition.

12. See Smith, pp. 327–28 for this last note.

13. *Letters,* II.121–28. However, the statement that "Percy was largely responsible for the addition of the notes to the second edition" (p. 121, n.4) is a considerable overstatement.

14. *Letters,* II.121–25 passim.

15. Third ed., 1775, I.xv and n.

Notes

207

16. See L. J. Lloyd, "Dr. Richard Farmer, 1735–97," *Book Collector,* 26 (1977), 524–36 for a description of many of the "*curious* and scarce Books."

17. ECA LIB 7 1. and 2.

18. Pp. 13–18, 160–64 and an added parallel for "haver" from John Davies (19, 164).

19. Pp. 48–51, 180–81 and the parallel from *Piers Plowman* for swearing on the sword (51, 181).

20. Pp. 52–56, 182–85, with further discussion of *Macbeth,* ending with the Latin quotation on 56 and 185.

21. Pp. 85–86, 198 and 87–88, 198–99.

22. Pp. 66–69 and 189–90.

23. P. 39 in the *Essay;* compare 1765, VII.[406] with 1773, IX.[4].

24. Benjamin Domville (formerly Barrington) was admitted a pensioner at Emmanuel on 8 January 1772. He became Doctor of Divinity (Dublin) and subsequently changed his name to Domville.

25. There is no index entry for Shakespeare's "books" or "library" in Samuel Schoenbaum's *Shakespeare's Lives* (1970) (Oxford University Press), for example.

26. Elizabeth Cooper, *The Muses Library* (1741) and *The Lives of the Poets . . . ,* 5 vols. (1753), nominally edited by Theophilus Cibber.

27. Numbers 7906–9.

Chapter 6. A Letter . . . to Mr. Steevens

1. Quoted in the New Variorum edition (p. 202), but without the parallel from Fairfax.

2. I have numbered the pages rather than giving references to the unwieldy signatures. This continues for the remaining chapters.

3. P. 4; see also pp. 24, 31, 33 for more on Capell.

4. Pp. 21, 24, 25, and 3, respectively.

5. Pp. 24, 25; the note on *Macbeth* is quoted in the New Variorum edition as is the passage in the *Essay.*

6. London and New York, 1973, VII.520.

7. *Narrative and Dramatic Sources,* III.92.

8. See, however, the following notes which are either first or the only notes cited or quoted in the New Variorum editions. The first page number is to the appendix: p. 2, on "long heath, brown furze" in *The Tempest* (pp. 20–21); p. 10, first to catch the allusion to *A Penniworth of Wit* in *Love's Labour's Lost* (p. 87); p. 11, the only note on "guards on wanton Cupid's hose" in the same play (p. 166); p. 15, first to correct Theobald's emendation of "sometimes" to "sometime" in *The Merchant of Venice* (p. 20); p. 21 on "that may blow" in *The Winter's Tale* (p. 10); p. 22 on "trol-my-dames" in the same play (p. 175); p. 36, on "barber-monger" in *King Lear* (pp. 117–18); p. 37, first to see the pun in "They stand so much on the new form, that they cannot sit at ease on the old bench" in *Romeo and Juliet* (p. 123); p. 38, first to suspect a "quibble" in Hamlet's "I am too much i' the sun" (p. 34); p. 39, first to correct Warner's emendation in Ophelia's "The courtier's, soldiers, scholar's, eye, tongue, sword" (p. 221); p. 40, on "for mine ease" in the same play (pp. 426–27).

9. P. 3; the idea is not bruited in M. M. Mahood, *Shakespeare's Wordplay* (London; Methuen, 1957).

10. For Theobald's note, see the 1773 *Shakespeare* (Modern Language Association of America), I.119.2.

208 Notes

Chapter 7. Further Notes on Shakespeare

1. See James M. Osborn, "Edmond Malone: Scholar-Collector," *The Library*, 5th Series, vol. 19 (1964), p. 12.

2. See immediately below, the letter from Malone to Charlemont.

3. Vol. I, part 1, p. 282.

4. "The Manuscripts and Correspondence of James, First Earl of Charlemont," vol. I. 1745–83, *Historical Manuscripts Commission*, Twelfth Report, Appendix, Part X, 373; hereafter "Charlemont MSS."

5. *GM* (November 1841), p. 495.

6. Edmund Bolton's *Hypercritica* is appended to Arthur Hall's ed. of Nicholas Trivet's *Annales sex regnum Angliae* . . . (1719).

7. Original in the James Marshall and Marie-Louise Osborn Collection, Yale University.

8. Quoted in the New Variorum ed. (p. 414), with the objections of later editors.

9. P. 21; see also p. 14 for one of Farmer's emendations. Two others are at I.414.1 and 565.3.

10. Editor, *Shakespeare's Sonnets* (Philadelphia, 1944), II.334–35.

11. See p. 143 and n. 5 above.

12. See Pope's *Windsor Forest*, 11.70–72, for one example of such desecration.

13. See also VIII.391.5, a pun on "honour" which is corroborated by Malone in 1790.

14. See p. 147. The note can be read in the New Variorum *2 Henry IV* (pp. 404–5).

15. Bronson, p. 180; p. 800 puts the year date of the letter at *circa* 1792. See *Diaries*, pp. 181 and 192–96 for Steevens's visits. He may have visited in 1791, but Reed was ill and there is no record of a visit in his diary.

16. 1794; I quote from the 1797 "New Edition Revised and Corrected with Many Additions."

17. Part 1, p. 39; see also pp. 33, 37–39.

18. Quoted in the *DNB*, *sub* Mathias.

19. Walter Whiter, author of *A Specimen of a Commentary on Shakespeare* (1794), of Clare Hall, an acquaintance of Farmer and Steevens, wrote, soon after Farmer's death,

> Death takes the good, too good on earth to stay,
> And leaves the bad, too bad to take away.
> Commentary
> And thus this confounder of odds and evens,
> Has taken poor Farmer & left us George Steevens.

20. IV.21.1, 46.4; V.383.1; XI.204.1, 239.6; XVIII.200.3; XIX.52.8 (Warburton had anticipated him); XX.112.3 (actually a folio reading).

21. No such proverb is listed in Morris Palmer Tilley, *A Dictionary of the Proverbs of England in the Sixteen and Seventeenth Centuries* (Ann Arbor, Mich.: University of Michigan Press) 1950. *Time's Whistle* is not listed in Alfred Harbage, *Annals of the English Drama*, revised by Samuel Schoenbaum (Philadelphia, 1964).

22. The note is on V.293.1 of *1 Henry IV* in his *Letter* to George Steevens (p. 27).

23. See Samuel Schoenbaum, *Shakespeare's Lives* (Oxford, 1970), pp. 189–233 for a full account.

24. K.S. had more to say on the subject in the January 1796 *GM*, pp. 7–8.

Notes

209

Chapter 8. Summing Up

1. *Richard Farmer,* p. 6.

2. Pp. 109, 119, 121, 133, respectively.

3. R. W. Chapman, ed., *Letters of Samuel Johnson,* 3 vols. (Oxford, 1952), letters 530, 673, 764.

4. *Transactions of the Cambridge Bibliographical Society,* VI (1973), 129–30. Dr. Stubbings gives a condensed version of Turner's account in the *Emmanuel College Magazine,* XLVIII (1965–66), 64–71.

5. Folger MS. M.A. 138, fol. 10ᵛ and fol. 17ʳ.

6. Quoted in Boswell's *Life,* I.554.

7. See Allen T. Hazen, *Samuel Johnson's Prefaces & Dedications* (New Haven and London: Yale University Press, 1937), pp. 158–68 for a full account; pp. 161–62 for the cancelled page.

8. *European Magazine* (March 1785) p. 191. See O. M. Brack, Jr. and Robert E. Kelley, ed., *The Early Biographies of Samuel Johnson* (Iowa City: University of Iowa Press, 1974), 301–2 for discussion of the authorship of the account. The rival candidate is George Steevens.

9. Marshall Waingrow, ed., *The Correspondence and Other Papers of James Boswell Relating to the Making of the "Life of Johnson"* (New York: McGraw-Hill, n.d. [1969]), 512–14.

10. "The Anonymous Letter Proposing Johnson's Pension," in *Transactions of the Lichfield Johnson Society,* December 1981, pp. 35–39. See also my *Birth of Shakespeare Studies, Commentators from Rowe (1709) to Boswell-Malone (1812)* (East Lansing, 1986), 168–69 for more on Blakeway.

11. Emmanuel MS. Lib. 7.2, p. 57.

12. The reader may wish to read the entire letter in Waingrow. See n. 9.

13. William Ingram was Esquire Bedell from 1592 to about 1605.

14. I.xlvi in the 1823 ed.

15. Farmer's connection with the letter goes unnoticed in G. B. Hill's edition of the *Lives* and in George Sherburn's edition of Pope's correspondence.

16. *Diaries,* pp. 138, 158, 174, 175–75; *Private Papers of James Boswell . . . ,* ed. G. Scott and F. A. Pottle (New York; Mount Vernon, privately published, 1928–34), XVII.85; XVIII.117, 264.

17. *Letters of Samuel Johnson,* I.140; Chapman expresses some doubts about the text of the letter.

18. J. P. Malcolm, ed., *Letters Between the Rev. Mr. James Granger . . . and Many of the Most Eminent Literary Men of his Time* (London, 1805), 33, 37.

19. *Lit. Anecd.,* VIII.633; see also VIII.572, 573.

20. Original in the James Marshall and Marie-Louise Osborn Collection, Yale University.

21. The definitive ed. of *Hudibras,* ed. by John Wilder for the Clarendon Press of Oxford (1967) lists five references to Nash and an *et passim* in the index. Neither Reed's nor Farmer's name appears therein. Reed's copy of Nash's ed. is item 6700 in the sale catalog of his library.

22. *Bodleian Quarterly Record,* VI. No. 72 (1931), 304; *Lit. Illustr.,* IV.738, partially quoted on p. 38; and *Bodleian Quarterly Record,* p. 306.

23. Richard Mant, ed., *The Poetical Works of Thomas Warton,* 2 vols. (Oxford, 1802), I.xlv.

24. *The British Museum Catalogue of Printed Books* lists one French translation only: "La Theseyde, contenant les amours des deux cheualiers Thebains Arcite et

210   Notes

Palemon, traduicte . . . par le Sieur D.C.C. . . . *Paris,* 1597, 12º." Warton describes the French translation as by "D.C.C. 1597. 11mo. Paris," but both his and Farmer's title differ from that in the BM Catalogue. Did Farmer have a different version? I find no such title in the sale catalog of his library.

25. I.4, notes k and i, respectively.

26. British Library, Add MS. 42561, ff. 123–24.

27. *Letters,* II.v. Subsequent page references in parentheses are to this volume.

28. Yeatman is Charles Yeatmen who became a Fellow of Emmanuel in 1748. He survived the influenza of 1762, dying in 1770. The "Thaxted gang" remains a mystery.

29. Horace, *Art of Poetry,* 7–8.

30. Folger PN/2598/G3/F5/Copy 4./Ex. Ill./vol. XV, p. 390.

31. *Letters,* VIII (1985), p. 50.

32. W. A. Craigie, ed., *The Maitland Folio Manuscript* (Edinburgh and London: W. Blackwood and Sons), Vol. II (1927), pp. 2 and 25.

33. *Restituta . . . ,* 4 vols. (London 1814–16), IV.244. Professor Bertram Davis informs me that Percy succeeded William Beresford who had been translated to the bishopric of Ossory. John Garnet, who died in 1782, was Bishop of Ferns and Leighlin. Read "Ekins" for "Elkins."

34. *Lit. Illustr.,* VII.35, and Bodleian MS. Percy c. 1, f. 184.

35. Rodney M. Baine, "Percy's Own Copy of the *Reliques,*" *Harvard Library Bulletin,* V (1951): 247. My page references are to the third ed. of the *Reliques,* unless otherwise stated.

36. The notes on Corbet's poem are at II.356; that on "Rebellion hath Broken up House" is at II.340.

37. Bertram H. Davis, *Thomas Percy* (Boston, 1981), p. 90.

Index

I practiced certain economies in the index to *The Birth of Shakespeare Studies: Commentators from Rowe (1709) to Boswell-Malone* (1821) (1986) and in that to *The Achievement of George Steevens* (1990), economies which I here continue.

The abbreviations for Shakespeare's plays and poems are those given in the *Shakespeare Quarterly* Bibliography, volume 6, number 6 (1985), pp. 691–92. A number of entries for the plays are for pages where the titles are not named but easily recognizable characters are. Articles in the titles of works indexed are omitted; many titles are abbreviated without benefit of ellipses, but are still identifiable by author and/or first words of those titles. Names of works abbreviated in quotations in the text are expanded in the index; i.e. Camden's *Remains* is expanded to *Remains of a Larger Work Concerning England*. Long titles in the text are abbreviated in the index. Farmer's *Essay on the Learning of Shakespeare* appears as *Essay*. Entries for Farmer and for Shakespeare are solely for their works. References to colleges are to Cambridge University, unless otherwise indicated. Some names are abbreviated: Chas., Geo., Robt., Thos., Wm., RF is Richard Farmer, S is Shakespeare. Easily expandable abbreviations are used in titles and in some other entries: *Hist., Wks., Eng.* (England or English), ed. [its], adm. [itted]. Place names are not indexed, nor are the notes.

Account of the Festivation, 49
Adams, John, *Index Villaris,* 110
"Agincourt, For the Victory at" (song), 195, 198, 200
Albe, Hammond (of Emmanuel), 77
"Alexander, Life of," i.e. the pseudo-Callisthenes *Life of Alexander of Macedon,* 187
Alfred (king of England), 188
Allenson, Edward (vicar of Swavezy), 57
Allot, Robt., *England's Parnassus,* 144
"Alphabetic List," 176
Alumni Cantabrigienses, 20
Ames, Joseph, *Typographical Antiquities,* 180, 187
Amyot, Jacques, *Vies des Hommes Illustres Grecs et Romains,* 114
Anacreon, 107, 113, 117
Anderson, Robt. (friend of Percy), 173
Andreas, Elias (trans. Anacreon), 117
Andrewes, Gerrard (RF's teacher), 18, 19, 20, 34
Andrews, James Petit, *Anecdotes,* 22
Annales d'Acquytayne, 108

Applethwaite (of Pembroke), 63
Arabian Tales, 108
Arbuthnot, Dr. John, 78, 153
Ariosto, *Orlando Furioso,* 108
Aristophanes, 22, 112
Arnolde, Richard, "Chronicle," 200
Ascham, Roger, *Toxophilus,* 108
Ash, Francis (his scholarship), 21
Ash, Dr. John (physician), 46
Ashby, Geo., *Essay on the Roman Military,* 87.
Askew, Mrs. (wife of Dr. Anthony Askew), 123
Askew, Dr. Anthony (RF's bibliographic friend), 23, 24, 42, 76, 85, 123, 185
Askew, John (of Emmanuel), 15, 48–49, 77
Astle, Thos. (antiquary), 86, 165, 193, 195, 196
Athenae Cantabrigienses, RF contemplates, 176
Aubrey, Atwater, *Hist. of Pembroke College,* 201
Aubrey, John, *Brief Lives,* 110

212 Index

Ausonius, 126
Ayscough, Samuel (of the British Museum), 165

Bacon, Lord Edmund, 49
Bacon, Sir Francis, 188; *Essays,* 132
Bacon, Montague, "Notes on *Hudibras,*" 181
Bagford, John (bookseller), 76
Baker, Sir Geo. (club member), 46
Baker, John (master of Christ's), 49
Baker, Thos. (antiquary of St. John's), 87, 103, 118, 171, 187; MSS of, 108; trans. "M.S. Hist. of St. Margaret's West," 196
Baldwin, Henry (publisher), 89
Baldwin, T. W., 96, 97
Bale, John, *Illustrium Maioris Britanniae Sciptorum,* 185, 192
Banks, Lady (Sir Joseph's wife) 45
Banks, Sir Joseph, 45, 76
Banks, Miss Sophia, 45
Banks, Thos. ("statuary"), 29
Barclay, Alexander, 108; *Ship of Fools,* 151, 155–56
Barnardiston, John (university librarian), 23
Barnes, Francis, 47, 79, 82–83
Barnes, Joshua, 184; ed. Homer, 183
Barnes, Juliana, *Gentleman's Academy,* 124
Barrett, Wm., *Hist. and Antiquities of Bristol,* 170
Barrington, Daines, his MSS, 191
Bassi, Andrea (Italian scholar), 104, 184
Bateman, Stephen, *Golden Book,* 108
Baudart, Wm. ("Baudasius"), 34
Baynes, John (friend of Reed), 45
Beadon, Richard (master of Jesus), 49
Beardmore, Dr. (club member), 46
Beattie, Dr. James, 192
Beaumont, Francis, and John Fletcher, *Maid's Tragedy,* 133, 139
Becket, Thos. (bookseller), 43
"Becket, Thos. a," song of, 195–96
Beecroft, John (bookseller), 90
Beehive of the Romish Church, 125
Bendish, Robt. (?) (friend of Dawes), 43
Bennet, Wm. (bp. of Cloyne), 25, 59, 74, 179, 195
Benskin, Miss (RF's "toast"), 19, 27, 29, 203

Benskin, Thos. (Miss Benskin's father), 19
Benson (of Emmanuel), 42
Bentley, Richard, ed. Milton, 108
Berridge, John (preacher), 57
Bethune, Maximilian de, Duke of Sully, 130
Betterton, Thos. (actor), 133
Beverly, John (Bedell), 44
Bible, *Ecclesiastes,* 193; *Proverbs,* 34; *Psalms,* 106, 153; *Zechariah,* 198
Bickerstaffe, Isaac; *Hypocrite,* 30
Bickerstaffe, Wm. (curate of St. Mary's), 19, 92–93
Birch, Thos. (historian), 178, 179
Bird, Wm. (of Trinity), 64
Blackall, Samuel (university proctor), 22, 42
Blagden, Dr. Chas., 45
Blakeway, Edward (of Magdalene), 174–75, 187–88
Boaden, James, *Letter to Geo. Steevens,* 165
Boccaccio, 105; *Teseida,* 104, 183, 184–85
Bolton, Edmond, *Hypocritica,* 143
Bond, Thos. (alderman of Camb.), 71
Book of Songs and Sonnets ("Tottel's Miscellany"), 118
Booth, Barton (actor), 133
Boswell, James, the younger, 45
Boswell James, the elder, 45, 46, 143, 144, 148, 171–78 *passim; Life of Johnson,* 173, 174, 177
Bowle, John (Hispanist), 147
Bowyer, Wm. (printer), 91
Boydell, Alderman John, 45
Boydell, John, Jr., 45
Braithwaite, Daniel (of the Post Office), 45, 46
Breton, Nicholas, *Toyes,* 159
Brokesby, Francis, *Life of Henry Dodwell,* 129–30
Brome, Richard, 164
Brooke, Arthur, *Tragic Hist.,* 132
Brooke, Zachary, *Defensio,* 23
Brooks, Cleanth, 104, 195
Broome, Wm., 171, 177
Brown, Dr. John, *Honour,* 188
Brownlow, Earl of, 49, 50
Brydges, Sir Samuel Egerton, 67; *Autobiography,* 39; *Restituta,* 193

Buchanan, Geo., 99–100, 107
Buckingham, second Duke of, 196; *Rehearsal,* a key to, 188, 190
Budgell, Eustace, 28
Bull, Geo. (bp. of St. David's), 28
Bullokar, John, *English Expositor,* 162
Bullough, Geoffrey, *Sources,* 131, 135, 145
Bulstrode, Sir Whitelocke, *Memorials of the English Affairs,* 197
Bunbury, Chas. John (rusticated), 63
Burbage, Richard, 125
Burgoyne, John, *Maid of the Oaks,* 43
Burleigh, first Baron Balfour of ("Lord Burghley"), 199
Burney, Chas., the younger, 75
Burney, Chas., the elder, 45, 46, 76
Burroughs, Sir James (master of Gonville and Caius), 189
Burton, Wm., *Description of Leicestershire,* 85, 89
Busche, Alexandre von den, called "le Sylvain," *The orator. See* Silvayn, Alexander
Bute, third Earl of, 174, 175
Bute, fourth Earl of, 174
Butler, Mrs. (wife of Samuel), 182
Butler, Jacob (his extraordinary epitaph), 56
Butler, Samuel, 145, 181–82; *Hudibras,* 112, 181–82,197; *Remains,* 182

C., R., *Time's Whistle,* 161, 162
Caddell, Walter (physician), 72–73
Caius, Dr. John (physician), 125
Caleb Shillocke, 148
Cambridge Chronicle, 50
Camden, Wm., *Remains of a Greater Work Concerning England,* 20
Capell, Edward, 59, 78–79, 102, 111, 121, 146, 160; *Prolusions,* 108, 113, 116, 117, 127
Carte, Mr. (vicar of St. Mary's), 84
Carte, Samuel (lawyer), 18
Carte, Thos., *General Hist., of England,* 188
Carter, Edmund, *History,* 55
Casaubon, Isaac, 184; *Lectiones Theocriticae,* 183
Castilio, Count Baldessar, *The Courtier,* 132

Cave, Sir Thos. (antiquary), 84–85
Cervantes, Miguel de, *Don Quixote,* 108, 163
Chafin, Wm. (of Emmanuel), 21
Chalmers, Alexander, 165
Chalmers, Geo., *Apology,* 201
Chapman, Geo., *Revenge for Honour,* 163
Chapman, R. W., 178
Charlemont, first Earl of, 141, 144
Charles I (king of England), 123
Charles II (king of England), 190
Charles, Marquis D'Albert and Duc de Luynes, 136
Charles the Bold, Duke of Burgundy, 33
Charlotte Sophia (queen of England), 24
Chase, Lord Richard, 49
Chatterton, Sara (the poet's mother), 58
Chatterton, Thos., 28, 169–70
Chaucer, Geoffrey, 121, 137; *Knight's Tale,* 183, 184; *Rondeau,* 196, 200
Chettle, H., *Robert Earl of Huntington* A. Munday, co-author), 117
Chevalier, John (of St. John's), 37
Churchyard, Thos., 108; *A Praise of the Bow,* 183; *General Rehearsal of Wars* ("Churchyard's Choise"), 162
Cibber, Theophilus ("biographer"), 118
Cicero, *de Officiis,* 22, 107, 115; *Rhetorica ad Herrenium* (attributed to), 147
Claudian, 126
Clayton, Giles, *Martial Discipline,* 129
Cleaver, John Banks (rescues a prostitute), 63
Clifford, Martin (master of Charter House), 186
Cockayne, Wm. (of Emmanuel), 49
Cole, Wm., 23–28 *passim,* 37, 38, 41, 48, 59, 67,68, 75–78 *passim,* 187, 190, 191, 193
Coleridge, Samuel Taylor, *Fall of Robespierre,* 44
Collier, John Payne (S editor), 160
Collignon, Dr. Charles (anecdote of Sterne), 43
Collins, Wm. (poet), 125, 185
Colman, Geo., the elder, 98, 101, 102, 105, 143, 164; *Clandestine Marriage* (with Garrick), 43; *Prose on Several Occasions,* 101; (trans. Terence), 100, 101

Index

Colman, Wm. (of Emmanuel), 26, 28, 45
Constable, Henry, 143, 144
Cooke, Dr. Wm. (provost of King's), 49
Cooper, Chas. Henry, *Annals,* 70
Cooper, Elizabeth (anthologist), 118
Cooper, John Gilbert, 20
Copley, Anthony (poet), 108
Corbet, Richard (bp. of Oxford), 197
Coronation of Edward the Sixth, 127
Cotton, Sir John, 41, 49
Courtenay, John (friend of Reed), 148
Cowley, Abraham, *Oliver Cromwell,* 150
Cradock, Joseph, *Memoirs,* 17, 18, 20, 22, 38, 84, 85, 92–99 *passim,* 105, 112, 194
Crashaw, Richard, *Epigrammatum,* 75
Creech, Thos. (trans. Theocritus), 184
Critical Review, 97, 98, 99

D., G. (poet), 183
Daborne, Robt., *Poor Man's Comfort* (?), 130
Dalrymple, Sir David, Lord Hailes, 182, 195
Daniel, Samuel, 108; *Civil Wars,* 168
Darker, Jonathan (MP for Leicester), 88
Davenant, Sir Wm., 153, 164
Davies, Sir John, 132
Davies, Thos. (bookseller), 121, 178–79; *Dramatic Miscellanies,* 121
Davis, Bertram H., 174
Davison, Francis (poet), 130
Dawes, Francis (senior Bedell), 43–44, 152
Dayrell, Marmaduke (expelled), 63
Dee, Dr. John (astrologer), 139
Dekker, Thos., 164; *Satiro-Mastix,* 110
Del Novelliero Italiano, 133
Denne, Samuel (of Corpus Christi), 176
Dennis, John, 103, 109, 169
D'Eon, Mme (transvestite), 46
De Quincy, Thos., 157
Devie, James (of Emmanuel), 45, 49, 50
Digges, Dudley (poet), 105, 106
Dodd, James A'Court (rusticated), 63
Dodd, Wm., *Beauties of S,* 111
Dodsley, James (bookseller), 88, 100
Dodsley, Robt., 192, 195; *Toy-Shop,* 108
Dodsley's Collection of Old Plays, 148

Dodson, Mr. (church warden at Swavesy), 57
Dodwell, Mr. (father of Henry), 129
Dodwell, Henry, 49
Domvile, Benjamin (dean of Armagh), 117
Donne, John, 130; *Paradoxes,* 163
Dorset, sixth Earl of, 137
Douce, Francis (S critic), 147, 165, 180
Douglas, Gawin, 108
Douglas, John (canon of St. Paul's), 25
Drake, Sir Francis, *Voyage Round the World,* 129
Drayton, Michael, 105, 106, 132
Driffield, John (has lectures on Theocritus), 184
Drummond, Wm., of Hawthornden, 117
Dryden, John, 164, 190; *Of Dramatic Poesy,* 96; Preface to *The Fables,* 104
Ducarrel, Dr. Andrew Coltree (antiquary), 88, 193
Duff, Wm., *Essay on Original Genius,* 117
Dugdale, Sir Wm., *Monasticon Anglicanum,* 184
Dunbar, Wm., 108
Dunning (lawyer), 72
Dyer, Sir Edward (poet), 144
Dyer, Geo., *Annual Necrology,* 15, 16, 21–31 *passim,* 38, 46, 54–59 *passim,* 66–74 *passim,* 87, 106; *Memoirs,* 54

Ecclesiasticus (Bible Apocrypha), 34, 163
Edward, Baron Herbert of Cherbury, *Autobiography,* 136
Edward III (S Apocrypha), 113, 127, 141, 160
Edwards, Richard, *Paradise of Dainty Devises,* 144
Ekins, Dr. Jeffery (dean of Carlisle) ("Dr. Elkins"), 30, 193
Eliot, John, *Ortho-epia Gallica,* 108, 134
Elizabeth I (queen of England), 28, 91, 96, 139, 161, 201; "Doubt of Future Woes," sonnet by, 196; her verses, 199, 200
Elliot, Sir John (physician), 194
Ellis, Clement, *Gentile Sinner,* 130
Elves, G. (printer), 127

Index

215

Essex, second Earl of, 182
Essex, James (architect), 75, 181, 182
Euclid, *Elements,* 22
Euripides, 108
European Magazine, 30, 68, 103, 159, 167, 168, 169, 173
Ewin, Wm. Howell (usurer), 64
Exercise of Armes, 151

Fabricius, A. ("bibliophilist"), 117, 183
Fairfax, Edward (trans. Tasso), 121, 137
Farmer, Bartholomew (RF's ancestor), 17
Farmer, George (RF's ancestor), 17
Farmer, Hannah, née Knibb (RF's mother), 17
Farmer, John (first son of Richard and Hannah), 17, 20
Farmer, John (RF's ancestor), 17
Farmer, Richard, *Charles the Bold,* 33; *Directions,* 154, 167–69; *Essay,* 24, 74, 84, 87–128 passim, 135, 140, 153, 165–71 passim, 182, 183, 184; *Leicester,* 16, 22, 84–93 passim, 116, 157, 171, 183; *Letter* to Reed, 103; *Letter* to Steevens, 95, 120–41 passim, 149, 163
Farmer, Richard (RF's father), 17
Farmer, Capt. Richard Byrom, 44
Farmer, Roger (adm. to Emmanuel), 20
Farmer, Seth (adm. to Emmanuel), 20
Farmer, Thos. (adm. to Emmanuel, 1641), 20
Farmer, Thos. (adm. to Emmanuel 1660), 20
Farmer, Thos. (RF's nephew), 20, 79–83 passim
Farmer, Thos. Cooke (RF's grand-nephew), 32, 33
Fawcett, James (of St. John's), 47, 201
Felton, Samuel (portrait of S), 22
Fenton, Elijah, 177
Fiddes, Richard, *Life of Cardinal Wolsey,* 108
Field, Nathan, 164
Fielding, Henry, *Journey from this World to the Next,* 133; *Tom Thumb,* 16, 45
Fleming, Abraham, 106
Fletcher, (John?) (Phineas?), 132
Fletcher, John, 145; *Maid's Tragedy*

(with Beaumont, Francis), 133, 139; *Two Noble Kinsmen,* 128
Florio, John, 150, 201
Ford, John, *Lover's Melancholy,* 131
Fox, Chas. (statesman), 24
Frend, Wm. (unitarian), 74
Fuller, Thos., *Hist. of Worthies of Eng.,* 185, 186

Gage (of Emmanuel), 42
Garland of Withered Roses, 188, 189
Garnett, John (bp. of Clogher), 193
Garnier, Robt. (French poet), 125
Garrick, David, 34, 98, 99, 100, 105, 111, 112, 132; *Clandestine Marriage* (with Colman), 43
Garwood, Edmund (sizar of Magdalene), 62
Gascoigne, Geo. (trans. Ariosto), 100; *Certain Notes,* 108; *Posies,* 196, 200; *Princely Pleasures at the Court of Kenilworth,* 188; *Supposes,* 100
Gascoyne, Richard (antiquary), 89
Gazam, Mr. (grocer), 53–54
George II (king of England), 35
George III (king of England), 22, 24, 25, 31, 50, 66, 67
Gesta Romanorum, 121, 130
Gildon, Chas. (ed. S's poems), 108, 109, 112, 117
Gillingham, Richard (his scholarship), 22
Gleig, Geo., *Encyclopedia Brittanica,* 24–29 passim, 38, 40, 66,67, 68, 87
Glenham (wounded by Dennis), 169
Glynn, Dr. Robt. (physician), 28
GM, 15, 16, 20, 28, 50, 54, 66, 71, 75, 84, 87, 91, 99, 165–71 passim
Godwin, Wm., *Political Justice,* 44
Godwyn, Chas. (of Balliol Coll., Oxford), 101
Gooch, James Wyard (of St. John's), 53
Gooch, Dr. John (prebendary of Ely), 49
Gorgeous Gallery, 132
Goslyn, John, in Milton's poem, "In obitum Procancellarii medici," 186–87
Gosson, Stephen, *School of Abuse,* 108
Gough Richard, 28, 59, 68, 75, 78, 88, 89, 92, 121, 165, 176, 179, 180; *British Topography,* 179; *Catalogue of Coins,* 179–80

216 Index

Gower, John, 117
Granger, James, 179; *Biographical Hist.*, 178–79
Gray, Thos., 37, 124, 171
Greek Anthology, 126
Greek Testament, 22
Green (friend of Reed's), 46
Green, Dr. (dean of Salisbury), 24
Green, Geo. Smith (*Paradise Lost* in blank verse, specimen of), 108
Greene Robt., 148; *Arcadia,* 140; *Dorastus and Faunia,* 136; *Friar Bacon and Friar Bungay,* 131; *Whole Contention,* 144
Greenham, Richard, "a sweet comfort," 197
Gregory, Saint, 76
Gregory, John (bookseller), 84
Greville, Robt., Lord Brooke, 162
Grey, Zachary, 111, 126, 136, 138; ed. Butler's Hudibras, 181–82, 198
Griffith, Elizabeth (S critic), 111
Grimald, Nicholas, 108
Grotius, Hugo, *de Veritate Religionis Christianae,* 22
Guilford, second Earl of ("Lord North"), 24, 42
Gunning, Henry, *Ceremoniès,* 65; *Reminiscences,* 27, 38, 50, 53–58 *passim,* 64–71 *passim,* 77
Guthlac, Saint, *Hymni,* 182
Guthrie, Wm., 100, 103, 104, 123; *Essay on Eng. Tragedy,* 97, 107, 111, 116
Guy, Earl of Warwick, 188
Guy of Warwick, 189

Hales, John (of Eton), 107, 108
Hales, Wm., *Inspector,* 59
Hall, Arthur (ed. Triveth, Nicolaus), 143
Hall, Edward, 151; *Union of the Noble and Illustre Families of Lancaster and York,* 120
Halliday, Francis Alexander (rusticated), 63
Hallifax, Samuel (bp. of Gloucester and Asaph), 18, 67, 69
Halliwell-Phillipps, James Orchard, 135, 150
Hanmer, Sir Thos. (ed. S), 96, 111, 114, 115, 130, 133, 136

Harding, Sylvester(portrait painter), 45
Hardwicke, second Earl of, 48, 50
Harington, Sir John (trans. Ariosto), 108; *Metamorphosis,* 118, 149; *Nugae Antiquae,* 118
Harris, Wm. (co-editor of 1803 S), 163
Harsnet, Samuel (archbp. of York), 182
Harte, Wm. (S's nephew), 137
Harvey, Gabriel, 151
Harwood, Busick (prof. of anatomy), 27, 47, 79, 82, 83
Hatcher, Thos. (vice-chancellor), 149
Hatton, Lady, 44
Hatton, Miss, 19, 26, 27, 28, 29
Hatton, Sir Thos. (father of Miss Hatton), 19, 26, 27, 28
Haughton, Wm., *Grim the Collier,* 161
Havard, Wm., *King Charles the First,* 42
Hawes, Stephen, 137
Hawkins, Sir John, 180
Hawkins, John Sidney, ed. Ruggles's *Ignoramus,* 180
Hayley, Wm., 46, 75
Hearne, Thos., 186; notes to *Thomae Caii Vindiciae,* 187
Heath, Benjamin, *Revisal of S's Text,* 111, 155
Henderson, John (actor), 45
Henley, Samuel (S commentator), 141, 166
Henry IV (king of England), 130
Henry VIII (king of England), 133, 185
Hentzner, Paul, *Journey into England,* 199
Herbert, Sir Thos. (Master of the Revels), 123
Herbert, Wm., 17, 181; ed. *Typographical Antiquities,* 180, 187. See Ames, Joseph
Hertford, Earl of, 199
Heydrick, John (RF's schoolfellow), 15, 17
Heyrick, Samuel (antiquary), 84
Heyrick, Tobias (M.A. of Trinity College), 90
Heyward, Sir John, *Hist. of Edward VI,* 133
Heywood, John, 164; *David's Tears,* 146; *Epigrams,* 115
Heywood, Thos., 132, 147, 159; *A Warning for Fair Women,* attributed to, 162

Index

217

Hickes, Geo., *Linguarum Vett. Sept-entrionalium,* 182

Hill, Aaron, 104

Hinchliffe, John (bp. of Peterborough), 49

Hist. of Glorianus and Gloriana, i.e. *Grobianus et Grobiana,* 171–72

Hist. of Lord Fauconbridge, 126

Hist. of Seven Champions of Eng., 183

Hoby, Sir Thos., trans. *The Courtier,* 132. *See* Castilio, Count Baldessar

Hogarth, Wm., 182

Holinshed, Raphael, *Chronicles,* 107, 108, 168

Holland, Wm. (publisher), 51

Hollick, Mr. (supports Peter Musgrave), 50

Hollond, John (expelled), 63

Holt, John, *Remarks on the Tempest,* 106, 111

Homer, 109, 183

Homer, Henry (of Emmanuel), 56

Honourable Entertainment to the Queenes Majesty . . . at Elvetham, 199, 200

Horace, *Epistolae,* 109

Howard, Baron, "Defensative," 131

Howard, John (prison reformer), 29

Howell, James, *Epistolae Ho-elianae,* 131

Howes, Edmund (continuation of Stow's *Summarie*), 108

Hubbard, Henry (Lady Margaret Preacher), 23, 37, 55, 76

Huddesford, Wm. (Oxford antiquary), 97, 99, 101, 184,185–86; *Lives,* 185–86

Hume, David, 59, 167–69, 175; *Hist.,* 154, 188

Humphry, Ozias (portrait-painter), 152

Hurd, Richard (bp. of Lichfield and Coventry), 23, 24, 38, 55, 67, 107, 112, 171, 183, 184; ed. Horace, *Ars Poetica,* 22, 23, 24; *Letters on Chivalry and Romance,* 192; *Marks of Imitation,* 109

Hymni Aliquot de S. Guthlacan, 182

Hystorie of Hamblet, 111, 118

Ingram, Wm., "Miscellaneous Collections," 176

Ireland, Wm. Henry, 164–66; *Vortigern,* 103

Irwin, Mr. (friend of Reed), 46

Islip, Adam (printer), 145

Jackson, Dr. (canon of St. Paul's), 29

Jackson, Mr. (Greek scholar), 18

James, Dr. Robt. (physician), 78

James I (king of England), 97, 139, 190, 200

James II (king of England), 190

Jebb, Dr. John (physician and theologian), 66, 69

Jeffreys, Dr. (canon of St. Paul's), 29

Jeffries, Geo. (of Trinity College), 28

Jenyns, Soame, 49

Johnson, Samuel (ed. S), 29, 38, 46, 88, 94, 95, 96, 100, 105–15 *passim,* 120, 121, 123, 128, 130, 133, 139–44 *passim,* 150, 151, 163, 164, 170–80 *passim,* 186, 192, 194; Dedication to Percy's *Reliques,* 173; *Dictionary,* 175; *Life* of Isaac Watts, 174; *Lives,* 171, 174, 177; (trans. Father Lobo), 173

Jones, John (engraver), 144

Jones, Stephen, ed. 1812 *Biographia Dramatica,* 103

Jonson, Ben, 100, 104, 132, 136, 145, 159, 164; *Bartholomew Fair,* 159, 160; *Magnetic Lady,* 148; *Sejanus,* 128

Juvenal, *Satire X,* 125

Kempe, Will, 125

Kendall, Richard (friend of Dawes), 44

Kendall, Timothy, *Flowers of Epigrammes,* 126

Kennicott, Benjamin (Hebraist), 189, 190

Kennilworth Ballad, 188, 189

Kenrick, Wm. (S critic), 123

Keppel, Augustus (admiral), 69–70

King, Wm., *Original Works,* 16

King and the Beggar, ballad of, 137

"King Lear," ballad of, 198

Kippis, Andrew, ed. *Biographia Britannica,* 28, 75, 103, 169

Knibb, John (RF's maternal grandfather), 17

Knight, Richard Payne (MP), 46

218   Index

Knolles, Richard, *General Hist. of the Turks,* 151

Kuster, Ludolph (Greek scholar), 108

Kyd Thos., 164; *Hieronymo,* 110, 158; *Soliman and Perseda,* 150; *Spanish Tragedy,* 132

Lacy, Henry, *Richardus Tertius,* attributed to, 140.

Lamotte, Antoine Houdart de, 108

Laneham, Robt., *A Letter . . . of the Entertainment untoo the Queen, at Killingwoorth Castle,* 130, 134, 199

Langbaine, Gerard, *English Dramatick Poets,* 111

Langland, Wm., *Piers Plowman,* 110

Lansdowne, first Marquis of ("Lord Shelburne"), 76

Lasco, Albert a ("Prince Laskie"), 139

Laud, Wm. (archbp. of Canterbury), *Diary,* 162

Law, Edmund (bp. of Carlisle), 25

Lawrence, Miss Elizabeth (and the younger Boswell), 144

Lawrence, Dr. Thos. (physician), 46

Leicester, first Earl of, 149

Leland, John, *Scriptoribus,* 185, 186, 192; *Itinery,* 108

Leman, Thos. (antiquary), 91

Lennox, Charlotte (S critic), 111

Lewis XVI (king of France), 32

Leycester, Geo. (of Trinity College), 172

Life and Death of St. George, ballad of, 161, 162

Lincoln-book (in Lincoln Cathedral), 189, 192

Ling, Nicholas, *England's Helicon,* 144

Little John Nobody, ballad of,196

Littleton, Lord Edward, 49

Lobo, Father Jerome, *Voyage to Abyssinia,* 173

Locrine (S Apocrypha), 146, 159

London Magazine, 163

London Prodigal (S Apocrypha), 146

Long, Wm. (friend of Reed), 46

Longinus, 121

Longueville, Wm. (Butler MSS), 182

Lord Cromwell (S Apocrypha), 146, 147

Lort, Michael (of Trinity), 25, 26, 27, 45–49 *passim,* 102, 103, 112, 148, 172, 179

Lowth, Robt. (bp. of London), 42

Luttrell, Narcissus, 46

Lydgate, John, 117, 123

Lye, Edward, *Dictionarium Saxonico et Gothico Latinum,* 182

Lyly, John, 105, 106, 159; *Endymion,* 164; *Euphues,* 97, 163; *Mydas,* 129; *Sapho and Phao,* 117

Lyttlton, Chas. (bp. of Carlisle), 87

Lyttleton, first Baronet of, 125

Macaulay, Catherine, 168; *Hist. of England,* 168, 169

Machin, Lewis (dramatist), 164

McKitterick, David, *Hist.,* 72

Maitland MSS, 191, 192

Malone, Edmond, 45, 47, 49, 80, 97, 103, 132, 133, 137–48 *passim,* 152–54, 157–66 *passim,* 200; *Essay,* 103; *Historical Account,* 158; *Inquiry into the Authenticity of Certain Miscellaneous Papers . . . attributed to S,* 165; *Letter to . . . Farmer,* 153; *Second Supplement,* 151

Mansell, Wm. Lort (public orator), 27

Manwaring, Edward, *Treatise,* 108

Markham, Gervase, *Book of Armory,* 172; republishes *Gentleman's Academie,* 124–25

Marlowe, Christopher, 143, 144; *Edward II,* 143; *H6* triad, attributed to, 159; *Jew of Malta,* 117; *Lust's Dominion,* 135; *Tamberlaine,* 159

Marston, John, 164; *What You Will,* 115

Martin, "Honest Tom" (antiquary), 85, 88

Martyn, Thos. (botanist), 19, 20, 27, 29, 56, 57, 58, 85–86, 98, 103

Mason, Geo., "Collections," 176

Mason, John Monck (S critic), 158

Mason, Wm., 193

Massinger, Philip, 164; *New Way to Pay Old Debts,* 45

Masters, Robt. (of Corpus Christi), 28, 41, 44, 47, 152, 179

Mathew, Wm. (Bedell), 44

Mathias, Thos. James, *Pursuits of Literature,* 83, 157

Mattaire, Michael ("bibliophilist"), 117

Matthew of Westminster, 125

Index

Mead, James (of Emmanuel), 42
Meen, Henry (of Emmanuel), 26, 30, 42, 68, 77–83 *passim*, 195
Melcombe-Regis, First Baron of, "Lord Melcome," 175
Memoire de l'Academie des Inscriptions, 189, 192
Memoires de Litterature, 108
Menage, Gilles, 105
Meres, Francis, *Palladis Tamia,* 113, 191
Merry Devil of Edminton (S Apocrypha), 117
Middleton, Conyers (historian), 23
Middleton, Thos., 164; *More Dissemblers Besides Women,* 131
Milton, John, 32, 107, 108, 168
Minshew, John, *Guide into the Tongues,* 131
Mirror for Magistrates, 151
"Miscellanies relative to . . . Camb.," 176
Monmouth Geoffrey, *Historia Regnum Britanniae,* 199
Monthly Review, 99
Morden, Mrs. (assaulted), 63
More, Sir Thos., his epigrams, 101
Morning Chronicle, 44
Mortlock, John (deputy mayor of Camb.), 70, 71
Munday, Anthony. *See* Chettle, Henry
Murphy, Arthur, 45
Musgrave, Peter (tailor), 50–54 *passim*
Musgraviana, 53
Myddelton, Mr. (junior proctor), 63

Nash, Treadway, ed. Butler's *Hudibras,* 181–82
Nashe, Thos., 140; *Christ's Tears,* 151
Neale, Thos. (amateur actor), 33
Neve, Peter le (antiquary), 85
New, Mr. (amateur actor), 33
Newbery, Francis (bookseller), 46
Newcastle, first Duke of, 31, 32
New Monthly Magazine, 172
News from Scotland, 150
Newton, Thos. (bp. of Bristol), 108
Nichols, John, 15–29 *passim*, 38, 43, 45, 46, 49, 55–59 *passim*, 66, 67, 75, 76, 84–92 *passim*, 97, 98, 167, 181, 183, 185, 194; *Anecdotes of Wm. Bowyer,* 91; *Barnwell Abbey,* 91;

Bibliotheca, 56, 91; *Hist. of Hinckley,* 177; *Illustrations,* 172; *Leicestershire,* 15–19 *passim*, 67, 84–86, 91, 177; *Progresses . . . of Queen Elizabeth,* 177; *Select Collection of Poems,* 177
Nicol, Geo. (bookseller), 45, 46
North, Frederick (MP), 46
North, Sir Thos. (trans. Amyot), 114
Northcote, Sir Stafford (fined), 42
"Nut-Brown Maid," ballad of, 200

Oldershaw, John (of Emmanuel), 42, 48, 74, 194, 195
Oldham, Wm. (of Peterhouse), 37
Omiah, of Otaheite, 92
Orelia and Isabella (i.e., *Aurelia and Isabella*), 125–26, 186
Orford, fourth Earl of, 28, 166, 169; *Wks,* 170
Osborn (printer), 173
Overbury, Sir Thos., *Characters,* 131
Ovid, 34, 97, 100, 112, 117, 125; *Heroides,* 100
Owen, John (satirist), 34

Paine, Thos., *Rights of Man,* 50
Painter, Wm., *Palace of Pleasure,* 133
Palamon and Arcite (author unknown), 104
Palliser, Sir Hugh (vice-admiral), 69, 70
Palmer, John (amateur actor), 33
Palmer, John (theater manager), 46
Paris, Matthew, 125
Parker, Matthew (archbp. of Canterbury), 182
Parr, Katherine (wife of Henry VIII), 133
Parr, Samuel (prominent Whig), 39, 157
Pavyer Thos. (printer), 148
Peacock, Geo. (bp. of Ely), *Observations,* 61–62
Pearce, Wm. (master of Jesus), 44
Peele, Geo., 113
Pegge, Samuel (antiquary), 45
Pellontier (unidentified), 189
Pennington, Dr. Isaac (physician), 16, 43, 78
Pepper, Dominus (actor?), 159
Pepys, Samuel, collection of old ballads, 192, 195, 196

220 Index

Percy, Anne (wife of Thos.), 171, 190–96 *passim*
Percy, Henry (son of Thos.), 194–95
Percy, Thos. (bp. of Dromore), 25, 27, 30, 45, 72, 78–89 *passim*, 94–112 *passim*, 123, 141, 142, 165–86 *passim; Essay on Ancient Eng. Minstrels,* 189, 19, 200; *Origin of Eng. Stage,* 200; *Reliques,* 94, 105, 106, 112, 130, 173, 187–200 *passim;* ed. Surrey's poems, 193, 195
Perkins, Wm., his "tables," 197–98
Perry, James (ed. *Morning Chronicle*), 44
Petrarch, 108, 118, 121
"Phillida and Corydon," ballad of, 199
Phillips, Ambrose, 34, 171
Pigott, Geo. (of Abington), 49
Pilkington, Gilbert, *Tournament of Tottenham,* 192
Pilot, Lazarus, trans. *The Orator. See* Silvayn, Alexander
Pinkerton, John, 165, 191–92; *Ancient Scottish Poetry,* 192
Pits, John ("Pitsius"), 192
Pitt, Wm., the younger, 24, 25, 29, 30, 49, 53, 92, 93
Plautus, *Amphitryon,* 22; *Trinummus,* 100
Plumptre, James (of Clare), 35
Plumptre, Richard, *Hints,* 61, 71, 72
Plumptre, Robt. (prof. of moral theology), 44
Plutarch, 100, 107, 114
Poems (1640), 146
Pomfret, Countess of, 17
Pomfret, first Earl of, 17
Poor Knight his Palace of Private Pleasures, 133
Pope, Alexander (actor), 45
Pope, Alexander (ed. S), 96, 104, 107, 109, 111, 131, 134, 183; *Dunciad,* 125; *Epilogue to Satires, II,* 125; *Epistle to Dr. Arbuthnot,* 153; *Memoirs of Martinus Scriblerus,* 104, trans. of Odyssey, 177
Porson, Richard, 165
Porto, Luigi da, *Giulietta e Romeo,* 132–33
Price, John (librarian), 187
Prince Arthur (popular pageant), 183
Progress at Elvetham, 200

Puritan (S Apocrypha), 128, 146, 147
Puttenham Geo., *Art of Eng. Poetry,* 196

Queen of Bohemia's actors, 159
Quincy, John, *Lexicon Physico-Medicum,* 81
Quintillian, *Instituto Oratorio,* 22

Rastell, Wm., *Collection of all the Statutes* (?), 126
Ratcliffe, Agremont, *Politique Discourse,* 151
Ratsey, Gamaliel, *Ratseis Ghost,* 160, 161, 162
Rawlinson, Richard, *Catalogue* of his library, 188
Reading, Mr. (of Leicester), 86
"Rebellion hath broken up House," from Butler's *Hudibras,* 197
Reed, Isaac (ed. S), 15, 16, 26–30 *passim,* 38, 40–49 *passim,* 65, 66, 67, 71–82 *passim,* 101, 102, 103, 108, 118, 119, 124, 136, 143–52 *passim,* 157, 158–59, 164–73 *passim,* 177–82 *passim,* 195; ed. *Biographia Dramatica,* 42, 169
Resnel, l'Abbe du, *Recherches,* 108
Return from Parnassus, 125
Rex Platonicus, 108
Reynolds, Sir Joshua, 45, 46
Richardson, Wm. (master of Emmanuel), 35, 180; "List of Graduates," 176,180
Ricroft, R. (killed in a duel), 63
Ritson, Joseph, 39, 45, 154, 164, 165, 166; *Cursory Criticisms,* 153, 154; *Remarks,* 39, 164
Roberts, Sir Sidney Castle (master of Pembroke), 68, 168
Robinson, Robt. (preacher), 54, 74
Rogers, Mr. (amateur actor), 33
Rollins, Hyder E. (S editor), 146
Romaunt of the Rose, 108
Romney, Geo., 29, 45, 46, 142
Ronsard, Pierre, 108
Rowe, Nicholas (ed. S), 96; *Account,* 111
Rowley, Thos. (Chatterton's creation), 170
Rowley, Wm., 164; *Birth of Merlin* (S Apocrypha), 117
Royle, John (rusticated), 63
Ruggles, Geo., *Ignoramus,* 180

Index

221

Ruggles, Thos., 180
Rushworth, John, *Historical Collections of Private Passages of State,* 197

S., K., 165,
S., R. [Stapleton, Richard?] *Phoenix Nest,* 144
Sachs, Hans, 118
Sackville, Thos., "Mirrour for Neighbours," i.e. *Mirror for Magistrates,* 134–35
Sainte-Palaye, Jean Baptiste, de la Curne, *Memoires sur l'ancienne chevalerie,* 192
St. James Evening-Post, 89
St. James's Chronicle, 89, 92
Sandwich, fourth Earl of, 92
Sappho, 121
Sarah, Duchess of Marlborough, "Apology," i.e. *Account of the Conduct of the Dowager Duchess of Marlborough,* 168
Sawbridge, Wanley (of Emmanuel), 21
Saxo Grammaticus, 116; *Amleth,* 96, 118
Sayers, James (associate of Reed), 45
Seale, John Barlow (Greek scholar), 180
Secker, Thos. (archbp. of Canterbury), 177
Seltzer, Christ. (on Chatterton), 169–70
Serving-Man's Comfort, 145
Seward, Wm., 29, 46; *Biographiana,* 66, 167
Sewell, Geo. (S critic), 97
Shakespeaare, Wm., *Ado,* 126, 162, 184; *Ant.,* 114, 151, 155; *AWW,* 104, 150, 158, 161; *AYL,* 16, 125, 140, 145, 156, 160; *Cor,* 107, 139; *Err.,* 118; *Ham.* 96, 103, 105, 107, 110, 113, 121, 125, 127, 133, 137, 140, 145, 149, 150, 154, 158, 159, 160, 161, 162; *1H4,* 115, 142, 151, 159, 160, 162, 163; *2H4,* 139, 147, 151; *1&2H4,* 148, 149; *H5,* 97, 108, 113, 128, 151, 153, 163; *2H6,* 52, 115, 134–35, 144; *3H6,* 142, 144; *H6Triad,* 113, 127, 128, 141, 143, 144, 145, 159, 177; *H8,* 110, 128, 149, 164; *JC,* 115; *Jn.,* 103, 124, 126, 128; *LLL,* 100, 101, 107, 124, 129, 130, 145, 150; *Lr.* 51, 135; *Luc.,*
107, 113, 139; *Mac.,* 99, 104, 107, 123, 124, 125, 131, 147, 150, 157, 162; *MM,* 96, 109, 149, 150, 158; *MND,* 110, 130, 135, 137; *MV,* 116, 121, 130, 136–37, 139, 145; *Oth.,* 127, 133, 138, 158, 163; *Per.,* 104, 113, 126, 127, 146, 153, 158; *PP,* 145; *R2,* 124, 153, 157; *R3,* 115, 120, 151; *Rom.,* 121, 124, 128, 132, 148, 155; *SHR.,* 100, 105, 107, 109, 113, 115, 128, 150, 163; *Son.,* 137–38; *TGV,* 51, 136; *Tit.,* 113, 127, 158, 160; *TN,* 126, 127, 130–31, 135, 149; *TNK,* 127, 128; *Temp.,* 96, 102, 118, 125, 129, 135, 156, 158, 162, 186; *Tro.,* 115, 121, 129, 130–31, 156, 160; *Ven.,* 102, 146; *Wiv.,* 112, 115, 116, 120, 123, 134, 140, 149, 152, 156; *WT,* 131, 136, 152, 156

Sharp, John (archdeacon of Northumberland), 171
Sharpe, Richard (friend of Reed), 29, 46, 73, 74
Shelton Thos. (trans. *Don Quixote*), 108
Shenstone, Wm., 171, 192
Sherard, Geo. (a row at Magdelene), 63
Sherley, Sir Robt., *Sir Robt. Sherley ambassadour of the King of Persia,* 149
Shirley, James, 164
Shore, Jane (portrait of ?), 193
Shuckburgh, E. S. (of Emmanuel), 17, 40, 68
Sidney, Sir Philip, *Astrophel and Stella,* 135–36
Sigebert, d. 637 ? (king of East-Saxons), 185, 186
Silvayn, Alexander, 145
Simmonds, John (vicar of St. Mary's, Leicester), 18, 19, 20, 84
Sir John Oldcastle (S Apocrypha), 146, 147
Sisson, Chas. (friend of Reed), 56
Sixtus V, 74
Skeat, Walter Wm., 131
Skelton, John, 107, 113, 137
Smart, Christopher, "Brief Enquiry," 97
Smith, Adam, 108
Smith, D. Nichol, 96, 97, 104, 107, 110, 111, 118
Smith, Wm. (S commentator), 138

222 Index

Solomon, 183
Sophocles, 108
Southampton, third Earl of, 142
Speed, John, 125; *Hist. of Gt. Britain,* 193; "Tables" *(Theatre of the Empire of Great Britain?),* 110
Spelman, Sir Henry, *Glossarium Archaiologicum,* 110
Spenser, Edmund, 120, 134; *Fairie Queene,* 112, 183
Stamford, fourth Earl of, 18
Stanyhurst, Richard (trans. epigram), 101
Stapleton, Sir. Robt., *Sleighted Maid,* 117
Statuta Hospitalis Hierusalem, 74
Staunton, Howard (ed. of S), 130
Staveley, "Wm.," i.e. Thos., 38, 84
Staveley, Thos. (antiquary), 19, 84, 88
Steevens, Geo. (ed. S), 26, 27, 30, 41–49 *passim,* 56, 65, 78–83 *passim,* 89, 95, 101, 102, 103, 108, 111, 113, 115, 118–66 *passim,* 170, 177, 180, 181, 182, 187, 195, 198; ed. *Twenty Plays of S.,* 198
Stephens, Henry (trans. Anacreon), 117
Sterne, Laurence, 43; *Tristram Shandy,* 114, 116, 136
Stevens, Harry, *Poetae Graecae Principes,* 183
Stobaeus, Joannes (Greek scholar), 108
Stow, John, 125, 168; *Summarie of Eng. Chronicles,* 108, 129
Strype, John, *Annals of the Reign of Queen Mary,* 196; *Memorials of Thos. Cranmer,* 196
Stubbings, Frank (of Emmanuel), 172–73
Suckling, Sir John, 134
Surrey, Earl of, 110, 118, 188, 189
Swift, Jonathan, 16

Talmud, 114
Tanner, Thos., *Bibliotheca Britannica,* 185, 192
Tarleton, Richard, *Jests,* 108, 123
Tasso, Torquato, 121; *Jerusalem Liberated,* 137
Taylor, John (the water poet), 108, 132
Taylor, John, "Lectures on Theocritus," 184
"Taylor, Peter," 52, 53

Temple, Sir Wm., 168
Terence, *Eunuch,* 105
Terrick, Richard (bp. of London), 56
Theatrical Review, 113
Theobald, Lewis, 96, 111–15 *passim,* 130–37 *passim,* 190; *Double Falshood* [sic], 104, 107
Thomae Caii Vindiciae, 1878. See Hearne, Thos.
Thomas, Hugh (vice-chancellor), 62
Thurlow, first Baron of, 92
Thyer, Robt (ed. Butler's *Remains*), 182
Tilly, Mr. (amateur actor), 33
Tollet, Geo. (S critic), 164
Tooke, John Horne (philologist), 29
Topham, Edward (club member), 45, 46
Torfaei, Thormodes, *Orcades, seu rerum Orcadensium Historiae Libri Tres,* 199
Triveth, Nicolaus, *Annales sex Regum Angliae,* 143
True Chronicle Hist. of Leir, 198
Tuffin, Chas. (?) (and St. Paul's Cathedral), 29
Turberville, Geo., 121, 134; *Tragical Tales,* 106
Turkington, John (master of Clare), 49
Turner, Baptist Noel (of Emmanuel), 171–72
Turner, Joseph (master of Pembroke), 201
Tweddell, John (of Trinity College), 27, 53
Tyrwhitt, Robt. (of Jesus), 67–8, 69
Tyrwhitt, Thos., 120, 130, 141, 142, 155, 157, 164; *Observations and Conjectures,* 111
Tyson, Michael (bursar), 40, 68, 78, 88, 89, 121, 179–80

Universal Visiter, 97
Upton, John, *Critical Observations,* 107, 109, 111, 112, 114, 115, 189–90; ed. *Fairie Queene,* 112
Urry, John (ed. Chaucer), 150

Vachell, Wm. (friend of Dawes), 44, 50
Venn, Henry (preacher), 57
Verdala, Hugh de Loubenx (cardinal), 74
Vezey, Mr. (Dawes's executor), 44

Index

223

Virgil, 112, 135; *Aeneid,* 96; *Georgics IV,* 97
Von, Mr. (amateur actor), 33
Vulgate, 132

Waingrow, Marshall, *Correspondence,* 174
Wakefield, Gilbert, 74; *Silva Critica Antica,* 73
Walden, de, fourth Baron of ("Lord Howard"), 43
Walker, W. S., *Critical Examination of the Text of S,* 124
Walkington, T., *Optick Glasse,* 103, 108, 118, 119
Wall, Adam (of Christ's), 185
Walton, Isaac, *Complete Angler,* 198
Wanley, Humfrey, "Catalogue" in vol. 2 of Geo. Hickes's *Linguarum veterum,* 182
Warburton, Wm. (bp. of Gloucester), 42, 109–15 *passim,* 120, 125, 130–39 *passim,* 151, 190
Warner, Richard (S critic), 102, 123, 164, 207; *Letter to Mr. Garrick,* 132
Warren, Lord John Borlase (admiral), 49
Warren, Thos. (publisher), 173
Warton, Thos., 38, 86, 97, 102, 105, 112,1 23, 125, 126, 140, 182–87 *passim,* 190, 192, 193; *Hist.,* 183, 184–87, 192; ed. Milton, 186–87; *Observations,* 183; ed. Theocritus, 183
Watson, Wm., 121
Watts, Isaac, 174
Webb, Daniel, *Remarks,* 111
Webster, John, 164
Wedderburn, Alexander (lawyer), 72
Westmorland, tenth Earl of, 24, 25, 49
Whalley, Peter, *Enquiry,* 96, 97, 109, 111
Whately, Thos., *Gazetteer,* 108, 110
Whichcote, Francis (his scholarship), 21

Whiston, John (bookseller), 18
White, Thos. Holt (S critic), 163, 166
Whitmore, Geo. (of St. John's), 63
Whytinton, Robt., 108
Wilcox, Francis (of Emmanuel), 24, 42, 47, 49, 77
William of Malmsbury, *Gesta Regum Anglorum,* 125
Williams, John (archbp. of York), 182
Willis, Browne (antiquary), 87
Wilson, Thos. (dean of Carlisle), 193
Wimbolt (printer), 180
Windham, Wm. (MP), 46
Winstanley, D. A., 20, 59
Winstanley, Wm. (compiler), 143
Winwood, Sir Ralph, *Memorials of Affairs of State . . . ,* 150
Withers, Geo., 132; *Philarete,* 162
Wolfe, John (printer), 199
Wolsey, Cardinal Thos., 48, 107, 110
Wombwell, T., *Optick Glasse,* attributed to 103, 118. *See* Walkington, T.
Wood, Anthony a, 143, 186; "Claruit," 113
Wooll, John, *Memoirs of the Rev. Joseph Warton,* 183–84
Worde, Winkin de (printer), 121, 130
World, 169
Wortham, Hale (married Miss Hatton), 27
Wright, Dr. Richard (friend of Reed), 40–41, 44, 45
Wyatt, Sir Thos., 118, 193; (trans. Petrarch), 121
Wynne, Edward (of Little Chelsea), 46

Yates, Lowther (vice-chancellor), 71
Yeatman, Chas. (of Emmanuel), 188
Yorke, John (?) (of Corpus Christi), 50
Yorkshire Tragedy (S Apocrypha), 104, 106, 146, 147